Beyond All Reason

Beyond All Reason

The Radical Assault on Truth in American Law

Daniel A. Farber
Suzanna Sherry

New York   Oxford
Oxford University Press
1997

Oxford University Press

Oxford   New York
Athens   Auckland   Bangkok   Bogotá   Bombay
Buenos Aires   Calcutta   Cape Town   Dar es Salaam
Delhi   Florence   Hong Kong   Istanbul   Karachi
Kuala Lumpur   Madras   Madrid   Melbourne
Mexico City   Nairobi   Paris   Singapore
Taipei   Tokyo   Toronto   Warsaw

and associated companies in
Berlin   Ibadan

Copyright © 1997 by Oxford University Press, Inc.

Published by Oxford University Press, Inc.,
198 Madison Avenue, New York, New York 10016

Library of Congress Cataloging-in-Publication Data
Farber, Daniel A., 1950–
Beyond all reason : the radical assault on truth in American law /
by Daniel A. Farber, Suzanna Sherry.
p.   cm.   Includes index.
ISBN 0–19-510717–9
1. Critical legal studies.   2. Discrimination.   3. Merit (Ethics)
4. Multiculturalism.   I. Sherry, Suzanna.   II. Title.
K370.F37   1997   97–20369
340'.112—dc21

9 8 7 6 5 4 3 2 1

Printed in the United States of America
on acid-free paper

To the memory of my grandparents,
Harry and Mary Shugan
D. A. F.

To the memory of my grandmother
Pearl Andelson Sherry
1899–1996
S. S.

Contents

Beyond All Reason

Introduction

I should be happier about this, the quietist option—and I shall have more to say about quietism later on—if I did not believe that it matters, it always matters, to name rubbish as rubbish, that to do otherwise is to legitimize it.

—SALMAN RUSHDIE

When Robert Bork was nominated for the U.S. Supreme Court, one of his former colleagues at Yale explained why the Senate shouldn't worry about Bork's somewhat intemperate scholarship. Since becoming a judge, the colleague explained, Bork had changed his reasoning style. Then came the zinger: This eminent professor testified that Bork's "abandonment of his slashing and extreme style in favor of a judicious incremental approach to thinking about the law . . . disqualifies him for a reappointment at Yale Law School." Apparently, only extremists make good legal academics. Reason, moderation, and common sense may be positive traits in a judge, but nowadays they are fatal flaws in a legal scholar.[1]

Perhaps this attitude explains the popularity of the extremists we examine in this book. If one academic extreme was represented by Bork, the other is represented by the scholars we focus on, who proclaim that reality is socially constructed. What they have in common is an abandonment of moderation and a dearth of common sense.

The work of former Harvard law professor Derrick Bell illustrates the nature of this kind of extremism. Bell—who is now at New York University Law School—views American society as totally and irredeemably racist. For instance, in his allegory, "The Space Traders," aliens offer the United States "untold treasure" in return for surrendering all blacks to the aliens. The American public votes to accept the deal by an overwhelming margin.

The story also expresses another theme of Bell's, that even the noblest principles merely conceal white self-interest. His development of this theme, however, reveals its disturbing underside. In the story, there is opposition to the deal, especially among the Jewish leadership. They condemn the trade as genocidal and organize the Anne Frank Committee to oppose it. But, Bell points out, their high-minded proclamation leaves out the true motivation of many Jews—a fear that "in the absence of blacks, Jews could become the scapegoats." The moral: Jews don't really desire black equality; they want to keep blacks around as convenient targets to deflect white gentile anger.

It seems the momentum of his avant garde scholarship has led Bell into something more traditional but less attractive: a failure to recognize anti-Semitism when he sees it. Indeed, although Bell sometimes seems to view Jews as among the victims of oppression, he does have something of a problem with the Jewish issue. As we'll see in later chapters, he thinks that discriminatory standards have given Jews an undue share of faculty jobs, and that Louis Farrakhan has been unfairly maligned for anti-Semitic remarks.

It would be convenient if we could simply condemn Bell's lapses as symptoms of an insensitivity to anti-Semitism. Unfortunately, we believe the problem is deeper. Bell's difficulty with the Jewish question is no aberration. Instead, it is a corollary of his widely shared theory that standards of merit are socially constructed to favor the powerful. That theory—sometimes called social constructionism—brings to mind a painting by Goya entitled *The Sleep of Reason Produces Monsters*. Social constructionism is an attack on the modern conception of Reason, and anti-Semitism is one of the first monsters produced when Reason dozes off.

In our view, the very nature of social constructionism poses serious risks to our intellectual and political community. One of those risks is legitimating anti-Semitism, but there are others as well. This book is an attempt to expose these risks in the hope of dimming some of the allure of social constructionism and related theories.

War and ideas are both difficult to contain, and so it should come as no surprise that the culture wars have spread from humanities departments to law schools. Over the past few years, a group of legal academics has been making startling claims about the nature of reality and its implications for law. Although these scholars are social constructionists, not all social constructionists are allied with this camp, nor do they all make such radical claims. To distinguish the subjects of this book from other scholars, we label them *radical multiculturalists.* Largely politically progressive, radical multiculturalism includes adherents of a broad assortment of theories, including critical race theory, radical feminism, and legal writing about gays and lesbians, often called "gaylegal" theory. It also includes the occasional iconoclast at the other end of the political spectrum who uses postmodern theories to support recognizing creationism as a valid alternative to evolution. This motley group is united primarily by their rejection of the aspiration to universalism and objectivity that is the fruit of the European Enlightenment. Reality, they suggest, is subjective and socially constructed.

As Bell's story illustrates, these radical multiculturalists believe in particular that western ideas and institutions are socially constructed to serve the interests of the powerful, especially straight, white men. This leads them to attack such core concepts as truth, merit, and the rule of law. Catharine MacKinnon, the well-known feminist theorist, says that traditional standards of merit for jobs and school admissions are merely "affirmative action for white males," reflecting what white males value about themselves.[2] This theme has been repeated by a number of other feminists and critical race theorists, who have seemingly been blind to its anti-Semitic implications. Others attack the concepts of reason and objective truth, condemning them as components of white male domination. They prefer the more subjective "ways of knowing" supposedly favored by women and minorities, such as storytelling like Bell's. As to the rule of law, it is an article of faith that legal rules are indeterminate and serve only to disguise the law's white male bias. In short, radical multiculturalism includes a broad-based attack on the Enlightenment foundations of democracy.

Not surprisingly, this movement has encountered resistance in the legal academy. Both law and the academic world have long been viewed as bastions of objective, reasoned argument within a broader world that relies less on reason and more on political power or manipulative rhetoric. Universities increasingly have come to be treasured as enclaves of reason in an unreasoning world, evolving from their beginnings as gentlemen's finishing schools to become scholarly communities dedicated to the proposition that "reason could grasp the essentials of human activity." Supreme Court Justice Felix Frankfurter praised his own alma mater as a place where reason and intellectual merit reigned supreme. Many today still see the academy as "an island of intellectual inquiry and robust discourse." Berkeley law professor Robert Post, for example, has applauded the "fidelity to reason" that underlies the university's longstanding commitment to the pursuit of truth. His colleague Edward Rubin characterizes scholarship as unique because of its dependence on the "cognitive faculty that we identify as reason." The conventional view is thus that, within the university, persuasion takes place "on the basis of reason and evidence," not "social standing, physical strength, or the raw vehemence of argument."[3]

Law, too, has often been seen as the province—whether in reality or only in aspiration—of reason rather than emotion, of principle rather than raw power. The image of even the least powerful among us using the reason of law to force capitulation by Goliaths of government and industry is captured in historic cases. There are the well-known cases, the stuff of documentaries: *Brown v. Board of Education*, in which the Supreme Court struck down segregated schools, and *Gideon v. Wainwright*, which insisted that even the poorest criminal defendant was entitled to a lawyer at trial. Other cases are virtually unknown to nonlawyers, but had substantial impact on American institutions: in *INS v. Chadha*, a suit by a single immigrant scheduled for deportation led to the invalidation of as many as two hundred federal laws; in *TVA v. Hill*, an ugly but endangered little fish—the snail darter—halted the construction of the Tellico dam on the Little Tennessee River, a project that had already cost the federal government $100 million. Like the university, then, the law has seen itself as a bastion of the Enlightenment tradition, in which power means nothing if it does not have the force of reason behind it. Radical multiculturalism launches a fierce critique against both.

So what's wrong with radical multiculturalism and its rejection of the Enlightenment? The standard answers are that it is impractical and that it necessarily deconstructs itself. Camille Paglia notes wittily that "if there were no facts, surgeons couldn't operate, buildings would collapse, and airplanes couldn't get off the ground." Physicist Alan Sokal invites those who believe that "the laws of physics are mere social conventions" to "try transgressing those conventions" from the windows of his twenty-first floor apartment. But these types of "facts" aren't the main target of the radical multiculturalists. As far as we know, they obey the same laws of physics as the rest of us.[4]

As for radical multiculturalism deconstructing itself, we are certainly not the first to ask: If there is no such thing as objective truth or knowledge, why should we bother listening to what the (powerless) radical multiculturalists have to say? After all, if reason and knowledge are only the belief systems favored by the powerful, whoever is in power will make his own belief the definition of reality, so it becomes difficult to find a basis for the powerless to criticize social arrangements. This is a significant philosophical problem for radical multiculturalists; but having philosophical problems does not necessarily distinguish radical multiculturalism from any other jurisprudential approach. As Stanford Dean (and sometime critical legal scholar) Paul Brest pointed out long ago, a critique of legal theory is often "rather like an aesthetic judgment issued from the Warsaw Palace of Culture: 'Why is the best view of Warsaw from the Palace of Culture? . . . Because that's the only place in Warsaw where you can't see the Palace of Culture.'" All jurisprudential theories have unresolved philosophical problems—that's what makes jurisprudence interesting.[5]

In any event, we are constitutional law professors, not philosophers or literary theorists. We will therefore address neither of these frequently noted flaws of social constructionism. Instead, we propose to examine the legal and societal implications of radical multiculturalist legal theories. Where do the radical multiculturalists' beliefs take them? In particular, we explore whether their beliefs serve or instead undermine the radicals' own progressive goals. We share their goals of increasing both social justice and individual freedom and improving the quality of public discourse. But these goals are not necessarily well served by radical multiculturalism. Indeed, we contend that the radicals' attachment to social constructionism and related doctrines hinders rather than furthers attainment of all these goals.

Before we do so, we should make several things clear at the outset. First, we are primarily interested in criticizing a body of thought, not the individuals who have accepted it. Radical multiculturalism is an "it," not a "they." It is, in other words, a complex of ideas, not a group of scholars. So when we argue that radical multiculturalism should be rejected, we don't mean that all the work of these scholars is worthless. When they are not in radical multiculturalist mode, many of these writers offer provocative, intriguing observations about some critical social issues. Rich and interesting scholarship has come from the pens of radical feminists, critical legal scholars, gaylegal scholars, and critical race theorists. They have much to add to discussion of issues like affirmative action, where the conventional debate has become stale and our society desperately needs some fresh perspectives.[6] We don't want to drive these scholars out of the law school world; we would be happy, however, if they abandoned what we think is the least fruitful and most troublesome part of their message. When we refer to radical multiculturalists, then, we mean to identify the scholars who have endorsed radical multiculturalist tenets, but we don't mean that radical multiculturalism is the essence of their thought. Mostly, they would be far better off if they dropped the radical multiculturalist slogans and went on with their intellectual work unabated.

Our second point is not quite so simple. Radical multiculturalism, as we define it, isn't a unified theory. No one has sat down to lay out systematically the assumptions of radical multiculturalism and to work out its implications—and if any one legal scholar did so, others would surely find plenty with which to disagree.[7] What has actually happened is something more like this: A number of legal scholars, who have a variety of social and intellectual ties, are appalled by society's treatment of women and minorities and by the legal system's ineffective response to that mistreatment. Those scholars, like the rest of us, are now engaged in a struggle to find a set of tools to understand and address issues of race and gender. Naturally enough, they latch onto some themes that are currently in academic circulation. Radical multiculturalists favor ideas relating to the social construction of reality, just as conservative scholars have latched onto other ideas about free markets. Some efforts to use these ideas are nuanced and sophisticated, but the ideas have the most punch when they are used more crudely—and so they often are used in the bluntest, most forceful way.

Perhaps the best term for radical multiculturalism is to call it an ideology: a set of relatively simple ideas and slogans that help hold a group together and give it a coherent view of the world. We don't mean this term to be pejorative. In this sense, centrists like us have our own ideology.

There are several ways to critique an ideology. Although not itself a theory, an ideology will typically be associated with fully developed theories, which in turn can be subjected to probing intellectual analysis. Such a critique lies outside our expertise and would to some extent be misplaced, because the legal scholars we are criticizing have relatively little interest in the nuances of philosophical theories.

An ideology can also be rejected at the outset on political grounds. For example, if minority groups and women do well under current conditions, we don't need radical multiculturalism; this is the tenor of many conservative attacks on multiculturalism. But we are not so sanguine about the social problems facing our society. Thus, we're not prepared to reject radical multiculturalism out of hand on the ground that our traditional society (before feminists, multicultural- ists, and gay activists came on the scene) was just fine.

Another approach—the one we are going to take—is to show that the ideology doesn't work: It fails to keep its promises. Such an ide- ology fails on its own terms because it cannot support the kind of world that it seeks to create or maintain. For example, we argue that although radical multiculturalism attempts to promote equality, its conception of equality is fatally flawed because of its inherently anti- Semitic and racist implications. It's not that the radicals necessarily have anti-Semitic or racist feelings themselves. Instead, they are toy- ing with an ideology that in the end is a fundamental misfit with their own values. We might call this attempt to grapple with social con- structionism on its own terms a *normative critique.*

Because we take the use of the labels "anti-Semitism" and "racism" seriously, we should pause for a moment to explain our meaning. We do not accuse radical multiculturalists of harboring even covert ani- mosity toward Jews or Asians. We nevertheless view their theories as anti-Semitic and racist in implication. Although anti-Semitism was traditionally based on religious aversion, modern anti-Semitism more often takes the form of rejection of Jewish success, and radical multiculturalism falls into this latter category.[8]

In the end, radical multiculturalists cannot answer an important question without invoking disturbingly anti-Semitic and racist expla- nations: If there is no such thing as objective merit, what explains the success of Jews and Asian Americans, both of whom, like blacks, have been victims of discrimination by white gentile America? We are not trying to play the victims' one-upmanship game or ask why some disadvantaged groups have succeeded where others have not. Nor are we accusing the radicals themselves of being personally racist or anti-Semitic. We are simply suggesting that their theory—which attributes all success to power—cannot account for groups that surpass white gentile America without resorting to racism and anti-Semitism.

The radical theories inescapably imply that Jews and Asians enjoy an unfair share of wealth and status. Thus, the necessary normative implication of the radical theory is that steps should be taken to redress the balance more in favor of white gentiles. In addition, the radicals cannot easily explain Jewish and Asian success. Although benign explanations for this success are available, they are logically inconsistent with radical multiculturalism; consequently, the radicals would be forced to explain Jewish and Asian success by deploying theories that parallel historic forms of anti-Semitism. In short, if the radical multiculturalists are not personally anti-Semitic or anti-Asian, it is only because they have failed to work fully through the logic of their own theories.

Their theories also play into the historic dynamics of prejudice against Jews and similarly successful minority groups. Because of their relative success and their group identities, Jews, Chinese, and other groups have always been attacked by the "have nots" (not to mention some of the "haves"). These attacks are generic reactions against the success of minority groups—reactions that existed long before the radical multiculturalists. The Enlightenment idea of merit provided a partial defense to these basic social antagonisms. Even though the radical multiculturalists may care nothing about Jews one way or the other, their theories have the potential to expose Jews to the traditional attacks by removing the shield of Enlightenment values. Particularly given the role of anti-Semitism and anti-Asian sentiment in some minority communities, the radicals are unwittingly supplying ammunition to less scrupulous group leaders.

We are confident that radical multiculturalists do not have any personal resentment toward Jews or Asians. But most people today would consider a theory racist if it implied that blacks are inherently inferior mentally. They would consider a theory sexist if it implied that women are incapable of pursuing professional careers. And they would attach these labels regardless of whether the holders of the theories had any personal anger toward blacks or women. By the same token, we consider radical multiculturalism anti-Semitic and anti-Asian.

Obviously, radical multiculturalists do not dislike Jews or Asians, nor is their goal to deprive them of their success. How, then, did they get to this point? How could they have failed to notice the pitfalls of their theory? The answers are deeply embedded in their world view. Although the anti-Semitism and racism claims may be the most serious of our charges against radical multiculturalism, we believe that radical multiculturalism suffers from additional grave flaws. In particular, it is corrosive to public discussion of racial and gender issues. It also encourages an evasive attitude toward historical reality. As a result, radical multiculturalists have adopted a position whose disturbing implications are not easily disclaimed.

In the first part of the book, we explore the tenets of radical multiculturalism. We begin by trying to establish that there are indeed a number of prominent legal scholars who are taking quite extreme positions about truth, merit, and legal reasoning. Given the natural reluctance of readers to believe that respectable scholars are taking seemingly crazy positions, we go to some length to document their views. Then we explore in more detail how those views relate to law. Radical multiculturalists have crusaded for significant legal changes—for example, a fundamental rethinking of the doctrines of free speech—and it is important to see how these proposals relate to their underlying ideology.

We then turn, in the second part of the book, to a three-pronged critique of radical multiculturalism. First, in our view, the radical attack on merit has implications that should appall the radicals themselves as well as others. If merit is nothing but a mask for white male privilege, then it becomes difficult to defend the fact that Jews and Asians are quite disproportionately successful. If their success cannot be justified as fairly earned, it can only be attributed to a heightened degree of entanglement with white male privilege. In short, we believe that radical multiculturalism implies that Jews and Asian Americans are unjustly favored in the distribution of social goods. These anti-Semitic and racist implications of radical multiculturalism are unavoidable, and lead us to condemn radical multiculturalism itself as unacceptable.

Second, radical multiculturalism leads to disturbing distortions in scholarship and public discourse. Because they reject objectivity as a norm, the radicals are content to rely on personal stories as a basis for formulating views of social problems. These stories are often atypical or distorted by self-interest, yet any criticism of the stories is inevitably seen as a personal attack on the storyteller. More generally, because radical multiculturalists refuse to separate the speaker from the message, they can become sidetracked from discussing the merits of the message itself into bitter disputes about the speaker's authenticity and her right to speak on behalf of an oppressed group. Criticisms of radical multiculturalism are seen as pandering to the power structure if they come from women or minorities, or as sexist and racist if they come from white men. This makes dialogue difficult at best.

Third, the radical multiculturalist attack on the concept of objective truth has other disturbing consequences. Besides leading the radicals on occasion to a nonchalant mishandling of evidence, it also provides no defense against even the most outrageous distortions of history, such as Holocaust denial. On less dramatic issues, it licenses the radicals to ignore uncomfortable facts about our present racial and gender situation. When the facts do not fit your preconceptions, it is handy to have a theory that says facts can be dismissed as social constructs.

In the last chapter, we try to clear up some loose ends. We show how the various tenets of radical multiculturalism fit together and reinforce each other. We also explore the mechanisms that allow the radicals to abandon common sense and adhere to a set of basically implausible beliefs. One factor is the distortion of discourse mentioned above, which helps them to brush off criticism. Other factors include a reliance on misleading or inaccurate "stock stories" that reinforce their view of society, and a self-sealing ideology that resists punctures by evidence or logic. In combination, these factors encourage a somewhat paranoid style of thought, which sees the covert influence of white male power behind every text, event, or institution, and which interprets any criticism or disagreement as a political power play. Finally, although we believe that radical multiculturalism is itself a dead end, we believe that progressive legal scholars have other valuable insights, and in the "Conclusion" we discuss the prospects for constructive dialogue between them and mainstream scholars.

Because experience has shown that some readers are likely to jump to conclusions about our viewpoint, we should emphasize what our argument is *not* intended to prove. We are not arguing against affirmative action, or in favor of blind adherence to existing standards of merit. We do want to debunk some bad arguments that have been used to advocate especially broad forms of affirmative action, but there are other kinds of affirmative action and other arguments supporting it, which we don't deal with here. (In fact, the two of us don't always agree about affirmative action.) Also, we have no illusions about the perfection of current education and employment standards, which are all too often tainted by irrelevant considerations such as preferences for children of alumni. What claim to be merit standards can also be excuses for exalting marginally relevant credentials into what economists call "barriers to entry." We are defending the accepted ideal of making decisions on the basis of merit, not all the specifics of how decisions are currently made.

We should also emphasize that our critique is not meant as a broadside against all left-of-center legal thought. Feminist and critical theorists come in many varieties. Our critique addresses some important positions taken by some key members of those groups, but certainly not by everybody in those groups. There are many whose views are more moderate and not subject to our critique. But people like Derrick Bell, Richard Delgado, Catharine MacKinnon, and Patricia Williams are far from being marginal figures, and their views on the points we discuss have not been seriously challenged by their peers. Indeed, one radical multiculturalist has suggested that any standard for evaluating the radicals' unconventional scholarship must "definitionally give high marks" to the work of these four scholars. It is tempting, no doubt, to explain away even the statements by Bell, Delgado, MacKinnon, Williams, and others as merely rhetorical excesses, but we find that defense patronizing and, ultimately, simply a way of avoiding an uncomfortable confrontation with disruptive new ideas.[9]

Our argument against radical multiculturalism is unavoidably harsh, because we view its flaws as serious, profound, and dangerous. We do not, however, bring this argument forward without misgivings. The people whose views we criticize are, after all, earnestly seeking to remedy some of the worst injustices of our society. Given our liberal Jewish backgrounds, we feel a particular sense of discomfort in attacking the work of progressive minority scholars, or of seeming to reopen old wounds between the Jewish and black communities. Moreover, we have a strong distaste for the growing incivility of academic disputes. And despite our insistence that we are targeting certain ideas, rather than attacking the individuals who happen to hold those ideas, we can hardly expect the individuals themselves to feel unscathed by our accusations.

All of this we regret. Several friends, over the past few years, have urged these arguments as reasons for avoiding this topic. In the end, however, we feel that the issues are too serious for us to remain silent.

1

Radical Multiculturalism
and Its Discontents

Postmodernist theory . . . is often ponderous rather than playful, and its jargon-filled texts are opaque to all who have not been socialized into its vocabularies. While it derides the idea that American universities should be outposts of British culture, it often has the effect of trying to transform them into the retail outlets for the latest Paris fashions.

—DALE JAMIESON

The past twenty years have been a time of great ferment in the academy. An approach sometimes labeled "deconstruction" has swept through universities, altering the landscape in discipline after discipline. The goal of the deconstructionist is to expose, or deconstruct, the underlying subjectivity and indeterminacy of everything we thought we knew. Radical multiculturalists adopt this approach, attempting to deconstruct such fundamental concepts as truth, merit, and law.

In scholarship, as in politics, one of the most common sins is to mischaracterize an opponent's position in order to attack it. In the hope of avoiding that failing, we use this chapter to make good on our claims about the positions taken by the radical multiculturalists.

To avoid distorting their views, we present their views using their own language whenever possible, either by direct quotation or by integrating some of their distinctive language into our own prose. In the interest of brevity and readability, we have limited many of the direct quotations from their works to a single sentence or less. Readers who are concerned about whether the quotations are taken out of context should keep in mind that we are not quoting a few isolated statements that might have a different meaning in context, but rather a constant theme repeated by many authors and in many different sources. For readers who want to investigate the radicals' writings more fully, the endnotes provide citations for every quotation and paraphrase. Additional documentation of the views of the radical multiculturalists is also found in later chapters.

Although we refer to these scholars as multiculturalists, they represent only the most radical wing of progressive multiculturalist scholarship. The unique features of this radical wing have been variously described. The philosopher Charles Taylor distinguishes conventional multiculturalists, who presume that all cultures "have something important to say to all human beings," from radicals who demand "actual judgments of equal worth" for every culture. Diane Ravitch draws a similar distinction between pluralistic multiculturalists, who seek an inclusive common culture, and particularistic multiculturalists, who "insist that no common culture is possible or desirable." According to sociologists Stephan Fuchs and Steven Ward, a similar difference exists between conventional and radical deconstructionists: while the former challenge "only certain moves of certain competitors," the latter want to "play a different game altogether." Law professor William Eskridge, a leader of the gaylegal studies movement, explains that the difference is between people who would "create new and better stories that fit safely within the system of prior narratives" and others who "tear up the manual and start writing anew."[1]

The common thread in all these descriptions is that the radicals would jettison our inherited culture in its entirety in the name of empowering the downtrodden. While we focus on somewhat different aspects of culture, we use a similar distinguishing feature to identify radical multiculturalists: dissatisfied with incremental change, they attempt to overturn the foundations of American legal thought.

The Origins of Radical Multiculturalism

The radical multiculturalists are located at the intersection of two intellectual trends. They are, first, indirect heirs of the legal realist movement that swept American laws schools from the late 1920s into the 1940s. Spearheaded by such luminaries as Karl Llewellyn at Columbia, and Jerome Frank and Morris Cohen at Yale, the legal realists attacked the formalist notion that law embodies neutral, general principles derivable from cases. The legal realists instead contended, in the words of one commentator, that "law is always the creation of some specific lawmaker, whether legislator, administrator, or judge, and it usually reflects the policy predilections of that lawmaker."[2]

The realists contended that legal doctrine was both indeterminate and incoherent: "For each legal rule that led to one result, at least one more rule pointed toward another result." Thus Walter Wheeler Cook of Johns Hopkins remarked that "legal principles—and rules as well—are in the habit of hunting in pairs." Cook argued that two accepted but conflicting principles can always be construed to apply to any given case. Llewellyn similarly maintained that in interpreting statutes, "there are two opposing canons [of construction] on almost any point." By way of illustration, he listed twenty-eight pairs of contradictory principles of statutory interpretation that had been used by courts and set forth in treatises.[3]

The realists suggested that judges are actually guided by subjective value choices, which are justified and rationalized in their "neutral" written opinions. The intense concern about the possible ideological tendencies of recent Supreme Court nominees shows that these realist ideas are now broadly accepted. But as anyone who follows the Court's work closely can testify, ideology is actually by no means the whole story; legal arguments can make the critical difference in decisions.

Although they believed that legal rules are indeterminate, the realists did not advocate that judges give free rein to their own biases. They suggested that the empirical social sciences should fill the void left by the realist attack on formalism. Instead of the formalists' "artificial logical concepts," realists urged reliance on scientific expertise and empirical data. Robert Maynard Hutchins, a prominent legal realist at Yale who later became the president of the University of

Chicago, wrote that scholars ought to do empirical studies to investigate the actual "operation of legal rules." Indeed, one scholar has recently characterized the heart of legal realism not as what realists believed but as what they did: empirical legal research.[4]

There was thus an affinity between legal realism and the contemporaneous political events of the New Deal. There is some dispute about the extent to which New Deal lawyers actually put legal realism into practice, but there is little doubt that New Dealers and legal realists shared an emphasis on efficiency, empiricism, and expertise. For all their rejection of formalism, then, the legal realists were not as much interested in societal transformation as they were in efficiency. It was left to the critical legal studies movement (popularly known as CLS) to turn the realist insights to progressive political goals several decades later.[5]

Even before CLS, however, legal scholars wrestled with the implications of legal realism. If legal principles are infinitely flexible and decisions depend on what the judge had for breakfast, "law" is just another name for arbitrary discretion. Teaching and writing about rules of law become difficult, frustrating, and ultimately irrelevant activities. In the 1950s and 1960s, legal scholars ultimately restrained the insights of legal realism by focusing on the need for orderly processes to decide legal issues, rather than on substantive legal rules. Herbert Wechsler at Columbia—once a stronghold of legal realism—was a leading proponent of process theory. In his highly influential 1959 article, *Toward Neutral Principles of Constitutional Law*, he argued that judges must be prepared to explain their decisions by reference to principles that "transcend the case at hand." Unlike legislators, courts are not free to function as "a naked power organ"; they must instead engage in a principled *judicial* process. "A principled decision," wrote Wechsler, "is one that rests on reasons with respect to all the issues in the case, reasons that in their generality and their neutrality transcend any immediate result that is involved." Formalists had demanded that decisions apply clear rules announced in advance. Process theorists were willing to live without clearcut rules and were prepared to settle instead for a fair process of decision making and a principled explanation for the ultimate decision. For process theorists, a fair hearing before an unbiased, principled tribunal is the best we can reasonably expect from the legal system.[6]

Wechsler's article simultaneously helped put to rest any remaining realist sentiments within the legal academy and posed a new problem. For Wechsler went on to apply his theory to the Supreme Court's then-recent decision outlawing segregated schools. That case, *Brown v. Board of Education*, decided in 1954 by a unanimous Court, provided Wechsler with the "hardest test" of his "belief in principled adjudication." Despite his fondness for the result, he found *Brown* an ultimately unprincipled decision. Blacks wanted to associate with whites, but many whites did not want to associate with blacks; how could a court choose which side to favor? No neutral principle could justify choosing between the freedom of association denied to blacks by segregation and the "repugnant" association forced on whites by integration. Constitutional scholars would spend at least the next twenty years trying to extricate *Brown* from Wechsler's critique without undercutting his rejection of legal realism.[7]

The failure to formulate a satisfactory version of legal process theory led, perhaps inevitably, to a recycled legal realism. But the CLS revival of legal realism, which began in the late 1970s, differed in several ways from its predecessor. First, as we noted earlier, CLS critiques of law were focused on progressive—even radical—political change rather than on efficient government. Critical legal scholars also recognized and exploited a contradiction within legal realism. As historian G. Edward White has explained, the realist practice of exposing the incoherence and indeterminacy of legal rules conflicted with their attachment to empirical social science: "Why did they assume that while arguments based on legal doctrines were necessarily value laden, arguments based on empirical observation could be value free?" Critical legal scholars abandoned the latter assumption, uncoupling the realists' link between indeterminacy as the problem and social science as the solution. They adopted only the indeterminacy half of the realist program, leaving behind as naive the realist reliance on objective empiricism.[8]

Thus, CLS scholars tended to embrace some of the nihilistic potential of legal realism, which the realists themselves had mostly avoided. Mark Tushnet (one of the founders of CLS), for example, once wrote that "critique is all there is." CLS scholars often focused on what came to be known as the "indeterminacy thesis": that "a competent adjudicator can square a decision in favor of either side in any given lawsuit with the existing body of legal rules." Thus, a sufficiently smart judge (or a judge with sufficiently smart law clerks) can always justify deciding a case either way. He can always twist the law enough to justify his decision. Much of CLS scholarship was aimed at deconstructing legal doctrine to show its indeterminacy.[9]

One frequent CLS target was the liberal idea of individual rights, which CLS scholars sought to show were unintelligible. In his 1984 *Essay on Rights*, Tushnet suggested that any appeal to individual rights is a "masquerade." The masquerade is sometimes successful, he continued, "because the language of rights is so open and indeterminate that opposing parties can use the same language to express their positions." Reliance on rights is also dangerous, Tushnet argued, because the same rights that operate on the side of the angels in one case can be used against them in the next case. He gave as an example the extension of the right of free speech to include advertising. The Supreme Court had first invalidated a ban on price advertising in the drug industry, arguing that it deprived consumers of useful information. But in the very next commercial speech case, Tushnet observed, the Court struck down government attempts to help consumers; the Court invalidated limits on the speech rights of a monopolistic utility. The right that seemed so progressive in the first case was turned against progressive causes in the second. Peter Gabel, another critical legal scholar, denounced rights as part of "an ideological framework that coopts [people] into adopting the very consciousness they want to transform." Envisioning individuals as holding rights necessarily presupposes the existence of the government as the grantor of rights, Gabel argued. Thus, he said, the idea of rights subtly "establishes the presumptive political legitimacy of the status quo."[10]

This "trashing" of rights had its critics among political progressives. The failure of CLS to recognize the real gains that individual rights theories produced for women and people of color led to a somewhat uneasy alliance between those groups and CLS. As Columbia law professor Patricia Williams, who helped inspire what eventually became critical race theory, put it in 1987: "'Rights' feels so new in the mouths of most black people. It is still so deliciously empowering to say." Kimberlé Crenshaw, another prominent critical race theorist who is now a colleague of Williams at Columbia, suggested the next year in the *Harvard Law Review* that CLS's "'trashing' rights consciousness may have the unintended consequence of disempowering the racially oppressed while leaving white supremacy basically untouched." Discontented with CLS doctrine, progressive lawyers were also frustrated at the legal system's resistance to drastic social change. Eventually, their dissatisfaction ripened into the beginnings of the new radical multiculturalist movement.[11]

Some straight white males also moved from CLS into the emerging radical groups. Although relations between CLS and the new groups were mostly cordial, the split did occasion some vituperative rhetoric on both sides. New radical and Georgetown Law School faculty member Gary Peller lambasted his colleague Mark Tushnet as "conservative" and "part of a larger group of white male progressives for whom the recent influx of minority and feminist scholars into legal education has been a source of anxiety." Tushnet responded by suggesting that Peller's attack contained an "oedipal element" compounded by Peller's insecurity about whether his contributions measured up to those of the older generation of CLS. More mildly, one critical race theorist chastised her CLS predecessors because they "exhibit the same proclivities of mainstream scholarship": they "seldom speak to or about Black people."[12]

Like most parents and children, CLS and its progeny share some characteristics and differ in others. While CLS and the newer movements share a left-leaning or progressive political outlook, the new movements tend to have a narrower focus. Where CLS deconstructed every part of the law—one of the most famous CLS articles is on eighteenth-century legal scholar William Blackstone and another is on contract law—the new radicals concentrate on race and gender issues, and particularly on how the law creates or contributes to unequal power relations.[13]

Critical race theory, according to Crenshaw, "focuses on the relationship between law and racial subordination in American society." Another prominent critical race theorist, Richard Delgado, lists eight themes of critical race scholarship, including "the belief that knowledge and ideas are powerful," a "critical examination of the myths and stories powerful groups use to justify racial subordination," and "criticism of liberal legalisms." He also asserts that critical race scholars must be ready to question the premises of civil rights law and to examine how legal doctrines impede reform. Other theorists assert that radical feminism is similarly an "attempt to describe and critique patriarchal jurisprudence." Likewise, gaylegal studies "investigates a particular but pervasive phenomenon that transcends multiple fields of human identity, experience, and knowledge and that negatively impacts all of our lives and many of our laws."[14]

In addition to their focus on race, gender, and sexuality, the new radical multiculturalists expanded the core ideas of CLS by emphasizing the thought of French postmodernists such as Michel Foucault and Jacques Derrida. This meant extending the insight that law is socially constructed into an argument that *everything* is socially constructed. Peller describes this extension as the crucial difference between old and new radicals: "When left academic politics were about demonstrating how misguided mainstream scholars were— how much smarter the left was—critical legal studies and similar organizations were comfortable places for this left faction. Now that the agenda has begun to consider the social construction of intellectual merit itself, many likely feel threatened."[15]

Although CLS was mostly interested in indeterminacy as a way of threatening law's legitimacy, the new radicals were more concerned with how indeterminacy conceals racism and sexism. This view had its roots in another strand of CLS scholarship. Although CLS scholarship had often focused on the inevitable incoherence of legal doctrine, some critical legal scholars also suggested that indeterminacy allowed judges to combine progressive-sounding rhetoric with oppressive results. Thus, legal discourse "conceals and reinforces relations of domination." The late Alan Freeman, for example, argued in one of the earliest CLS articles that antidiscrimination law actually undermined the cause of racial equality and legitimated discrimination.[16]

The radical multiculturalists focused on this legitimating function of law, finding confirmation in Foucault's writings. Where some had found doctrinal incoherence, the new radicals found instead a deliberate concentration of power in the white male establishment. Law (as well as everything else) is constructed by the powerful to maintain and enhance their own power. Derrick Bell, for instance, argues that *Brown v. Board of Education* actually served the interests of whites at least as much as it furthered the interests of blacks. Indeed, he contends that as a general matter, "the interest of blacks in achieving racial equality will be accommodated only when it converges with the interests of whites." Radical feminist Robin West contends that our legal, political, and social cultures are "pervasively misogynist." The radicals thus focus on the roles played by race and gender in the social construction of reality. Their mission is to expose the specific power relations that underlie legal doctrine and practice.[17]

The Social Construction of Reality

The radicals' core beliefs go by many names: social constructionism, postmodernism, deconstructionism. Don't let all the *isms* fool you; their basic theory is both simple and astoundingly powerful. Stated baldly, their thesis is that reality is socially constructed by the powerful in order to perpetuate their own hegemony. As one radical feminist puts it, "feminist analysis begins with the principle that objective reality is a myth." Before you respond that this must be nonsense— that, as the philosopher John Searle notes, Mount Everest exists and is covered with ice and snow at its peak independent of human action or perception—let us explore the more particular claims of the radicals. Most of them, after all, are entirely uninterested in the climatic conditions of Mount Everest, and while their theory might require them to deny the peak's objective reality, they have no particular stake in doing so.[18]

What they do have a stake in is making claims about social aspects of the world. Here their claims have greater plausibility. The statement "Mount Everest has snow at its peak" is different from the statement "Farber and Sherry have written a careful and scholarly book," or even the statement "Farber and Sherry are law professors." It isn't simply that a value judgment creeps into the middle statement that isn't present in the other two. Neither statement about the authors makes sense in the absence of particular human institutions: universities, law schools, scholarly books (as opposed to novels, collections of cartoons, or tabloid articles), standards of judgment about appropriate levels of care, and even what it means to "write" a book (which may or may not include using a pen or pencil, and may attribute authorship to only a limited subset of those who contribute to the final product). In that sense the statements necessarily reflect, at best, only a socially constructed truth.

But, as Stanley Fish among others has suggested, that reality is socially constructed doesn't tell us much by itself: "If everything is socially constructed then the fact that something . . . is socially constructed cannot count as a reason for dismissing it." Tables are socially constructed—they're never found in the wild—but they're certainly real. What difference does it make that reality, or any particular part of it, is socially constructed?[19]

Here is where the radical multiculturalists, drawing on Foucault and other modern French thinkers, make their most significant claims. Foucault at times suggested that underlying what counts as objective knowledge is a power relation, one category of people benefiting at the expense of another category of people. The radicals thus see the social construction of reality as a device to reproduce and perpetuate existing hierarchies. Derrick Bell, for example, writes that "law—and by extension, the courts" are "instruments for preserving the status quo" and only "periodically and unpredictably" serve as a "refuge of oppressed people." Our particular American reality, for Bell, is neither random nor generally benign and adaptive: it is constructed so as to benefit those currently in power. Thus it is no coincidence that Wechsler's call for neutral principles coincided with a defense of segregation: our social practices are constructed in such a way that support for the oppressed is perceived as non-neutral. To be neutral is to side with oppression, which is built into the very order of things.[20]

The beneficiaries of this covert oppression are usually described as straight white males, or, more pompously, as "the white male establishment." Everyone else is either a victim, a collaborator, or an unwitting dupe. The background assumption of the new radicals is well stated by Richard Delgado: "Racism is . . . natural and normal—the ordinary state of affairs. . . . It is the 'normal science' of our day, part of the baseline, the from-which-we-reason. Conversation begins with racist premises." Jerome Culp also finds racism both pervasive and the root cause of all social ills: "Without the racism of The University of Chicago and Northwestern and Duke University, Cabrini Green cannot exist."[21]

Radical feminists take an analogous approach: "With the tools provided by social constructionism, feminists have uncovered the deep connections between our culture's understanding of the human relationship to reality, on the one hand, and our culture's commitment to gender difference and gender oppression, on the other hand." The goal of the radical multiculturalists is thus to expose the racism, sexism, and other pathologies of accepted legal doctrines and social practices, and to suggest changes to help current victims.[22]

Radical multiculturalists especially focus on and criticize such concepts as knowledge, reason, and merit. These concepts are both fundamental and seemingly unbiased; they claim a universal validity. All of them involve standards of judgment, which according to the radicals are socially constructed and culturally contingent, and thus suspect. As critical race theorist Alex Johnson writes, "the presumed norm of neutrality actually masks the reality that the Euro-American male's perspective is the background norm or heuristic governing in the normal evaluative context." Stanley Fish, a Milton scholar who holds a joint appointment in the law school and the English department at Duke, similarly contends that "like 'fairness,' 'merit,' and 'free speech,' Reason is a political entity," an "ideologically charged" product of "a decidedly political agenda." Justice, too, is substantively contentless; one critic of the radicals suggests that they view "talk of 'injustice'" as "a rhetorically disguised demand for capitulation."[23]

The view that talk about justice merely masks group interests and dominance hierarchies is well illustrated by a passage in Derrick Bell's story, "The Space Traders." This passage, which we mentioned in the Introduction, deserves a closer look. Recall that the story's premise is that aliens offer white Americans great benefits in return for an agreement to allow the aliens to take all of America's blacks away. One of the few groups that courageously takes a stand on behalf of the blacks is the Jews, who denounce the alien proposal as genocidal and form a secret Anne Frank Committee to organize resistance. It all seems very noble, but it turns out there is a hidden agenda that has nothing to do with "injustice" and everything to do with keeping Jews from being at the bottom of the social hierarchy. As Bell explains, "A concern of many Jews not contained in their official condemnations of the Trade offer, was that, in the absence of blacks, Jews could become the scapegoats for a system so reliant on an identifiable group on whose heads less-well-off whites can discharge their hate and frustrations for societal disabilities about which they are unwilling to confront their leaders. Given the German experience, few Jews argued that 'it couldn't happen here.'"[24] Or to put it another way, this purportedly noble claim on behalf of blacks is instead rooted firmly in group self-interest, and a rather ugly interest at that—for it appears that what the Jews really need is to be sure that blacks remain available as targets for white racism. Rather than wanting to rescue blacks from being held hostage by white society, the Jews really want to use them as human shields to fend off gentile attacks. So much for abstractions like morality and justice.

This wholesale condemnation of purportedly objective standards stems from the radicals' rejection of the very notion of objectivity. Objectivity itself is a sham, perpetrated by the powerful. Radical feminist Ann Scales describes "the process of objectification: the winner is he who makes his world seem necessary." Or, as another radical feminist puts it: "'objectivity' is only a cover for a male viewpoint." To claim an objective viewpoint is, at best, to mistake a particular for a universal truth. "There is," writes one radical multiculturalist, "no objective reference point, separate from culture and politics, available to distinguish truth from ideology, fact from opinion, or representation from interpretation." We can thus have no universal or common standards of judgment. Anything that masquerades as universal is merely a "mas[k] for the will to political power of dominant hegemonic groups." All "normative orderings . . . reflect the views of the powerful," and all "standards are nothing more than structured preferences" of the powerful. One opponent accurately captures the radicals' beliefs: "Rationality, objectivity, accuracy and standards of intellectual quality and merit are slogans or masks of oppression designed to convince the oppressed that subordination is justice."[25]

Catharine MacKinnon offers a succinct summary of the radical position:

> If feminism is a critique of the objective standpoint as male, then we also disavow standard scientific norms as the adequacy criteria for our theory, because the objective standpoint we criticize is the posture of science. In other words, our critique of the objective standpoint as male is a critique of science as a specifically male approach to knowledge. With it, we reject male criteria for verification.

Or, as she puts it a few pages earlier, "the feminist theory of knowledge is inextricable from the feminist critique of male power because the male point of view has forced itself upon the world, and does force itself upon the world, as its way of knowing."[26]

The Attack on Knowledge and Merit

At least since the Enlightenment, knowledge has been thought of as universally accessible and objective. Something counts as knowledge not because of its pedigree but because of its content. That the Pope or the president or the *New York Times* says it does not insulate it from challenge. Moreover, you and I can know the same thing. We can convey that knowledge to others, and we can be persuaded through reason to reassess what we know. Some things even count as "common knowledge."

Objectivity is a tricky concept. (Ask any philosopher.) In using the term *objective knowledge*, we have in mind something more modest than eternal, unchanging truth, or what philosophers sometimes call the God's-eye view of the universe. Knowledge as understood at any given time is not necessarily the same as ultimate truth. We sometimes think we "know" things that seem well-established but turn out not to be true, as when everyone knew that the sun revolved around the earth, or that chocolate caused hyperactivity in children. These things have since been disproved, and we now have knowledge of— or at least a very well-justified belief in—their converses. Knowledge is nevertheless objective in the sense that it reflects something beyond fiat or a parochial viewpoint. We would, for instance, tend to discount an unsupported statement by the chocolate industry denying any relationship between chocolate and hyperactivity. This is because we generally believe that there are independent standards for evaluating claims to knowledge and for mounting challenges to established knowledge. Moreover, these standards are crucial to our common vision of knowledge as both objective and subject to change. What keeps knowledge from being stagnant is its universal vulnerability to challenge. Objectivity is the aspiration to eliminate beliefs based on bias, personal idiosyncrasy, fiat, or careless investigation.

The radical multiculturalists deny the objectivity of knowledge. As one radical feminist puts it, "knowledge is socially constructed rather than objectively determined." Gary Peller notes that there can be "no neutral theory of knowledge," because knowledge is itself "a function of the ability of the powerful to impose their own views." Another radical—of the religious rather than the feminist or racial camp— suggests that "the allocation of creationism to the marginalized world of subjectivity, and evolution to the privileged world of objectivity, is merely the exercise of social power rather than a natural, value-neutral distinction." In other words, all statements about the world are the equivalent of the chocolate industry's hypothetical statement on hyperactivity: they all reflect the desires of their authors. There is no difference, for the radicals, between the chocolate industry's public relations department and a reputable scientific laboratory, except perhaps in their awareness of the subjectivity of their statements. Peller makes this idea explicit, suggesting that he and other radicals "deny . . . that there is a difference between rational, objective representation and interested, biased interpretation."[27]

More broadly, radical multiculturalists question the use of such standard tools for expanding knowledge as abstract rationality and linear reasoning. Catharine MacKinnon labels these tools a specifically male approach to knowledge, and Richard Delgado describes them as "what the victors impose." Another radical feminist condemns a preference for statistical and empirical proofs as inherently male. The radicals also reject "narrow evidentiary concepts of relevance and credibility." In the words of one careful scholar of the radical feminist movement: "The Cartesian knower is male. The characteristics associated with the knower—objectivity, reason, universality, intellect—are associated with men." A sympathetic observer notes that the creationist branch of the radical movement sees the cultivation of objective judgment and critical thought as a form of indoctrination. Like all social constructions, the idea of reason cannot be understood in the absence of the background knowledge about power relationships: social constructionism "teaches that terms like . . . 'reason and analysis' are uncontroversial only so long as the background assumptions that seem to make their meaning obvious remain unexamined."[28]

Even on a level as mundane as library indexing systems, Delgado suggests, hierarchy replicates itself: the absence of entries for hegemony, legitimation, or false consciousness hinders transformative movements like critical race theory. And he concludes that the oversight is not merely accidental. He and his coauthor note approvingly that a radical feminist friend, whom they describe as sophisticated in the ways of patriarchy, blamed her difficulties in researching a particular feminist topic on index categories "rooted in the structure of male-dominated law."[29]

Objectivity, reason, and universality are, of course, the crown jewels of our Enlightenment heritage. At least some radicals, following

Foucault, directly condemn the Enlightenment itself, as well as its progeny: liberalism and democracy. Delgado suggests that "enlightenment-style Western democracy is . . . the source of black people's subordination" and "racism and enlightenment are the same thing." "Enlightenment is to racism," he continues, "as sexuality is to women's oppression—the very means by which we are kept down." He thus recommends that "if you are black or Mexican, you should flee Enlightenment-based democracies like mad, assuming you have any choice." (Strangely enough, actual migration patterns seem to go in the opposite direction.) Foucault also sometimes suggested that liberal democracies are actually more oppressive than medieval despots or even modern totalitarianism.[30]

Modernity—the era of the Enlightenment—is over, replaced by postmodernism. University of Texas law professor Sanford Levinson declares that "what Michel Foucault devastatingly labeled 'the monologue of reason' has been, for many contemporary intellectuals, displaced by an emphasis on the socially contingent and power-driven nature of conceptions of reality and the ubiquity of often incommensurable perspectives. No longer can those with even radically different views be facilely denounced as irrational."[31]

If reason and knowledge cannot be objective or universal, what is left? For radical multiculturalists, knowledge is intensely personal. Personal perspective, however, is not individual. Instead, it is based on membership in a group. Like everything else, knowledge is also political in the sense that it is a method of maintaining established hierarchies. Knowledge thus cannot be evaluated apart from the social roles—and, in particular, the race and gender—of those who claim to know. Alex Johnson argues accordingly that "society largely constructs social reality," and "matters of race affect this construction."[32]

According to the radicals, knowledge is a facet of "mindset": "the bundles of presuppositions, received wisdoms, and shared understandings against a background of which legal and political discourse takes place." (Mindset turns out to be a very powerful concept for justifying changes in legal discourse and even constitutional rules, as we'll see in the next chapter.) Since mindset depends on individual experience, which differs by race and gender, women and people of color have different sorts of knowledge. Indeed, many of the radicals suggest that women and people of color not only know different things, they know them—and communicate them—in different ways.[33]

In 1982, Carol Gilligan published an intriguing book, *In A Different Voice*, in which she asserted that men and women may approach moral questions somewhat differently. Subsequently, scholars in a variety of disciplines, including law, have expanded on and radicalized Gilligan's ideas. Gilligan put forth a rather tentative suggestion—since then subjected to empirical criticism for poor methodology, and later limited and softened somewhat by Gilligan herself—that there may be more than one approach to moral reasoning, and that women may be more inclined than men toward a situational "ethic of care" rather than the use of abstract moral principles. Without further research, many radical scholars have used Gilligan to argue that women have an entire world view that differs substantially from that of men and that is in some sense generally inaccessible to men. Minority scholars, drawing on the feminist literature, have argued that there is also a distinctive "voice of color."[34]

The radical claim is more than that life experiences—or even genes—may have a subtle effect on beliefs, attitudes, or approaches. (Indeed, one of us has previously defended that moderate view.) The claim is that some people can know things that others readily cannot. Yale law professor Stephen Carter describes, and criticizes, the radical view: radical multiculturalism "proposes . . . that writers who are white and writers who are not are at opposite ends of an unbridgeable chasm, that their experiences of reality diverge so sharply that beyond a certain, limited point, a shared understanding is virtually impossible." Or, as Delgado puts it, when it comes to certain kinds of knowledge, "minority status constitutes virtually a presumption of expertise." Another radical suggests that male scholars should reconsider the legitimacy of their scholarship on feminist topics if feminist women disagree with them. The radicals, in keeping with their view that objectivity is impossible and claims to objectivity are merely power plays in disguise, argue that knowledge itself depends on the race or gender of the knower.[35]

Because the scholarship of women and people of color reflects their distinctive knowledge, the radical multiculturalists argue, it cannot be judged or tested by traditional standards. Instead, they imply, it should be judged according to its political effect: it should be judged "in terms of its ability to advance the interests of the outsider community," because "outsider scholarship is often aimed not at understanding the law, but at changing it." Eskridge defends a reconceptualization of scholarship as "community-building."[36] Knowledge and power are thus conflated.

The view that knowledge is subjective also affects the methods by which it can or should be communicated. For the radical multiculturalists, knowledge is communicated not so much by dispassionate reasoning as by telling stories that inspire faith. Narratives are powerful means for both creating and destroying mindset. The dominant majority tells "stories" about the world, which although they are accepted as an accurate depiction of reality, are actually just the myths of the powerful. The radicals thus try to explode the dominant myths or received knowledge, disrupt the established order, shatter complacency, and seduce the reader. The goal of scholarship is transformation; knowledge is communicated with a flash of recognition that resonates with the recipient's experience. (Most of these descriptive terms come from their works.) The focus is on rhetoric rather than logic; indeed, rhetoric, according to one radical multiculturalist, is "a magical thing" that "transforms things into their opposites" and makes "difficult choices become obvious."[37]

The attack on objectivity also encompasses an attack on the concept of merit. Radical multiculturalists deny that merit standards can ever be fair or objective. They thus reject the possibility that one person could *actually* be a "better A" than another: any statement of the form "x is better than y" is only another way of saying that the dominant power structure prefers x to y. Merit, therefore, can play no role in accounting for the relative positions of different groups in society. Rather, causation runs in the opposite direction: conceptions of merit are invented by the powerful to reinforce their dominant position. What purport to be neutral standards of merit are simply tools of social subordination: "merit is not merely contingent, it is racially biased."[38]

For example, Harvard law professor Duncan Kennedy, a founder of CLS, has expressed "a pervasive skepticism" about current societal standards: "We just don't believe that it is real 'merit' that institutions measure, anywhere in the system." "Judgments of merit," he says, "are inevitably culturally and ideologically contingent." Thus there can be no objective standard of merit applicable to all groups within the society. Fish states unequivocally that "there is no such thing as intrinsic merit." Note that these statements aren't limited to attacks on particular merit standards as erroneous, nor are they limited to academic standards. All standards, everywhere in society, are merely social constructs.[39]

Like other "objective" criteria, moreover, merit standards are created by the powerful to perpetuate their own power: "Any society's elite class will deem what they do well as constitutive of merit, thus assuring that their own positions become even more secure." MacKinnon contends that current standards simply reflect "what white men value about themselves," and another radical feminist describes merit as "defined by white men to reward what white men become." Delgado suggests that standards of merit are merely preferences for favored groups: "Merit is that which I . . . use to judge you, the Other. The criteria I use sound suspiciously like a description of me and the place where I stand." He considers merit standards to be "like white people's affirmative action. . . . A way of keeping their own deficiencies neatly hidden while assuring only people like them get in." Merit, he also says, "is a prominent example" of the "kind of racism evident in facially neutral laws."[40]

Similarly, other radicals argue that current standards are a "gate built by a white male hegemony that requires a password in the white man's voice for passage," and that "cultural bias sets standards for performance in terms of the tendencies, skills, or attributes of white America." "Facially objective and disinterested standards," writes Jerome Culp, a critical race theorist at the Duke Law School, "in fact serve the interests of the white majority." Words such as experienced and qualified are, according to Patricia Williams, "con words, shiny mirrors that work to dazzle the eye."[41]

Again, these claims raise questions about how to conduct evaluations in the absence of some concept of objective merit standards. Most radical multiculturalists tend not to address this question; they condemn the current standards of evaluation but offer no substitute. Delgado, however, has suggested replacing current merit standards with a standard that guarantees racial and gender proportionality. Williams seems to espouse similarly result-driven changes: she proposes that standards should be restructured "for rather than against—to like rather than to dislike—the participation of black people." Duncan Kennedy once proposed that students should be admitted to law school by lottery, with quotas for various groups.[42] These suggestions affirm the fundamental tenet of radical multiculturalism: that all of reality is socially constructed to create and maintain power. The only way to succeed is to demand more power. In the context of academia, power is defined by having a sufficient number of like-minded colleagues to set the so-called objective standards so as to favor one's own mindset. These proposals by Delgado, Williams, and Kennedy are thus strategies for achieving success in a socially constructed world.

If objectivity is a myth, and knowledge and merit are socially constructed, where does that leave those who cling to traditional Enlightenment aspirations? The answer: at some risk of being labeled racists and bigots. Attacking Judge Richard Posner's defense of merit, Culp called him a racist and compared him to "white slaveowners in the antebellum South who were kind to their slaves." Delgado says that "today's most strident meritocrats are the straight-line descendants of the late nineteenth and early twentieth century ones," who were "fascinated by the idea of proving racial differences, particularly ones involving intelligence and cranial capacity." He considers the agenda and arguments of the two generation of meritocrats as "in some respects . . . exactly the same." Fish similarly couples racism and objectivity: "Individualism, fairness, merit—these three words are continually in the mouths of our up-to-date, newly respectable bigots who have learned that they need not put on a white hood or bar access to the ballot box in order to secure their ends."[43]

We can now summarize the fundamental tenets of the new radical multiculturalism. If the modern era begins with the European Enlightenment, the postmodern era that captivates the radical multiculturalists begins with its rejection. According to the new radicals, the Enlightenment-inspired ideas that have previously structured our world, especially the legal and academic parts of it, are a fraud perpetrated and perpetuated by white males to consolidate their own power. Those who disagree are not only blind but bigoted. The Enlightenment's goal of an objective and reasoned basis for knowledge, merit, truth, justice, and the like is an impossibility: "objectivity," in the sense of standards of judgment that transcend individual perspectives, does not exist. Reason is just another code word for the views of the privileged. The Enlightenment itself merely replaced one socially constructed view of reality with another, mistaking power for knowledge. There is naught but power.

2

Transforming the Law

*A free society requires some confidence in the ability of men to reach
tentative and tolerable adjustments between their competing interests
and to arrive at some common notions of justice which transcend all
partial interests. A consistent pessimism in regard to man's rational
capacity for justice invariably leads to absolutistic political theories; for
they prompt the conviction that only preponderant power can coerce the
various vitalities of a community into a working harmony.*
—REINHOLD NIEBUHR

Radical multiculturalism may have spread from one university
department to another, but it took on a different character once
it left the humanities departments and reached the law schools,
where the cloistered world of the academy meets the world of law
and coercion.

In the rest of the university, the direct effects of radical multiculturalism are mostly internal to the academy, for better or worse. Perhaps literary multiculturalism results in fewer students taking Shake-
speare classes, or offers interpretations of classical literature that
offend traditionalists, or overglorifies some works by women or minorities. In the long run, the result might be a significant cultural
change.

But legal multiculturalists want to change the law immediately—to censor some forms of speech, to expand legal protections for minority groups, and to revamp affirmative action—legal changes that would have a substantial and direct effect on our entire society. Legal multiculturalists (like legal scholars generally) may lack some of the sophistication of the best theorists in other disciplines, but they make up for it with a potential for more immediate practical effect. If literary theorists, historians, and philosophers are like theoretical physicists, then the radical multiculturalists in law are the equivalent of the engineers who convert scientific theory into operating machinery.

In chapter 1, we attempted to locate the views of the legal multiculturalists in the culture wars within the modern academy. As we have seen, they have allied themselves with fundamental challenges to such basic concepts as truth, objectivity, and merit, which they portray as devices for racial and sexual domination. In this chapter, we focus instead on the legal dimension of their scholarship. Our goal is to show how the generalities of radical multiculturalism translate into legal insights. We begin by showing how radical multiculturalism solves a basic problem posed by critical legal studies (CLS) about the nature of the legal system. We then consider the application of radical multiculturalist theory to specific legal issues such as free speech and discrimination.

As we will see, various pieces of multiculturalist legal thinking fit nicely together. The indeterminacy thesis holds that the conscious process of legal reasoning is not really what accounts for a judge's decisions. Since judicial decisions are nevertheless often predictable, we are left with the question of what supplies this predictability or determinacy. The radical multiculturalist view of the world points to an answer: despite an appearance of rationality, law is actually driven by unconscious mindsets or tacit understandings. Because these understandings are below the level of consciousness, they are initially learned—and can later be changed—through images and stories rather than through rational arguments. Thus the radicals favor storytelling by the oppressed over more traditional forms of argument for change. For the same reasons, they advocate government suppression of oppressive "stories" such as hate speech and pornography. In support of these measures, they have argued for fundamental reconceptualizations of both free speech law and discrimination law.

After considering the legal implications of radical multiculturalism we turn to a broader issue. Radical multiculturalist legal theories draw on a theme of opposition to the world view of the Enlightenment tradition. That tradition is the basis of conventional scholarship and the foundation of important parts of the legal system, such as the first amendment's protection of free speech. In the final portion of this chapter, we consider the problem of how to conduct a useful debate across this great intellectual divide.

Indeterminacy and Persuasion

Of all the aspects of CLS, perhaps none gave rise to as much dispute as the indeterminacy thesis. The conventional view of legal reasoning is that a lawyer can persuade a judge to rule in her favor through the use of valid legal arguments drawing upon authoritative legal texts such as precedents and statutes. It is this picture of persuasion that the indeterminacy thesis challenges. In simple terms, the indeterminacy thesis holds that "legal reasoning does not provide concrete, real answers to particular legal or social problems." Instead, "the ultimate basis for a decision is a social and political judgment incorporating a variety of factors." In short, the judge's decision "is not based on, or determined by, legal reasoning." Obviously, lawyers do use legal arguments, but the indeterminacy thesis holds that these arguments lack the power to compel a particular conclusion.[1]

If these flaws in legal reasoning are ubiquitous, legal reasoning as a whole lacks logical force. In the jurisprudential equivalent of Newton's law of motion, every legal argument is matched by a logically equal and opposite legal argument. If the indeterminacy thesis is correct, then it is unclear how legal arguments ever have any persuasive effect, because all arguments are equally sound.

Yet we know in reality that arguments by lawyers do affect outcomes, which is why lawyers are sometimes paid large amounts of money to make those arguments. Also, sometimes the legal arguments do seem to point to a single conclusion—some cases at least *seem* easy, whether or not this appearance is correct. Not surprisingly, critical legal scholars concede that in fact judges will not find all arguments equally plausible. Sometimes a case seems easy because opposing arguments, while logically valid, are unacceptable to actual judges. Thus, there is a certain degree of determinacy in the operation of the legal system, but it does not derive from the content of legal rules or arguments. What then is the external source that supplies the legal system with predictability?[2]

Critical legal scholars have found it difficult to answer this question. Joseph Singer points to the context of the judicial decision, which includes "the institutional setting (for example, court or legislature), the customs of the community (such as standard business practices), the role of the decisionmaker (judge, legislator, bureaucrat, professor), and the ideology of the decisionmaker." Others speak of stabilizing conventions or cultural values.[3]

These varying formulations suggest an account of how language does its most important work. On the surface, people make assertions and offer arguments, which they then assess in some purportedly rational way. But at a more fundamental level, language bypasses this process of rational consideration; it instead creates the structure or mindset that forms the backdrop for the process society calls rational thinking. In some sense, when language is doing its real work, it proceeds outside of what is considered rational thought.

This view of how language operates in law is intimately related to the radicals' view that objectivity and neutrality are merely shams concealing a dominance game. As Derrick Bell puts it, law is "not a formal mechanism for determining outcomes in a neutral fashion— as traditional legal scholars maintain—but is rather a ramshackle ad hoc affair whose ill-fitting joints are soldered together by suspect rhetorical gestures, leaps of illogic, and special pleading tricked up as general rules, all in the service of a decidedly partisan agenda that wants to wrap itself in the mantle and majesty of law." Specifically, Bell argues that although courts proclaim a veneer of high principle, judges rule in favor of black interests only when the interests of whites are thereby served; the ultimate agenda is white self-interest. But the mechanism by which the mindset of racial dominance influences judicial opinions may also be subtler. In her analysis of affirmative action law, Patricia Williams argues that racism "empowers the mere familiarity and comfort of the status quo by labeling that status quo as 'natural.'" "One consequence," she adds, "is that any change will be felt as unnatural and thus as extremely unsettling," so the costs of change "are inflated to terrifying proportions." Hence, even well-intended judges subconsciously steer away from the fundamental legal changes needed to achieve racial justice.[4]

Thus, behind the purportedly objective reasoning deployed by judges and lawmakers, operate mindsets that mold the results. But dominance mindsets like sexism and racism are learned rather than genetic. This view of the legal system suggests two strategies for change. First, what was once learned can later be unlearned through legal storytelling. Second, messages like hate speech and pornography, which transmit these mindsets, can be intercepted before they do their harm. The first of these strategies seeks to transform legal scholarship, and the second would rewrite constitutional doctrines, but both stem from the radicals' view of thought as driven by stories rather than by reasoning.

Storytelling as Legal Scholarship

As Singer points out, the indeterminacy thesis makes the enterprise of persuasion problematic. Singer suggests that stories can provide a method of persuasion that avoids this dilemma.[5] Although Singer discusses the use of stories only in one narrow situation, his comments have considerably broader implications. They suggest that the tacit understandings that determine mindsets may be transmitted through stories. The suggestion seems plausible, particularly if the term "stories" includes narratives, images, and similar types of communication. From the mindset theory of law, it is only a small step to the view that dominance mindsets are created by, and changed through, stories.

This view implies the need for a basic redefinition of legal scholarship. But the issue goes beyond the narrow question of what topics legal academics should study or what should be published in law reviews. It involves fundamental issues about the role of reason in the creation of public policy. Most law review articles are intended as contributions in the quest to identify improvements in the law. Should we assess proposals for legal change on the basis of reasoned argument and empirical data, or on the basis of stories?

Traditional legal scholarship was primarily doctrinal. It attempted to synthesize confusing or complex areas of law, offering harmonizing principles, clarifications, or reform proposals. In the past two decades, this form of scholarship has increasingly been supplemented by interdisciplinary work, often arguing for significant legal reforms. This interdisciplinary work retains the conventional forms of scholarship, familiar to professors of law and other disciplines alike. Most recently, however, a new form of legal scholarship has arisen. Rather than relying solely on legal or interdisciplinary authorities, empirical data, or rigorous analysis, legal scholars have begun to offer stories, often about their own real or imagined experiences. Today one can open a leading law review and find a dialogue between the author and an imaginary radical friend, or a recollection of some incident in the author's past. Often, the story recounts how the author was mistreated because of race, gender, or sexual orientation.[6]

Although few dispute that these stories are more readable than typical law review fare, the consensus about their value stops there. Advocates of storytelling believe that stories can play a fundamental role in advancing social reform. Only through stories, they contend, can society's essentially racist, sexist, and homophobic structures be confronted and changed. Critics, including ourselves, have raised concerns about the storytelling movement. In particular, critics have been concerned about the risk that stories can distort legal debate, particularly if those stories are atypical, inaccurate, or incomplete. The critics have called for greater care and rigor in the use of narratives within the framework of scholarly analysis.[7] In turn, storytelling advocates have argued that these criticisms implicitly posit the very conceptual framework that stories are designed to challenge.

The new storytellers believe that stories have a persuasive power that transcends rational argument. Indeed, one of the standard claims about stories is that "there are some things that just cannot be said by using the legal voice," but only by telling stories. Outsider stories recount the experiences of those who have "seen and felt the falsity of the liberal promise." Storytelling is also described as psychic therapy. Descriptions of storytelling often use metaphors of sensory experiences or physical effects, confirming that storytelling exerts its effects outside the level of reason.[8]

Storytelling advocates contrast rational argument with the more emotional power of stories. As critical race scholar Gerald Lopez tells us, "stories and storytelling de-emphasize the logical and resurrect the emotive and intuitive." Feminist narratives, according to Kathryn Abrams at Northwestern Law School, show that there are ways of knowing other than "scientific rationality." Radical feminists—especially those using narrative as a methodology—thus reject the linearity, abstraction, and scientific objectivity of rational argument. Robin

West, for example, questions whether purportedly rational theories
are not instead rooted in emotion. She writes that "images, sometimes articulate, sometimes not, of what it means to be a human
being . . . become the starting point of legal theory," and that those
images derive from such noncognitive experiences as "school yard
fights, armed combat, sports, games," and "the male child's memory
of his mother." All of this should seem quite familiar after chapter 1.
A key tenet of radical multiculturalism is that concepts like reason,
objectivity, truth, and merit pretend to offer neutral principles but
instead embody only the world view of privileged groups. The radicals advocate storytelling as a substitute for (or at least a crucial supplement to) logic and empirical research, the traditional focal points
of scholarship.[9]

The debate among legal scholars about storytelling has focused on
methodology—what techniques may be legitimately used in legal
scholarship, for what purposes, and how these techniques may be
evaluated. But the same view of how language creates mindsets has
substantive implications as well. Not all stories are necessarily benign. Radical multiculturalists have asserted that existing mindsets
like racism and sexism have been created by stories told by dominant
groups; these assertions in turn serve as a basis for demanding government intervention to eliminate these malignant stories. We will
consider two areas of law in which this demand has been made: free
speech, and discrimination law.

Censoring Pornography and Hate Speech

We begin with pornography. Since the early 1980s, a debate has raged
between radical feminists and civil libertarians about the regulation of
pornography. This debate has centered on proposed legislation designed by Catharine MacKinnon and Andrea Dworkin to regulate
pornography as a civil rights violation. Our present concern is less
with the merits of this debate than with how the legislation's supporters view pornography. We will focus on Catharine MacKinnon, who
is unquestionably the leading advocate of this viewpoint in the academy, as well as the single most influential radical feminist theorist.[10]

In MacKinnon's view, pornography plays a central role in the construction of gender inequality. Her view is based on a more general
perspective on language that she shares with the legal storytellers.

Society, she says, is "made of language," and language provides the foundation for oppression. "Social inequality is substantially created and enforced—that is, *done*—through words and images." Subordination is "embodied in meanings and expressed in communications" in which "saying it is doing it." Or, putting it another way, "so-called speech can be an exercise of power which constructs the social reality in which people live, from objectivication to genocide." According to MacKinnon, language is the key to oppression: "Words and images are how people are placed in hierarchies, how social stratification is made to seem inevitable and right, how feelings of inferiority and superiority are engendered, and how indifference to violence against those on the bottom is rationalized and normalized." Subordination is created "through making meanings"; to unmake subordination requires unmaking the meanings. In short, oppression is ultimately constructed through language.[11]

Of the oppressive uses of language, pornography is the most effective, according to MacKinnon. Pornography transmits the inferiority and subordination of women. It is especially potent in creating misogyny because of its connection with sex, which allows it to circumvent the conscious mind and exercise its effects without any awareness of the ideas being transmitted. It is naive, MacKinnon says, to think that "anything other words can do is as powerful as what pornography itself does." Pornography changes people rather than persuading them. It bypasses the brain for the penis, for "an erection is neither a thought nor a feeling, but a behavior." Pornography makes rational discussion of gender impossible: "Try arguing with an orgasm sometime." Because of pornography, "consumers see women as less than human, and even rape them, without being aware that an 'idea' promoting that content, far less a political position in favor of the sexualized inequality of the sexes, is being advanced." To put it another way, pornography is the ultimate exercise in noncognitive storytelling.[12]

Thus, MacKinnon views sexism as a dominance mindset that is inculcated through stories that bypass conscious thought. Like the legal storytellers, she views the creation of societal mindsets as fundamental to social structure, though her focus is on evil rather than benign stories. Because pornography does not operate at the level of reason but at this deeper and more powerful level, she views it as a form of conduct in need of government regulation, rather than as speech deserving first amendment protection. Ultimately, for MacKinnon, pornography does not merely cause sex inequality, it *is* inequality.

Although MacKinnon views pornography as uniquely powerful, she believes that other forms of inequality are also based on societal mindsets created by speech acts. In a brief she coauthored in a Canadian hate speech case, she argued that "stereotyping and stigmatization of historically disadvantaged groups through group hate propaganda shape their social image and reputation, which controls their access to opportunities more powerfully than their individual abilities ever do." In short, "hate speech and pornography do the same thing: enact the abuse." Both kinds of "stories" create subordination, though MacKinnon thinks that pornography is more powerful because of its connection with sexual arousal.[13]

Other radical multiculturalists have focused their attention on racist speech rather than pornography. One distinctive tenet of critical race theory has been its advocacy of the suppression of hate speech. Critical race theorists contend that systems of oppression are inseparable from these verbal acts: "We do not separate cross burning from police brutality nor epithets from infant mortality rates. We believe there are systems of culture, of privilege, and of power that intertwine in complex ways to tell a sad and continuing story of inside/outsider." This argument, like MacKinnon's, views hate speech as fundamental to creating subordination. Or, to put it another way, "racist speech constructs the social reality that constrains the liberty of nonwhites because of their race." By providing unconscious cues, hate speech subtly distorts thinking and behavior.[14]

The evil effects of hate speech have nothing to do with rational persuasion. Hate speech produces physiological shock reactions in its victims, subtly distorting their views of their worlds and themselves. Nor can its malignant effects on the white majority be countered through the marketplace of ideas, for (like pornography) it does not operate at the level of conscious reason. Instead, "like a computer virus," it alters our programming without our knowledge: it is "an epidemic that distorts the marketplace of ideas and renders it dysfunctional."[15]

Among the invidious effects of hate speech is that it shapes the results of legal reasoning. For instance, the "all deliberate speed" mandate for desegregation may have "relied on some assumptions that were significant in the dominant racist ideology" as reasons for avoiding immediate integration. Again, as with the indeterminacy thesis, the focus is on the role of dominance mindsets, rather than logic, in shaping judicial decisions.[16]

Hate speech and hard-core pornography are nasty stuff, and radical multiculturalists are not the first to argue for legal controls. But radical multiculturalism shifts the terms of the debate in three ways. First, according to radical multiculturalism, these forms of speech are not simply painful symptoms of racism and sexism but indeed the fountainheads of all the evils of racism and sexism. So banning these forms of speech is not merely advisable but a high priority.

Second—fortunately enough—banning these kinds of speech is also costless in the sense of requiring no important trade-offs. We need not worry that censorship will eliminate works of genuine value, because conceptions of literary merit are as bankrupt as other determinations of merit. As MacKinnon puts it, "existing standards of literature, art, science, and politics, examined in a feminist light, are remarkably consonant with pornography's mode, meaning, and message."[17]

Nor do we have to worry about balancing the harm caused by pornography and hate speech against our commitment to free speech. The idea of "freedom of speech" is just another one of those illusions the law uses to rationalize the outcome of cases. Once we deconstruct the idea of free speech, we realize that it is a vacuous concept rather than a genuine concern. To quote the title of a book by Stanley Fish, *There's No Such Thing as Free Speech and It's a Good Thing, Too.*

Radical multiculturalism also eliminates another concern about regulating hate speech. A traditional first amendment argument is that we must be evenhanded. We are not allowed to choose which speech to suppress on the basis of our personal preferences. In short, we supposedly need to regulate on the basis of neutral principles. But radical multiculturalism holds that first amendment rulings never have and never will rest on anything more than personal preferences. (The indeterminacy thesis again.) As Fish tells us, "decisions about what is or is not protected in the realm of expression will rest not on principle or firm doctrine but on the ability of some persons to interpret—recharacterize or rewrite—principle and doctrine in ways that lead to the protection of speech they want heard . . . and the regulation of speech they want silenced." Just because we decide to tolerate the speech of Marxists on the left doesn't mean that we need to allow the speech of neo-Nazis on the right. In other words, if you don't like it, ban it.[18]

Just as left-wing demagoguery need not be treated the same as right-wing demagoguery, we can also transcend neutrality by taking into account the identity of the speaker. As Fish puts it, "discrimination is not a problem in logic but a problem in historical fact, and it is a fact about discrimination that it is usually practiced by the powerful at the expense of the relatively powerless." Thus, he says, we should not worry about racist talk by the powerless directed at the more powerful.[19]

Although critical race theorist Mari Matsuda worries about anti-Semitic speech, even by other oppressed groups, Derrick Bell suggests that we need not be overly concerned about Louis Farrakhan's brand of anti-Semitism. To begin with, although "anti-Semitism is a horrible thing, . . . not every negative comment about Jews—even if it is wrong—is anti-Semitic." Anyway, Jewish concern about black anti-Semitism is just scapegoating: "a misguided effort to vent justified fears on black targets of opportunity." Moreover, Farrakhan's harsh rhetoric should not be condemned by other blacks. Although his statements are "bold, impolitic, and sometimes outrageous," this is only because "they are intended for those blacks whose perilous condition places them beyond the courteous, the politic, even the civilities of racial and religious tolerance." These blacks need to hear their rage articulated, and they need "reassurance that others, not they, are the cause of the wretched circumstances in which they live." Thus, despite some possibly regrettable lapses, Farrakhan deserves support. He performs a vital service: "Using direct, blunt, even abrasive language, he forthrightly charges with evil those who do evil under the racial structure that protects them and persecutes us, that uplifts them regardless of merit and downgrades us regardless of worth."[20]

In short, there is hate speech, and then again there is speech that is merely hateful, and those who have learned to transcend neutral principles know how to tell the difference. Similarly, MacKinnon wants to ban pornography that reinforces male dominance, but not equally erotic material that furthers feminist views of sexuality. This abandonment of the idea of neutrality may be the most significant innovation in radical multiculturalist arguments for regulating speech.[21]

The fundamental argument for neutrality is that we have to hear both sides to decide what to believe. But mindset theory says that the two sides are not symmetrical: one reinforces oppressive mindsets and the other does not. Speech is no different from any other product; the government should ban harmful speech and promote healthful speech. What gets lost is the notion that we should use our own reason to determine which idea to accept.

In contrast, many of the most eloquent opponents of hate speech regulations view reasoned deliberation as more central than the use of language for emotional effect. Robert Post, for example, grounds his regretful rejection of most university hate speech regulations on a view of democracy that begins with the concept of "public reason." Feminist Carlin Meyer's impassioned denunciation of the antipornography movement ends with a call to analyze and reform sexist ideology rather than to ban sexist images. New York University law professor and longtime ACLU activist Burt Neuborne opposes attempts to ban campus speech that causes "bruised emotions, even rage or anguish" unless the speech also causes "a demonstrable, tangible adverse effect on academic performance." All these scholars endorse a view of language and thought that elevates the rational aspects of language over the emotive.[22]

Put in a broader context, the debates over the regulation of hate speech or pornography are in part conflicts over the legitimacy of the "marketplace of ideas" as a justification for the first amendment. This famous metaphor of Justice Oliver Wendell Holmes assumes that ultimately truth will win in a fair contest. Many advocates of hate speech regulations, in contrast, reject the idea that speech persuades by rational argument, and thus have no faith in the marketplace of ideas. The domain of public speech is not a free market, but rather an oligopoly: whoever has control of the most insidious and successfully emotionally manipulative language will prevail, regardless of the "truth" of the ideas.[23]

Discrimination Law

In a thought-provoking article, Georgetown professor and leading critical race scholar Charles Lawrence has made a sustained effort to work out the implications of mindset theory for discrimination law. He begins with an exploration of the formation of mindsets, drawing on psychological theory to explain how hate speech shapes mindsets. He views racism as primarily an unconscious phenomenon. (In support of his description of racism as irrational, he cites studies showing that racists and anti-Semites give hostile responses even when asked about entirely fictitious groups.) Freudian mechanisms such as repression, denial, projection, reaction formation, and reversal are involved in racism. Lawrence also makes use of cognitive psychology, which teaches that social categories are learned early in life through tacit lessons and emotional identification with parents. Thus, racist beliefs take the form of tacit understandings or mindsets rather than conscious beliefs that could be changed through argument.[24]

Not surprisingly, Lawrence finds in mindset theory a strong basis for banning hate speech. He has also made creative use of the theory in rethinking discrimination law. He begins with an innovative reading of *Brown v. Board of Education*, which invalidated segregated schools. Observing that the *Brown* opinion stressed how segregation stigmatized black children, Lawrence contends that precisely this stigma constitutes the direct harm of hate speech to its victims. Thus, in essence, *Brown* was a hate speech case, in which the Court not only allowed but actually *mandated* the suppression of a racist message of inferiority. The real question in the segregation cases was not racial separation as such. Rather, the issue was the messages of inequality communicated by particular forms of separation in a specific historical context.[25]

Lawrence also uses mindset theory to revise the role currently played by the concept of intent in discrimination law. Under current precedent, unless a statute refers to race on its face, it is unconstitutional only if enacted with discriminatory intent. This rule has been sharply criticized by a number of commentators. Lawrence shares these criticisms, but offers his own alternative to the intent test. In his view, the real question is not the legislature's intent but the message carried by a statute—its "cultural meaning." If a statute is understood by the public to invoke notions of racial inequality, then the court should presume racist intent. Such a statute not only has dubious origins, but functions much like hate speech: "Actions that have racial meaning within the culture are also those actions that carry a stigma for which we should have special concern."[26]

Lawrence's work is noteworthy in its creative application of the arguments in the hate speech debate beyond the area of first amendment doctrine. In doing so, he has shown how mindset theory can be used to justify a broader agenda for legal change. It would allow government actions to be struck down whenever a court detected a "racial meaning," even if the drafters of the law never consciously considered (let alone desired) any racial impact. For example, closing a bridge between a white and black community would only be allowed if a judge agreed that closing it was unavoidable, even if the city had made the decision purely on the basis of traffic flows or repair costs, without reference to race.

Radical multiculturalism also casts a different light on another issue in discrimination law, affirmative action. Mainstream scholars typically worry about how to reconcile affirmative action with principles of merit; they resolve the issue in various ways, depending on their perceptions of the urgency of affirmative action and the extent of the sacrifice involved. Radical multiculturalists, however, reject the idea that affirmative action involves any such tradeoffs at all, because they say existing standards of merit are implicitly geared to whites and males.

As Delgado says, radical multiculturalists "envision racial justice quite differently. In their vision, persons of color would not need to resemble successful whites to fit in, but would achieve success without sacrificing what is distinctive about themselves." Instead of affirmative action, Delgado favors "an overhaul of the admissions process and a rethinking of the criteria that make a person a deserving law student and future lawyer." Such a retooling will lead to "a proportionate number of minorities, whites, and women gaining admission." Similarly, Derrick Bell argues that current merit standards "are often irrelevant or of little importance and therefore serve mainly as barriers to most minorities and a great many whites as well."[27]

Thus, the tradeoff between merit and equality that worries many mainstream scholars does not arise for radical multiculturalists. Instead, their major argument against affirmative action is that it doesn't go far enough—rather than using affirmative action to supplement conventional standards so as to ensure diversity, we should abolish the conventional standards entirely, in favor of new standards that will guarantee racial proportionality without the need for affirmative action.

Debating across a Gulf

On one level, the issues that separate traditional law professors from radical multiculturalists are rather narrow—a matter of what role narrative should play in scholarship, or of some adjustments to first amendment doctrine or discrimination law. The debate may seem

heated out of proportion to the scale of the issues, but that heat becomes more understandable as we comprehend the fundamentally
different world views of the two sides.

While the radicals view language as most powerful outside the
realm of reason, many who oppose their proposals celebrate the use
of language as a tool of rational argument. Note that "reason" does
not mean only deductive logic. It also emcompasses ways of thought
that scholars, scientists, judges, and the rest of us use when we deliberate carefully.

The belief in the primacy of reason rather than rhetoric underlies
much of the resistance to both the message and the medium of storytelling. San Diego law professor Larry Alexander, while not addressing storytelling specifically, condemns much recent feminist
and critical race theory scholarship because it "fails the test for rational discourse." Harvard literature professor Henry Louis Gates Jr.
makes an analogous point when he accuses critical race theorists of
replacing "the citizen at the center of the political theory of the Enlightenment" with "the infant at the center of modern depth psychology and its popular therapeutic variants."[28]

Thus, legal scholars today propound two fundamentally contrast-
ing views of how humans react to language. These opposing views, in
turn, have spawned two quite different views of both law and scholarship. According to radical multiculturalists, language is used most
powerfully for subconscious or rhetorical effect; scholars in their
writing and government in its legislation should recognize and respond to this primarily noncognitive aspect of language. For defenders of the Enlightenment, on the other hand, language is (or should
be) primarily a tool for rational argument. Of course, no one disputes
that people have biases or that their thinking may be confined by the
limitations of their cultures. But these failings should be addressed
through argument and critical thinking. For that reason, scholars
who seek to persuade others should rely on rational argument, and
the government—which draws its legitimacy from the consent of the
governed—should not limit the very tool that allows the populace to
reach considered judgments.

Given the gap between these two world views, it is unsurprising
that radical multiculturalists and Enlightenment traditionalists have
been unable to resolve their differences. Indeed, the occasional ran-
cor of the debate is understandable, because each side disputes not

only the claims of the other but also whether the very form of those claims is legitimate.

In this chapter, we have attempted to show how various strands of the radicals' legal theory can be woven together. Each, in its own way, challenges the Enlightenment view of reason and its role in human institutions. The indeterminacy thesis holds that legal rules can provide no footing for logical argument. Hence, the legal system cannot be guided by rational thought; instead, its predictability derives from the unconscious mindsets of lawyers and judges. Legal storytelling seeks to break the hold of these mindsets, not through rational argument but through narrative power. In the realm of constitutional doctrine, this view about mindsets and how they are formed leads to demands for the suppression of malignant "stories" such as hate speech and pornography.

In contrast, the Enlightenment view emphasizes that the legal system can and should rely on the use of reason to resolve disputes, that viewpoints are best changed through reason rather than rhetoric, and that all forms of communication are presumptively immune from government regulation. This Enlightenment confidence in the power of reason is sharply challenged by the radicals, who find it a weak reed on which to rely in law, scholarship, or political discourse.

All of this is, of course, an oversimplification of complicated intellectual terrain. To speak of the Enlightenment tradition is to invoke dozens of major thinkers whose mutual quarrels may nearly equal their agreements. Harvard philosophy professors John Rawls and Robert Nozick are both within the Enlightenment tradition, for example, but their views of government and society are at odds. And radical multiculturalism also contains a diversity of viewpoints, many of them individually complex. Our discussion deliberately ignores these nuances in the interest of providing a usable roadmap to contemporary legal scholarship. We mean our description to be taken as a rough overview of two idealized modes of thought, not as full-blown intellectual history. Still, we believe that this overview provides insight into the intellectual issues at stake in the ongoing debate between radical and mainstream scholars.

If we are right, disputes about constitutional issues such as hate speech or methodological issues such as storytelling often reflect global disagreements about the operation of language and thought. Consequently, attempts at dialogue may often misfire because the disputants share less common ground than they may believe. It is not easy to know how to continue a productive dialogue under these circumstances. Of course, it is fairly easy for each side, operating in the safety of its own intellectual framework, to attack the other. We believe, however, that the community of scholars should not readily abandon the idea of productive debate between opposing viewpoints. How, then, might one proceed in the face of such a deep intellectual divide?

One possibility would be to debate the truth of the radical multiculturalist ideas. The problem, of course, is that the two sides espouse different theories of truth and commitments to different forms of persuasion. It is the very concept of "truth" that is in dispute.

We have decided instead to take a different tack. Rather than asking whether radical multiculturalism is good philosophical theory, we prefer to ask whether it is wise politics. We don't mean politics in the sense of political parties, or even in the broader "Left versus Right" sense, but rather in the broadest sense of seeking the best way of life for a community. In agreeing to debate whether radical multiculturalism provides a viable political vision, rather than whether it is true, we are in effect agreeing to fight on the radicals' own terms—perhaps at the risk of taking on some of their characteristics ourselves.

Although framing the debate in the radicals' own terms involves certain risks, it seems more useful than framing it in terms of a concept of truth that they reject. If we shared no political values with the radical multiculturalists, this would be an equally pointless inquiry. But in fact we believe that we do share some premises with them, or at least with many of their sympathizers. In particular, we will base our discussion in the next three chapters on the following three premises:

- A valid conception of equality should condemn racism not only against blacks and Hispanics but also against Asians and Jews.
- Advocates of equality need to be able to engage in constructive discussions with each other and to contribute to public discourse in society at large.
- In order to learn from experience, society should aim for the fullest possible understanding of the past, free from overt political pressures, and should reject any standard for truth that allows suppression of the memory of genuine suffering.

These are aspirations that we believe are widely shared across the ideological spectrum.

What these premises amount to is a modest vision of some of the requirements of a democratic society. We will argue that radical multiculturalism, when closely inspected, is inconsistent with this vision. Of course, if our opponents (or our readers) turn out not to share these premises, or to interpret them in a way widely at variance from ours, our arguments won't get past step one. If so, however, we will at least have learned something useful (if frightening) about the tenuous hold of democratic ideas in our society. We believe, however, that these premises do command a broad consensus. In the next chapter, we begin our analysis by showing how the radical view of merit contradicts the first of our premises because of its anti-Semitic and anti-Asian implications.

3

Is the Critique of Merit Anti-Semitic?

Anti-Semitism sometimes changes its name, but never its story.
—ALAIN FINKIELKRAUT

Radical multiculturalists accuse meritocrats of basing their arguments "implicitly and explicitly, on racial superiority and xenophobia." They have it exactly backwards. The concept of objective merit provides a way out of regimes—like the Jim Crow South—that allocate benefits on the basis of race or other irrelevant characteristics. The radical critique of merit, on the other hand, points us back toward the dark ages of anti-Semitism.[1]

In this chapter, we consider whether radical multiculturalism can provide a viable conception of equality. We argue that after jettisoning the concept of merit, the radicals are left with a reductionist conception of equality, in which having more than the average is almost automatically to be an oppressor, and having less is to be oppressed. But this reductionist vision of equality is unacceptable. In particular, we suggest that the radical attack on merit inevitably has racist and anti-Semitic implications. The anti-Semitism inherent in radical multiculturalism, moreover, is not an accident, but a predictable component of any assault on the Enlightenment tradition. If we are right, that is reason enough to reject radical multiculturalism.

After fleshing out the radical critique of merit, we turn to the impact of that critique on Jews and on Asian Americans. Because Jews have fared so well under meritocratic regimes, they pose a problem for the radical condemnation of meritocracies. Indeed, we will suggest that if they stick to their theories, the radicals cannot avail themselves of *any* benign explanations for Jewish and Asian success. Instead, they will ultimately be forced to resort to modern versions of ancient anti-Semitic or racist myths. We conclude, finally, that the distressing implications of radical multiculturalism should not be surprising: to the extent that the radicals reject the traditions of the Enlightenment, they invite the recurrence of pre-Enlightenment evils.

Debating Merit

We begin with their critique of merit. Recall that the radicals argue that merit does not exist, so it can play no role in accounting for the success of individuals or groups. Indeed, rather than viewing success as a consequence of merit, they view merit as a consequence of success: the powerful define standards of merit to reinforce their own dominance. Where might such a belief lead?

We should note first that we do not claim that *current* standards of merit are ideal, or even completely objective and apolitical. We agree that merit is a slippery concept, and that it can be and has been abused in the service of racism and other ugly views. Sometimes an obsession with paper credentials, even where they are not truly relevant, supplants more reliable indicators of merit like actual performance.

In fact, we agree with some of the criticism of our own profession's merit standards. Law schools rely on certain paper credentials in hiring beginning teachers. These credentials are designed to predict performance in advance: unlike graduate students in most other disciplines, who have had some experience in both teaching and scholarship before they join a faculty, most beginning law teachers have had neither. So law faculty hiring depends heavily on such things as law school grades, participation on law review, and prestigious judicial clerkships. Unlike the radicals, we believe that these predictors are probably quite useful at this stage, although their value is always open for discussion. We do agree with the radicals that at later stages of a law teaching career—such as decisions regarding tenure, promotion, or lateral hiring—there should be less obsession with paper credentials and more focus on what the candidate has actually done so far. Too often, faculties may identify potential law teachers early in their student careers and then subject them to little further screening. But whatever is wrong with current standards of merit, we don't believe that it stems from racism or sexism.

Merit is also notoriously hard to measure, even when we carefully limit it to performance within a narrow field: Is a good law professor one who writes more articles or teaches more students? Does it matter whether the articles have a lot of footnotes? Where they are published? How often they are cited? Do we care whether the students like the teacher or only whether they learn from her? Should the students primarily be learning legal doctrines, honing their analytic or practical skills, or improving their ethical standards? The same sorts of questions arise in any discussion of merit: Is shooting or rebounding more important in a basketball player? To what extent must technical virtuosity be complemented by passion in a cellist?

Despite these difficulties, we nevertheless can and do make widely shared judgments of merit. Michael Jordan and Yo-yo Ma are where they are because of talent and hard work, not because American sports or European classical music were constructed to favor blacks or Asians.

We can now begin to understand how standards of merit can be in some sense objective. We are, in fact, constantly refining the standards of merit in hopes of making them fairer and more objective. We can thus aspire to a meritocratic society even if we can never quite attain it. The meritocratic ideal is that positions in society should be based on the abilities and achievements of the individual, rather than on characteristics such as family background, race, religion, or wealth. This ideal requires that merit be objective in the sense of being definable without regard to those personal characteristics. John Rawls has described this meritocratic ideal as one of "careers . . . open to talents," a concept that replaced the aristocratic world view.[2]

Under this conventional view, the ultimate conception of merit is color-blind and gender-blind. Its advocates believe that people are treated unjustly and discriminated against "when their merit is assessed according to their status rather than according to the value of their traits or products." Thus, for instance, under this conception of merit, racial discrimination "is irrational and unjust because it denies the individual what is due him or her under the society's agreed standards of merit."[3]

Notice that allegiance to the meritocratic ideal does not preclude support for affirmative action. Only the most dogmatic would say that no factors other than individual merit can ever be considered. Allegiance to meritocratic ideals does not preclude an argument along the following lines: Since racial criteria were used extensively for centuries, leaving some talented individuals unable to compete on their merits, a pure meritocracy may be temporarily inappropriate while the affected groups regain lost ground. Nevertheless, this argument for the necessity of affirmative action still aspires to an eventual meritocracy. Harvard's Randall Kennedy, for example, a firm supporter of affirmative action, is also one of the most outspoken defenders of the traditional conception of merit. He believes that although many sins have been committed against true meritocracy, the proper response is "not to scrap the meritocratic ideal" but to reaffirm it. In Kennedy's view, race consciousness, although sometimes necessary, should not "lose its status as a deviant mode of judging people or the work they produce." The traditional concept of merit is thus not necessarily fatal to progressive goals.[4]

Is the radical critique of merit also compatible with the progressive goal of racial justice? Radical multiculturalists certainly think so. Indeed, they use their theory as a convenient explanation for differing rates of success among racial groups. Denouncing the concept of merit altogether is much more satisfying than simply charging that objective standards of merit are applied in a discriminatory fashion, as unfortunately they sometimes are. Indeed, if the radicals were to rely on garden-variety discrimination ("I don't want any blacks working for me") or disadvantage ("black schoolchildren receive an inferior education because of their poverty"), their complaint would lose most of its sting.

That's partly because many of them concentrate their efforts on the levels of achievement of minority university professors. In universities, changing attitudes and the breadth of affirmative action programs undermine any ordinary claims of ongoing racial discrimination against minorities. For example, a recent study showed that between 20 and 25 percent of new faculty hired by law schools are people of color, and that minority candidates have a much better chance of being hired than do white candidates. Faculty of color are also paid more than whites at some universities—an expected consequence of small supply and great demand. So if some minority professors achieve less success than they would like, it's hard to blame the problem on a climate of discrimination. The claim that "merit" is itself racially biased circumvents the problems created by these inconvenient statistics.[5]

Attributing differing success rates to discrimination or disadvantage poses another problem for the radicals. The argument that current discrimination is the cause of differential success rates between blacks and whites rings increasingly hollow. It ignores the rise of the black middle class as discriminatory barriers have been lifted, and it fails to explain why the black underclass has grown despite the partial lifting of those barriers. It also suggests that what blacks—and by extension other disadvantaged groups—need to do is to continue battling discrimination. Far from being radical, this is the course that Thurgood Marshall proposed and nine white men adopted in 1954. The view that blacks suffer primarily when they don't get a fair chance to meet existing standards is a liberal position, not a radical one. Blaming discrimination thus does not justify the drastic legal changes many radicals advocate.[6]

Finding conventional explanations of differing success rates unsatisfactory, the radical multiculturalists change the focus of the inquiry. Unequal success rates, rather than a phenomenon in need of an explanation, are in and of themselves proof of unjust treatment. Why blame the losers for a lack of merit when it is the winners who design and control the game? Rejecting the idea of merit avoids hard questions about the causes of differential success rates, while also allowing the radicals to treat those differences as sufficient justification for remedial action.

But does it work? What happens if we eliminate merit as even a partial explanation of success? What happens is that the success of some racial or ethnic groups becomes extremely problematic. The radical multiculturalists cannot account for the extraordinary success of Jews and Asian Americans, so, as we show in the remainder of this chapter, their theories ultimately have strong anti-Semitic and racist implications. If merit is merely the exercise of group power, then Jewish success becomes the fruit of Jewish power. That way lies madness.

The Radical Multiculturalist Dilemma

There is no doubt that Jews and Asians, considered as groups, have achieved extraordinary success in our society, on average outperforming white gentiles on many measures of success. Income information is difficult to obtain, especially for Jews, who are not considered as a separate group for census purposes. Nevertheless, available figures show that both Jews and Asian Americans earn significantly more on average than white gentiles. In 1970, average Jewish family income was 172 percent of the average American income, average Japanese American family income was 132 percent, and average Chinese American family income was 112 percent. By 1980, American-born Chinese Americans were earning 150 percent of the non-Hispanic white average, with Japanese and Korean American families not far behind. As of that year, unemployment rates for Chinese, Japanese, and Korean Americans were also about half those of the general population, and poverty rates run significantly lower for many Asian American groups. Jews, too, continue to enjoy economic success. In 1982, 23 percent of the wealthiest 400 Americans, and 40 percent of the wealthiest 40, were Jewish, although Jews account for less than three percent of the American population.[7]

Educational attainment has accompanied this economic success. Jews and Asian Americans are disproportionately represented in higher education. In 1982, Jews graduated from college at nearly twice the rate of the general population; in 1990, the percentage of Jews with some college education was almost twice that of the rest of the population. During this period, Asian Americans also completed college at twice the rate of the general population. Americans of Japanese, Chinese, and Korean ancestry make up about one-fifth of the student body at many prestigious universities, although they are less than two percent of the national population. In California in 1986, 33 percent of Asian American high school graduates were eligible to attend Berkeley—the most selective institution in the California state university system—while only 16 percent of white high school graduates were. Although many universities used quotas to limit Jewish students and faculty from the early 1920s through at least the early 1960s, by 1975 Jews "constituted 10 percent of all faculty members but 20 percent of those teaching at elite universities." At Yale University alone, 22 percent of the faculty were Jewish in

1970, despite the fact that no Jew had ever held the rank of professor at Yale until 1946. Internationally, Jews also enjoy intellectual recognition: of the 513 Nobel Prizes awarded since 1901, Jews have won 17 percent, and Jews make up 40 percent of the American Nobel Prize winners in science and economics.[8]

The radical multiculturalists cannot account for this success without attributing it to the exercise of power by Jews and Asian Americans. Consider law school faculties. As Judge Richard Posner has observed, "If any group is overrepresented in law schools, it is not WASPs, but Jews." By 1970, Jews made up 25 percent of the faculties at American laws schools and 38 percent of the faculties at the most prestigious law schools. The figures are comparable today. According to the radicals, however, "faculties distribute political resources (jobs) through a process that is political in fact, if not in name." If this statement is accurate, Jews must have extraordinary influence to be awarded more than a quarter of the jobs while constituting less than 3 percent of the population. Or consider the assertion that merit standards are affirmative action for the dominant group, a method of "keeping their own deficiencies neatly hidden while assuring that only people like them get in." The intended reference was to whites, but at elite law schools one might as well be referring to Jews, which gives the statement a rather chilling overtone.[9]

The question of Jewish success has not gone entirely unnoticed in radical multiculturalist attacks on the concept of merit. As we mentioned in the "Introduction," Derrick Bell has raised questions about Jewish success. His view on the subject deserves careful study.

Bell argues that merit standards in law schools, "bearing little correlation to effective teaching or significant scholarship," create "almost unassailable barriers of class and race." Excluding white ethnics as well as racial minorities, they produce a class of law professors congruent with the "wealthy white men" who have always dominated law schools. He says he finds few if any Irish, Italians, Greeks, or Poles on the Harvard faculty. But the standards apparently do benefit one group, which stubbornly insists on maintaining its current advantage: "There are a substantial number of Jewish professors on the faculty, but despite Harvard's once exclusionary policy toward members of that group many of its more fortunate members do not recognize that rigid adherence to standards that now favor them are any less discriminatory to others." So the standards "favor" Jews at the price of being "discriminatory to others," including not only minorities but some white gentile ethnic groups.

Note that Bell isn't just arguing that standards should be changed in the future in a way that might happen to be less favorable to Jews. Instead, he is saying that current Jewish success is the result of standards that are as unfair to other groups as quotas used to be unfair to Jews. This leaves Jews today in the same untenable position as gentiles who exploited anti-Jewish quotas in the 1920s. Obviously, Jewish success is something of a problem for radical multiculturalists like Bell.[10]

The troublesome implications of the radical critique of merit are not limited to law schools. One liberal historian, adopting some of the premises of radical multiculturalism, criticizes the meritocratic beliefs expressed by Justice Felix Frankfurter in the 1930s. Frankfurter played an influential role in staffing many New Deal agencies, making a point of bringing into government young men whom he considered particularly bright. Historian G. Edward White contends that the premises behind Frankfurter's actions—"the idea of meritocracy" and "the assumption that merit could be objectively determined"—are "vulnerable to the claim of latent cultural bias." In light of this critique, it is somewhat jarring to recall that the beneficiaries of the placement network were disproportionately Jewish. Frankfurter's placement activities have one aura if he was in fact hiring the most talented lawyers, who simply happened to be Jewish. But if this meritocratic ground is invalid, as the radicals suggest, Frankfurter's conduct could look disturbingly like special favoritism for members of his own ethnic group.[11]

No Escape

These two examples of the troubling implications of the radical critique of merit are not flukes. If objective merit is wholly irrelevant, it is difficult to account for Jewish or Asian success. Indeed, the normative underpinnings of radical multiculturalism leave its adherents with no neutral explanations for that success. To see why, let us begin by exploring what is actually the most plausible explanation for Jewish or Asian success: Because these cultures happen to emphasize many of the values that turn out to be needed in modern society—like education and entrepreneurship—they are more likely to succeed in that society. Although it's plausible, this explanation can't get the radicals off the hook. Though there are several benign (that is, not racist or anti-Semitic) readings of this explanation, none are available to the radical multiculturalists, because the radicals deny the possibility of objective merit. The radicals are thus forced either to reject this explanation entirely or to give it a more racist or anti-Semitic interpretation.

One benign reading of this explanation is that certain traits are in fact useful in modern society, and that valuing them is adaptive rather than oppressive. But this reading is unavailable to radical multiculturalists. This reading suggests that Jews, Asians, and white gentiles have a different *but not necessarily oppressive* set of values or standards from some other groups. This interpretation implicitly concedes that standards have legitimate uses and do not function solely as a way of perpetuating existing hierarchies. This idea is directly inconsistent with the radicals' claim that merit standards are constructed to solidify existing power arrangements—that they reflect "what white men value about themselves."[12]

Another benign reading is that the congruence between the standards evilly imposed by the dominant majority and the values innocently adopted by Jews and Asian Americans is simply happenstance. Again, this reading does not rescue the radical multiculturalists. Either white gentiles impose standards of merit to solidify their own power, or they do not. (The possibility that elites actually gain by allowing other groups to succeed is addressed later.) If the elite do construct the standards for their own benefit, then white gentiles might allow Jews and Asians to *succeed*, but they would not allow them to *surpass*. A "gate built by a white male hegemony" is not likely to open wider for Jews and Asians than for members of the dominant culture. If, as critical race theorist Patricia Williams suggests, merit can be structured either to "like" or to "dislike" any particular group, one wonders how it came to be structured to prefer Jews and Asians to white gentiles and why those in power—themselves white and gentile—allowed it to remain so structured. Even if standards of merit are not infinitely malleable, it should be possible for a determined white gentile elite to mold the standards enough to prevent excessive Jewish or Asian success.[13]

Indeed, early in the twentieth century, when existing merit standards were thought to allow too many Jews into elite universities, those universities *did* change the standards of admission, successfully reducing the number of Jewish students. Merit, which had been defined solely in terms of academic performance, came to include "character" and "geographic diversity"; something similar may be happening to Asian Americans today. We can all agree that these policies were and are a betrayal of the ideal of a meritocracy. Unlike the radicals, however, we believe that it is an aberration rather than an inevitability. The radicals cannot explain why, if maintaining established power relationships is part of the fabric of social reality, widespread exclusion of Jews has not continued.[14]

Aside from this difficulty in explaining *why* Jews and Asian Americans succeed if standards of merit are the socially constructed creations of a racist society, the radicals must necessarily condemn Jews and Asians *for* succeeding. For to the extent that Jews and Asians do even better than white gentiles at the merit game, they are that much more implicated in racist values than are others. Radical multiculturalists cannot condemn the values as a racist power play without also assigning blame. Even this purportedly benign explanation of Jewish and Asian success ultimately turns nasty, then, when we remember that the radicals maintain that standards of merit are not only subjective but also racist and sexist. If Jews and Asians are even better at playing the crooked card game than the dealer, Jews and Asians must be even more crooked than he is.

So any way you look at it, radical multiculturalists can't rely on the happenstance of a congruence of values to explain Jewish success. If they want to contend that merit standards are created by the powerful to reinforce their own success, the radicals will have to come up with some other explanation for this success.

The Remaining Explanations

But if the benign explanation of Jewish and Asian success is unavailable to radical multiculturalists, we find only four other possibilities. All four are unacceptably racist or anti-Semitic, and we deal with each in turn.

1. *Jews and Asians succeed because there is a powerful and pervasive conspiracy behind American society.*

There are certainly Americans who believe that there is such a Jewish conspiracy. Jews have been blamed for everything from violence on television to the spread of AIDS. The existence of a powerful Jewish

conspiracy would obviously explain why Jews as a group are successful even if success has nothing to do with merit. Indeed, the radical
multiculturalist thesis posits that success is merely the fruit of power,
thus creating a direct linkage between Jews and power. When some
radicals argue that success is the result of the machinations of the
powerful, they come perilously close to endorsing a Jewish conspiracy theory.[15]

But if the existence of a Jewish conspiracy lurks in the background
of the radicals' rhetoric, it is also one of the most ancient anti-Semitic
myths. With roots dating back at least to medieval Christianity, the
Jewish conspiracy theory persisted through the Reformation and into
modernity. Martin Luther, for example, viewed Jews as a menace to
Christianity and as (in the words of one Reformation historian) the
"storm troops of the devil's forces." Luther had little doubt about the
appropriate remedy:

> First, [I advise you] to set fire to their synagogues or schools and to
> bury and cover with dirt whatever will not burn, so that no man will
> ever again see a stone or cinder of them. . . . Secondly, I advise that their
> houses also be razed and destroyed. . . . Instead they might be lodged
> under a roof or in a barn, like the gypsies. . . . Third, I advise that all
> their prayerbooks and Talmudic writings, in which such idolatry, lies,
> cursing and blasphemy are taught, be taken from them. Fourth, I advise
> that their rabbis be forbidden to teach henceforth on pain of loss of life
> and limb.[16]

The Jewish conspiracy theory has spawned such beliefs as the myth
that Jews used the blood of Christian babies in the Passover seder
and that Jews caused the Black Death by poisoning wells. It takes its
most powerful modern form in the fraudulent *Protocols of the Elders of
Zion*, which purports to document a Jewish conspiracy to destroy the
Christian world. Although the Protocols have been thoroughly dis-
credited, and were admitted to be a forgery by their American pub-
lisher, Henry Ford, in 1927, many Americans still believe in them. A
similar pamphlet, *The Secret Relationship Between Blacks and Jews*, has
been assigned recently in a course on African American history at
Wellesley College. *Secret Relationship* alleges that Jews were the primary villains in both the African slave trade and the "brutality against
and enslavement of" Native Americans. Columbus himself was al-
legedly financed by Jewish investors: "The history books appear to

have confused the word *Jews* for the word *jewels*. Queen Isabella's *jewels* had no part in the finance of Columbus's expedition, but her *Jews* did." Whatever is wrong with the world, conspiracy theorists surmise, the Jews caused it.[17]

Similar myths of an Asian conspiracy also abound. Fears of a "yellow peril," an Asian conspiracy to obliterate white civilization, were rampant in the first decades of this century. Even today, Japanese economic success is sometimes attributed to deviousness or a desire to dominate the world. The *Protocols of the Elders of Zion* finds its anti-Asian counterpart in the *Tanaka Memorial.* The *Tanaka Memorial* was a document purportedly presented by Prime Minister Tanaka to Emperor Hirohito in 1927, outlining Japanese plans for world domination. Like the *Protocols*, it was widely accepted as genuine, although it too was fraudulent.[18]

Conspiracy theories are a powerful tool for those who wish to portray themselves as innocent victims of a successful or feared Other. Such theories have been used to justify everything from university quotas on both Jews and Asian Americans to the Holocaust and the forced relocation and internment of Japanese Americans during World War II. Conspiracy theories were also used, with tragic success, to justify increasingly harsh treatment of black slaves in order to prevent slave revolts. While radical multiculturalists surely abhor conspiracy theories and agree that they have no place in academic thought, their reliance on postmodern notions of social constructionism and power unhappily entangle them in support of such theories. And, as we show in chapter 5, their critique of truth deprives them of any firm ground on which to reject such theories.[19]

2. Jews and Asians succeed because they are such good mimics that they can adapt to the structures of any society.

Another conceivable explanation for disproportionately high rates of success among Jews and Asians is that they are chameleons who, with no culture of their own, take on the cultural coloration of the society around them. Indeed, they are so successful at imitating cultural norms that they outperform "authentic" members of the society. The negative aspect of this stereotype is not the purported adaptability of Jews and Asians, which could be considered a positive trait. Rather, it is the specific form of that adaptation, which is described as purely imitative with no creative component. While it is logically possible to argue that Jews and Asians are both creative and imitative, most portrayals of imitators commonly imply a lack of creativity as well. For instance, radicals certainly never argue that Jewish culture ought to be included in a multicultural curriculum, as they should if Jews are more than imitators.[20]

A negative portrayal of Jews as parasitic, unimaginative imitators who succeed on the backs of the truly deserving is typical of anti-Semitism. Historically, Jews have been portrayed as soulless parasites on the surrounding culture. In the mid-nineteenth century, French scholar Ernest Renan claimed that Jews had "no mythology, no epic, no science, no philosophy, no fiction, no plastic arts, no civic life; there is no complexity, nor nuance," and Pierre-Joseph Proudhon, an early French socialist, characterized "the Jew" as "unproductive, . . . an intermediary, always fraudulent and parasitical, who operates in business as in philosophy, by forging, counterfeiting, sharp practices." The composer Richard Wagner similarly portrayed Jews—especially assimilated Jews—as the most heartless of all human beings, lacking passion, soul, music, or poetry. In the early twentieth century, an American anti-Semite belittled Jewish academic success as simply another sign of the "acquisitiveness of the race," describing Jews as "clever, acute, and industrious rather than able in the highest sense." In publications that have now become notorious, the deconstructionist Paul de Man took a similar position during World War II about the contribution of Jews to western literature.[21]

Asians, especially the Japanese, have similarly been described as imitative and without a culture of their own. In 1944, an American missionary with extensive experience in Japan wrote: "The Japanese have lost much irreparably by not having a great art, a great poetry, a great drama, to introduce to the Western world." A U.S. Navy publication of the same era described even premodern Japan as a third-hand culture, adding that the Japanese response to modernity had been "borrowing this and copying that, never inventing, but always adapting western machines, western arms, and western techniques to their own uses." Portrayals of the Japanese as primarily good mimics continued after World War II, and are still occasionally found today. The prevalent stereotype of Asian Americans as technically skilled but without social skills or leadership abilities—as "academically successful but narrow and not well-rounded"—is similarly dismissive of Asian abilities.[22]

Thus, to suggest that Jewish and Asian success is the result of their superior adaptive ability is to attribute to them a clever but ultimately unimportant trait. Copying is a neat trick, but it is in some sense parasitic and does not deserve the same respect as an act of creation. Like the conspiracy explanation, then, this explanation for Jewish success has both an anti-Semitic cast and a long anti-Semitic heritage.

3. *Jews and Asians succeed because the powerful elites allow them to; elites can use this success to assuage their own guilt and responsibility and to corroborate the meritocratic myth in order to quell dissent and rebellion against the meritocracy.*

This explanation places Jews and Asians squarely among the ranks of collaborators. Either Jews are unwitting pawns, too blind to see that they are being used for nefarious purposes, or they are willing to trade self-respect for the filthy lucre handed them by the establishment. They are in some broad respect race-traitors, selling out their fellow victims for a piece of the pie. As one chronicler of anti-Semitism describes it: "Jews are charged with being too successful because they abide all too well by the modern spirit of capitalism, too powerful because they utilize all the tools of leverage in a democracy."[23]

Those who have been too successful are often the target of this type of hatred. Traditional resentment of Jews and other "middleman" groups—including Japanese and Korean Americans—is often greater than resentment against the governments that have forced them into such trades. Indeed, historian Benzion Netanyahu argues that it was resentment of Jewish success—specifically the success of converts to Christianity—that gave birth to the idea of racism: since conversos no longer practiced their religion, their detractors focused instead on "blood purity."[24]

Viewing Jews and Asians as pawns or collaborators is a variant on the conspiracy thesis, except that in this version they are not calling the shots. Thus the widespread myth that Jews participated disproportionately in the American slave trade can also be seen as an allegation that Jews did the white man's dirty work. Again, Jews are not unaccustomed to this allegation: one historian suggests that Jews

often served as "the surrogate symbol of oppressive social forces for
. . . groups such as the Russian peasantry."[25]

Accusations of being in league with the oppressor are not limited
to Jews, of course. Christopher Darden writes that "the most offensive thing" one black could say to another is that he is "being used by
the man," that he is "an Uncle Tom." Being called an Uncle Tom by
another black, Darden suggests, is "the equivalent of publicly being
called a nigger by a white lawyer." Recent attacks on black conservative Shelby Steele condemn him as "a traitor to his race," who benefits "by ratifying the social prejudices of the wealthy and powerful."
One black gang leader explained why he and his friends ostracize
successful or ambitious black students: "Everyone knows they're trying to be white, get ahead in the white man's world. In a way, that's a
little bit of disrespect to the rest of us." It is, it seems, much worse to
be successful if you are not white and gentile; it is worse to be a traitor than to be merely an enemy. And, indeed, minority groups may
sometimes use charges of collaboration with the dominant majority
as a method of pressuring members not to succeed. There is even a
special form of hate speech consisting of derogatory names for people who are "white on the inside" but another color on the outside.
To suggest that Jews or Asian Americans are being used by the white
gentile majority for its own purposes is to condemn them.[26]

4. *Jews and Asians succeed because American culture embodies Jewish or Asian values.*

Given that the radical multiculturalists condemn American culture as
a racist, sexist creation of the powerful, this explanation for Jewish
and Asian success also has a distinctly bitter flavor. Blaming Jews for
the evils of mainstream culture has a long historical pedigree. The
rise of both capitalism and communism has been blamed on Jews. In
the early twentieth century, Germans and Austrians—in countries
where anti-Semitism had always flourished and would soon explode—lamented the "judaisation" of German and Austrian culture.
American universities blamed Jews for dampening their intellectual
atmosphere in the 1920s. Not surprisingly, given the role of Jews in
influential institutions such as universities and the media, the same
charges have been made about contemporary American culture.

Given their growing success, we can expect to hear similar charges against Asians.[27]

Attributing societal problems to despised minorities is a common technique. In the nineteenth century, Chinese immigrants were sometimes accused of threatening to destroy the American working class and its culture. Blacks have been blamed for causing cultural decay by introducing other Americans to everything from crime and drugs to family breakdown. Gays are charged with destroying family values. Like the other explanations, then, this theory portrays Jews negatively, and resembles the racist arguments that have been traditionally used against Jews and other minorities.

Suggesting that the fundamental "Jewishness" of American culture explains Jewish success also creates more questions than it answers. Since Jews constitute less than 3 percent of the population, how did Jewish culture become so dominant in American society? Either Jewish culture happened to have features that were superior in some ways to the majority culture, or Jews insidiously remade that culture in their own image. The former explanation conflicts with the radicals' denial of independent standards of merit and their embrace of multiculturalism. The latter explanation collapses back into the conspiracy theory of Jewish success. If anything, these explanations are even less tenable as applied to Asian Americans.

A Fallback Position?

Radical multiculturalists might try to escape the implications of their critique by modifying it. The trouble seems to come primarily from the assertion that standards of merit are the offspring of racism and sexism. Suppose the radicals were to move to the more moderate position that the standards are merely arbitrary. (This thesis is one reading of Foucault's work, although the legal theorists we are focusing on tend not to adopt it.) This modification might allow them to make an argument that avoids the charges of anti-Semitism and racism: Jews and Asians have merely had the good luck to profit from these arbitrary rules. So far, so good. The trouble is that this theory also eliminates any basis for criticizing how the standards apply to blacks and other minorities, who are by the same token merely suffering from bad luck. The arbitrary rules could just as easily have favored them rather than the Jews and Asians; things just didn't happen to turn out that way. Radical multiculturalism doesn't supply any basis for criticizing such a situation. To see why, let's assume for a moment that standards of merit *are* arbitrary.

Success often includes an element of luck, and by positing arbitrary standards the radicals would suggest that group success is entirely luck. In that case, however, merit standards are fair and objective: whoever draws the right cards wins, and everyone has had an equal chance to draw. Unlike chess, no one can control his own opportunity to win, but neither can he decrease another's chances. The random rules may be inefficient, but they are not unfair. The radicals cannot escape this dilemma by arguing that some groups don't have an equal chance to win. If someone is holding one group back, we would call that discrimination. But radical multiculturalists don't want to allege mere discrimination—and anyway, we have rules (and enforcement mechanisms) against that kind of discrimination. No radical reformulation of the legal system is necessary if discrimination is the main obstacle to success.

The problem is that it is hard to condemn an outcome as inequitable if it is merely the arbitrary result of a game that isn't rigged. Suppose that some group—let us say, gentiles—complains that current standards are providing disproportionate success to Jews, thereby depriving their own group of wealth or power. What responses are available to this complaint if the standards are random or arbitrary?

One response—the one most congenial to those who believe that such concepts as justice can have no objective meaning—is that no standard is better or worse than any other. If so, the disproportionate success rate is not an argument *against* current standards. Of course, there is also no argument *in favor of* keeping current standards, and force becomes the only arbiter. Unless they can appeal to some standard of justice, all the radicals can do is to say that they personally don't like a particular outcome. But since the dominant society apparently *does* like the outcome—and by definition has more power than its opponents—this is a losing argument.

So the radicals must invoke notions of fairness and justice, despite their denial that such concepts have any objective meaning. But even that won't help them. Continue to assume, with the radicals, that fairness is unrelated to the standard of merit itself, since the latter is random. They will have to define fairness in a way that doesn't incorporate merit. That turns out to be very hard to do. Conventionally, we define a rule as fair if it gives everyone what they deserve, what they've earned through merit. The radical multiculturalists cannot resort to this definition.

Perhaps they could define fairness instead in procedural terms: a standard is fair if the complaining group has had an equal chance to participate in its adoption. Maybe such a theory could be made to work. But if there is one thing the radicals hate, it's process-based theories. Such theories, far from being radical, take us back to the liberal jurisprudence of the legal process school; they incorporate the ethics of liberal philosophers like John Rawls, and the constitutional theories of liberals like Stanford's John Hart Ely. Radical multiculturalists have been attacking these sorts of theories since the advent of CLS.[28]

Alternatively, the radicals might define fairness in terms of outcomes: a standard is fair if and only if all groups achieve roughly proportionate success under that standard. This version of the argument, however, implies that it is *prima facie* unfair if any group, such as Jews or Asian Americans, achieves disproportionate success. Hence, anti-Semitic and racist strategies, such as quotas against Jews and Asian Americans, would allocate social resources more fairly. So that approach doesn't work either.

Here is the radicals' dilemma: they cannot explain why it is acceptable for Jews and Asians, but not for white gentiles, to be disproportionately successful, without either endorsing merit-based justifications or abandoning their radical views in favor of liberal process theory.

Anti-Semitism and Attacks on the Enlightenment

It is troubling, but not unprecedented, that one of the pivotal propositions of radical multiculturalism—that merit is constructed to serve the interests of the powerful—has anti-Semitic implications. Radicals have often ended up targeting Jews, whether intentionally or not. Anti-Semitism has served as "a convenient way of attacking the existing order without demanding its total overthrow and without having to offer a comprehensive alternative." The Left has a long and continuing history of anti-Semitism. In particular, blacks have often lashed out at Jews; anti-Semitism "not only allows [blacks] to identify with the white majority but it provides as well a socially acceptable outgroup on whom they might vent their frustrations." As a practical matter, then, it seems difficult for the Left to extricate itself from this, the longest hatred.[29]

But there is also an intellectual linkage between radical multiculturalism and anti-Semitism. Attacks on the Enlightenment, and on the norms and techniques of objective science, have long been associated with anti-Semitism and other prejudices. Eighteenth-century French counter-revolutionaries and German Romantics, condemning the Enlightenment and its fruits, argued that reason was bad because it defeated prejudice. "The most ignorant nation," wrote a German Romantic, "the one with the most prejudices, is often superior." Joseph de Maistre, writing against the French Revolution, explicitly traced the "noxious" influence of Jews to the Enlightenment.[30]

In this century, Nazi theorist Carl Schmitt condemned both liberalism and Marxism, labeling them, in the words of one biographer, as "offshoots of a single and spiritually hollow Enlightenment tradition." Schmitt linked "modern Jewish liberalism" to the Enlightenment, and traced to Jews all of Germany's ills.[31]

Aggressively Christian crusaders, who may or may not be outspokenly anti-Semitic but to whom Jews represent an anathema, have also attacked the Enlightenment. Intellectual historian David Hollinger draws a connection between Christian and radical multiculturalist critics of the Enlightenment. He points to "the recent, increasingly assertive claim of conservative Christians that Kuhn and Foucault and their followers have disproven the objectivity of science and thus have rendered an orthodox version of the biblical episteme cognitively legitimate once again." Thus, defenders of creationism can argue that there is no good reason to privilege Darwin's descriptions of human origins over fundamentalist Protestant ones.[32]

The Enlightenment world view, by contrast, allows and encourages deviation from the Christian orthodoxy. It also directly casts doubt on that orthodoxy. As Hollinger notes, "the simple notion that the Enlightenment diminished the place of Christianity in the West may be banal, but it is also true." Hollinger also points out that the role of Jews in the secularization of America is often overlooked. He documents the contributions made by an influx of "Enlightenment-inspired Jews" to the rise of secularism and the decline in pre-

Enlightenment beliefs: "Jews who managed to find a place for themselves in the public intellectual life of the nation . . . reinforced the most de-Christianized of the perspectives already current among the Anglo-Protestants." This interrelationship between Jews, the Enlightenment, and the decline of Christianity once led T.S. Eliot to contend that "any large number of free-thinking Jews" is "undesirable" in a Christian society.[33]

Jews have been especially committed to Enlightenment beliefs, and thus have been instrumental in secularizing and universalizing American culture. As one commentator wryly puts it, "the 'chosen people' broke their ancient ties and placed their bet on the universal."[34] It is a reciprocal relationship; the Enlightenment focus on intellect and away from pedigree, on achievement rather than biography, on universal rather than local standards of merit, helped open doors that had previously been closed to Jews. To attack that meritocracy necessarily implies that Jewish success is ill-deserved. Viewing merit as being arbitrary or worse deprives successful minority groups—like Jews and Asians—of any way to defend their attainments.

And if merit is socially constructed, it can be socially annihilated. Thomas Keneally tells a story in *Schindler's List* that illustrates this danger. Once, at a Nazi labor camp called Plaszów, a woman named Diana Reiter argued that the foundation of a new barracks needed to be torn out and replaced. Although Reiter was an architectural engineer, she was also a prisoner and a Jew, and the commander of the camp considered it a "first principle that you never listened to a Jewish specialist." He ordered her shot on the spot. His explanation? "The shooting of this Diana Reiter, the cancelling of her Western European diploma, had this practical value . . . that if Miss Diana Reiter could not save herself with all her professional skill, the only chance of the others was prompt and anonymous labor."[35] In hell, it seems, all reality is socially constructed, and merit does not exist.

4

Distorting Public Discourse

> *Reagan was a great communicator because he was a great storyteller. That is why he preferred the Bible's story of creation to Darwin's lineup of fossil charts. That is why he liked prophecies and astrological assurances. . . . The stories about our past were always better than any evidence about it.*
>
> —GARRY WILLS

Obviously, something has gone terribly wrong with the radical multiculturalists' understanding of how merit operates in our society. What is less obvious is how they have gotten so badly off track. Part of the explanation, no doubt, is that radical multiculturalist ideas are in the air. Another part of the explanation, as we saw in chapter 2, is that their rejection of the concept of objective merit provides a particularly simple and powerful argument for increasing minority representation, which they strongly favor.

These factors may explain why some scholars felt an initial attraction to the radical critique of merit, but they don't explain its continuing appeal. After all, the idea that merit is *only* a move in a power game really is not very plausible. Does anyone actually believe that graduate training is irrelevant to being a scientific researcher, or that *C* law students on average would teach advanced courses as well as *A* students, or that a residency at a great teaching hospital adds nothing to a physician's ability to practice medicine? We suspect that radical multiculturalists are perfectly capable of giving sensible answers to such questions, and of realizing that their theory of merit is a bit extreme. Their failure to do so is a clue that something may have gone badly wrong with the way this and other issues have been discussed within the community of radical scholars.

In fact, we believe that the radical multiculturalist perspective has warped discourse within their own community. One major theme of radical multiculturalism is that scholarship, as well as knowledge more generally, is personalized rather than objective. Thus, for example, minority scholars (or at least some of them) are said to write in a unique "voice of color" that makes their race part of their scholarship. Radical multiculturalists also celebrate storytelling as a form of scholarship. They embrace the retelling of personal experiences as an integral part of scholarship, viewing stories as at least equal partners with traditional scholarship. These views of scholarship make it much harder to draw a line between the scholar and the writings; indeed, they are intended to blur that line. But one consequence is to hinder debate among radical scholars themselves, let alone constructive dialogue between them and the mainstream. In addition, the storytelling technique itself poses considerable risks. Although under the right circumstances it can add an important level of concreteness to legal scholarship, unless used carefully and checked rigorously by other methods of scholarship, storytelling makes it easy for scholars to avoid critical examination of their ideas by themselves or others.

As we will see, radical multiculturalist discourse discourages fruitful debate in several ways while at the same time making it easier for these scholars comfortably to reaffirm their preconceptions. First, the stress of legal storytelling on personal experience means that the often atypical experiences of law professors—and those with whom they have the most contact, lawyers and litigants—take center stage. As we show in the next section of this chapter, this atypically has badly distorted the debate on merit. Second, after typicality has been rejected as a standard, it tends to be replaced by demands for authenticity. The question of authenticity turns into a struggle over group definition, as scholars quarrel over who has the true authority to speak on behalf of women, gays, or people of color. Third, unlike conventional arguments, stories don't have straightforward conclusions—they can be read in many different ways. This makes it hard to argue with a story; it also means that discussions of a story can easily get sidetracked into bitter disputes about the legitimacy or illegitimacy of different interpretations. Finally, stories lend themselves to several conversation-stopping moves. Attempts to dispute stories and their implications almost inevitably turn *ad hominem*—because the storyteller is inextricably part of the story—and the argument becomes brutally personal and angry. Each side accuses the other of silencing it or of ignoring the voice of the true victim or of assuming the mantle of the oppressor. No wonder that discourse within this community has failed so badly at weeding out false and even destructive ideas.

In this chapter, we explore each of these pitfalls of radical multiculturalist discourse in turn. The individual scholars who are now aligned with radical multiculturalism have the potential to contribute to a vigorous, forward-moving debate about issues of race and gender. The issues about which they write—discrimination, affirmative action, hate speech, sexual harassment, rape—have much more than a narrow academic significance. Whether their methods deserve academic recognition is less important than whether the methods improve or degrade our society's ability to address these issues. Our fear is that legal storytelling, and the allied notion that some women or minority scholars possess a unique "voice," will only weaken or disrupt public discourse about these critical social issues.

Of course, radical scholars are far from being the only, or even the main, threat to public discourse. Manipulative advertising, irresponsible talk shows, demagogic politicians, and the like also contribute to its degradation.[1] But the world of scholarship has always sought to present a contrast of reasoned discourse, aspiring to provide a reality check against the excesses of political debate. Experiential scholarship abandons that reality check, to the detriment of society as a whole.

We begin by showing how the storytelling mode has contributed to the radicals' embrace of an untenable theory about merit. Essentially, the storytellers fail to ask whether their stories are typical of the larger universe of law school or university hiring. We then show how stories, and other scholarship purportedly reflecting a group's special voice, can frustrate dialogue even among the radical multiculturalists themselves. Radical multiculturalists can also fail to maintain a dialogue with the mainstream because of claims that only they have access to unique modes of understanding. This short circuits any need to reply rationally to mainstream views. Stories can also misfire because their purposes are unclear, so further discussion lacks a foundation. Finally, just because stories are personal, they pose a grave risk of turning any further discussion into a donnybrook of mutual accusations and recriminations. In the end, radical multiculturalism provides a poor platform for constructive discussion of pressing social issues.

Telling Stories about Merit

We can begin to see the problems with this mode of scholarship by examining three stories about merit, each written by a leading critical race theorist.

The first story is by Derrick Bell. In 1985, he was invited to write the prestigious Foreword to the *Harvard Law Review*'s annual issue about the Supreme Court. His contribution took the form of a series of stories, one of which is called "The Chronicle of the Devine Gift." In this story, a successful black businessman provides funding to hire highly qualified minority scholars as faculty at a leading law school. The program is highly successful, leading to the hiring of six such scholars. The following year, a seventh recruit is identified. His credentials are impeccable: superb work as a law review editor at a top law school, a Supreme Court clerkship, a fast track to partnership at a major New York law firm. But seven is one too many. While admitting that the candidate may be better qualified than anyone of any race currently on the faculty, the school's dean says that further minority hiring would impair the school's identity as "one of the oldest and finest law schools in the country. It simply would not be the same school with a predominantly minority faculty." So much for the pretense of hiring on the merits.

After recounting these events, the narrator engages in a discussion with Bell himself about the implications. In the course of this conversation, the question arises whether the story is realistic. We are told that most white law teachers would insist otherwise. But Bell rebuffs this suggestion: "The record of minority recruitment is so poor as to constitute a prima facie case that most faculties would reject the seventh candidate."[2]

The second story is told by Patricia Williams. The story itself is very brief, but it is set at the beginning of *The Alchemy of Race and*

Rights and establishes a theme that runs through much of the book.[3] Williams recalls that she was having trouble getting started on her book and began flipping through television channels in search of a stimulus for writing. She hit a news report which grabbed her interest:

> Then I see it. A concise, modular, yet totally engaging item on the "MacNeil/Lehrer News Hour": Harvard Law School cannot find one black woman on the entire planet who is good enough to teach there, because we're all too stupid. (Well, that's not precisely what was said. It was more like they couldn't find anyone smart enough. To be fair, what Associate Dean Louis Kaplow actually said was that Harvard would have to "lower its standards," which of course Harvard simply cannot do.)[4]

The news story proved to be the inspiration she needed: "So now you know: it is this news item, as I sit propped up in bed with my laptop computer balanced on my knees, clad in my robe with the torn fringe of terry bluebells, that finally pushes me over the edge and into the deep rabbit hole of this book."[5]

The third story, by Richard Delgado, is more complex. It provides varying accounts of an unsuccessful law school interview of a minority faculty candidate, as told by white faculty members, the candidate, a militant protester, a judge, and a student leaflet. The "stock" story told by the white faculty is that the candidate was turned down after a lengthy, careful discussion, because he was vague about his research plans, had teaching interests in peripheral areas where the school already had enough faculty, and seemed to lack analytical rigor. This version of the story, Delgado tells us, measures the black candidate through "the prism of preexisting, well-agreed-upon criteria," but fails to consider that merit criteria may "conceal the contingent connection between institutional power and the things rated." In contrast, the militant accuses the faculty of ignoring dozens if not hundreds of qualified black candidates. Another "counterstory" is presented in a leaflet. It points out that every year, the faculty begins by looking for superstars, but they prove unavailable, so the faculty turns to other candidates a "notch or two below." The quality of these fallback candidates is established by personal recommendations from reliable sources. "Persons hired in this fashion are almost always white, male, and straight." So whites have two chances to be hired (through outstanding formal credentials and through the old boys' network), while minority candidates only have one.[6]

In different ways, all of these stories cast doubt on the idea of merit in law school hiring. Bell's story suggests that, at best, merit takes second place to white supremacy in hiring. If Williams is right, either Harvard wasn't really looking very carefully for black women or had defined merit in a way that eliminated them—"none of us are smart enough." Delgado's message really has two levels. At one level, the format he uses to tell the story communicates that although "merit" seems objective, it's really all a matter of perspective. There are many ways of telling the story, and no reason to privilege the dominant society's version. At another level, he is suggesting that law schools delude themselves when they think their hiring decisions are really based on objective standards, because they end up relying on subjective appraisals by themselves or others whom they trust. All three storytellers make it clear that minority candidates have a tougher time in the hiring process than whites. Their narratives function to reinforce, rather than challenge, the view held by these authors and other outsider scholars about how society makes hiring decisions. Repeat the stories often enough, and it becomes easy to endorse statements about the social construction of merit.

The problem is that the stories are not representative. It is surely not implausible to think that minority candidates generally might fare worse in the hiring process, but it turns out not to be true. The Association of American Law Schools (AALS) has carefully tracked law school recruiting. About half of all new faculty are hired through the association's annual hiring conference. Whites who participate in this process are only about half as likely to end up with faculty positions as are minority participants. Among faculty who are hired outside of the AALS process, the percentage of positions filled by minorities is even higher. Other statistics show that the percentage of black women on law school faculties is much higher than the percentage of black women lawyers. In the face of these statistics, whatever other forms of discrimination may still persist in law schools, it's hard to make the case for a biased hiring process.[7]

The stories nevertheless seem plausible to outsider scholars because, as one astute and sympathetic commentator about legal storytelling put it, they create a flash of recognition among the audience. Based on this resonance with the audience's experiences and intuitions, it is natural to draw conclusions about how the world works. But this is a dangerous way of proceeding, because it plays into a glaring weakness of the human mind: our tendency to assume that vivid or familiar events are typical.

This reliance on atypical examples is not due to any special intellectual failing of the radical multiculturalists, for studies by cognitive psychologists demonstrate that humans tend to over-rely on atypical examples. Because people assume that dramatic or easily remembered events are typical, they often overestimate the likelihood of such events. (For example, although plane travel is actually safer than car travel, many people assume the contrary, partly because plane crashes are so much more dramatic.) Even when they correctly appraise a situation as typical, they assume it is more common than it really is—in other words, people frequently engage in stereotyping. Finally, people are too quick to assume the presence of a pattern from a small number of cases. These are human failings that we can't eliminate, but which are only made worse by the uncritical use of storytelling. Storytelling is all too likely to function as a way by which like-minded people reassure each other that their shared perceptions of local events are representative of the world at large.[8]

Scholarship, Authenticity, and Community

In the traditional view, scholars speak as individuals, and their works stand or fall on the merits of their arguments, without regard to their authorship. In this view of the world, the question of whether an example is typical makes sense, without regard to who offers the example. But radical multiculturalism implies another view of scholarship. In this alternative view, the identity of the author is relevant because members of different groups can speak with distinctive "voices." The critical question then becomes not whether a story is typical in some statistical sense, but whether it is authentic. Does it really capture the distinctive experience of those who belong to the group? In a sense, however, this phrasing does not quite capture the radical multiculturalist view, for it suggests that the role of scholarship is merely to reflect an existing group identity. Instead, radical multiculturalists contend, scholarship at its best engages in the task of community building. As we will see later, this view of scholarship creates great difficulties in terms of debate between members of *different* groups. For the moment, however, we want to focus on the problems it creates for discourse within a *single* group—among critical race theorists or feminist scholars, for example.[9]

The problem of authenticity arises most easily in connection with storytelling. Georgetown law professor William Eskridge illustrates the transformative power of narratives with a series of eloquent narratives about gays in the military. For example, he tells and then retells the story of Perry Watkins, the plaintiff in a well-known case challenging the military's policy on gays. He shows how the facts portrayed in court left out Watkins's flamboyant sexuality and its threat to the military's version of masculinity. Watkins was not just an average service member who happened to chose same-gender sex partners; instead, his lifestyle was a challenge to conventional gender roles and sexual attitudes.[10]

Eskridge tells us that Watkins represents "a prevalent phenomenon." Eskridge's view clearly contemplates that gays share something more than a preference regarding sexual partners; rather, he seems inclined to posit a unified community with a coherent viewpoint. For example, he repeatedly uses the first person plural to refer to himself and all other gays collectively, and he speaks of the core stories told by gays, which suggests that if gays are distinguishable in their experiences, there is still clearly an archetypal gay experience. A recent critic, however, has persuasively argued that Eskridge's stories distort military life and do not reflect the experiences of the average gay or lesbian member of the armed services. She calls the Watkins story "so unrepresentative as to be useless."[11]

What is at stake in this dispute is not purely an empirical matter but also an argument about what it means to be gay. Eskridge sees society's attitudes toward homosexuality as bound up in the basic fabric of gender relations. Gay narratives have the potential to rupture and transform existing social norms. For his critic, however, homosexuality is seemingly a discrete trait, with no necessary implications regarding broader attitudes toward sexual norms or gender roles. The question, then, is which author speaks more on behalf of the group. Whose stories are truly representative of whatever it is that defines the group? Whose stories will be told? Or, to put it another way, what constitutes the group's identity?[12]

One possible answer is that the group's identity is based on a unique culture and world view. The group's viewpoint may or may not be espoused by the average group member, because the force of the dominant culture may lead many, perhaps most, members of the group to suppress their own unique identities. For instance, Jerome Culp says, blacks may put on whiteface, concealing their true selves in order to succeed. To the extent that stories about members of the group resemble those of the dominant narrative, they add nothing to the discussion, and merely replicate existing oppressive norms. As Alex Johnson puts it, the "Voice of Color is about articulating or il-luminating the unique insights that come from the duality inherent in the existence of any person of color who resides in the United States." Moreover, the voice of color must invoke a race-conscious perspective, as opposed to a majoritarian or colorblind one. In this view, the opposite of authenticity is assimilation.[13]

This view poses obvious dangers for the possibility of debate within a group. For to disagree with radical multiculturalists is not merely to be incorrect but to be a traitor or apostate. The risk is illustrated by the furor caused when Randall Kennedy, a black member of the Har-vard law faculty, published a critique of radical theories of legal schol-arship. Efforts were made to dissuade him from publishing the article, and his decision to go ahead was "regarded as a betrayal by many mi-nority professors and some liberal white law professors." After the ar-ticle appeared, efforts were made to exclude Kennedy from profes-sional forums where he could express his views. He was accused of selling out his people to the whites. His motives and sincerity were questioned. One Native American speaker compared him, in an elab-orate story, to an Indian warrior who first reveals the tribe's military weakness to the whites, resulting in a massacre, and then heads off to get a "new job at the school inside the fort." The bitterness of the dis-pute can be witnessed even several years later, when Derrick Bell ac-cused minority critics such as Kennedy of feeding white hatred of mi-nority rebels.[14]

Another victim of this phenomenon is our colleague Jim Chen, who published an article suggesting that some tenets of critical race theory seemed to lead to the rejection of racially mixed marriages. In a special symposium organized by his attackers, they accused him of producing "an attack ad with scholarly pretensions," a "kind of acad-emic mugging," and "not scholarship at all, but rhetorical assault in pseudo-scholarly disguise." One author wrote that Chen's article re-minded him "a great deal of the kind of similar journalism currently practiced by certain far-right magazines." This violent rejection of dissenters is obviously not conducive to open inquiry and discussion of highly charged issues.[15]

Similarly, Catharine MacKinnon has characterized feminist criticism of her pornography theory as a betrayal of women. The vehemence of her attack can only be communicated by reading some of her actual language:

> Why are women lawyers, feminists, siding with the pornographers? To be a lawyer orients you to power, probably sexually as well as in every other way. . . . [W]e were let into this profession on the implicit condition that we would enforce the real rules: women kept out and down, sexual access to women enforced. . . . It keeps the value of the most exceptional women high to keep other women out and down and on their backs with their legs spread.[16]

When prominent feminists such as Betty Friedan and Adrienne Rich opposed her pornography ordinances, she accused them of "fronting for male supremacists" and compared them to the black movement's "Uncle Toms and Oreo cookies." According to MacKinnon, feminists who disagree with her views are "collaborators" because they are "siding with the pornographers." As critics have observed, this is an "astonishing metaphor, conjuring up visions of Vichy France under the Nazis." Presumably, this characterization of other feminists is not meant as an invitation to dialogue: it is best classified as an authoritarian, conversation-ending move.[17]

Indeed, MacKinnon is quite candid about her lack of interest in dialogue. MacKinnon declines to debate feminists of opposing views. She says such debates merely play into "a pimp strategy to hide behind feminist women" in order to legitimize "a slave trade in women." She declares: "I do not need to be sucked into the pornographers' strategy, period." If a woman disagrees with MacKinnon, she is a traitor to the community of women, as defined by MacKinnon.[18]

Like MacKinnon, other commentators also connect group identity with victimhood. For example, Eskridge suggests that the label of homosexuality is socially constructed as a means of oppression. In some sense, then, what all gays may truly have in common is their status as targets of homophobia. A community founded on victimhood poses certain problems. As feminist Harvard law professor Martha Minow has observed, it may divert attention from the political to the therapeutic. Victimhood also has "passive and helpless connotations" that can be disempowering, and can encourage people to define their identities based on single traits. Indeed, Minow observes, the very idea of privileging the victim's perspective "requires a ranking of oppressions that is itself rendered problematic by the asserted authority of subjective experience." Thus, discussion can degenerate into the "victim talk world" where "people exchange testimonials of pain in a contest over who suffered more." Making a similar observation, Henry Louis Gates Jr. wryly suggests that perhaps academics should "institutionalize something that we already do implicitly at conferences on 'minority discourse': award a prize at the end for the panelist, respondent, or contestant most oppressed; at the end of the year, we could have the 'Oppression Emmy' Awards."[19]

This jockeying for victim status, with the concurrent struggle over whose stories can be told, threatens to block discussion altogether. A vivid illustration is provided by a national conference about feminism and the law that was sponsored by *Signs*, the leading feminist journal. At the conference, a white representative of prostituted women argued that prostitution is inevitably involuntary and linked with violence against women. She was criticized by a black woman and a disabled white woman for failing to reflect the varying experiences of prostitutes, some of whom might have found a life of prostitution their best available option. At that point, the prostitution activist "left the roundtable, visibly upset." One of the conference organizers (who was white) left the room to talk with the prostitution activist. She returned with the message that the activist had felt "discounted" and "silenced" and would not be returning. The black woman who had participated in the discussion found these comments accusatory, and the discussion "became clearly polarized into . . . activists versus academics, and a white woman versus a black woman."

In a later session at the same conference, minority women complained about the way that they felt their stories and work were excluded by the white academics who run the leading feminist journals. Then the white conference organizer intervened to criticize the group for "throwing out" the prostitution activist rather than listening to her. Now the minority women felt silenced, because they felt that the issue of minority access to feminist journals had effectively been suppressed. They resented the fact that the white conference organizer "had raised the issue of prostitution just as they had decided to use the short remaining time to discuss racism in publishing."

Understandably, the conference organizers found these developments painful and ironic. The minority organizer felt "frustration at what she experienced as a 'derailment' of race issues by mainly white women." The white organizer "acknowledged that a 'derailment' had occurred but felt nonetheless that most participants and some members of the audience had failed to confront their own investment in maintaining the institution of prostitution." In the end, though unhappy about the experience, the organizers constructively decided to treat it as a learning experience about the need to understand each others' viewpoints, and with commendable candor they published a full account of the dispute.[20]

This was not the first academic conference to come unglued because of disputes among participants. What is noteworthy, however, is how difficult the group found it to maintain a constructive discussion of either prostitution or minority access to feminist journals because of competing claims about whose victimization deserved priority in the discussion, and who was silencing whom. The way the dispute began is especially noteworthy: it started as a challenge to the activist's claim to present the stories of all prostitutes, a claim that was alleged to be an exercise of power on her part. Some might view the conference as a warning about the fragmenting effect of identity politics, but our point is much more mundane: the conference never did lead to a full discussion of the substantive issues. We view this approach to political and legal discourse as most unpromising. If outsider scholars cannot even manage to debate difficult issues among themselves, their ability to contribute to the larger social discourse is surely compromised.

It is little wonder, in the presence of such barriers to candid discussion, that important points go unraised. Imagine that a leftist scholar belonging to an oppressed group had raised the argument we made in the previous chapter, regarding the anti-Semitic and anti-Asian implications of the critique of merit. If the speaker had been black or Hispanic, the endorsement of traditional views of merit would have been received like Randall Kennedy's, as an assimilationist betrayal of group identity. If the speaker were Asian or Jewish, the charge might instead have been that she was favoring the stories of these relatively privileged groups over those of the most truly victimized. In such circumstances, even if the argument had occurred to an "outsider" scholar, she would have done well to keep silent. In such circumstances, who would speak out?

Even if our anti-Semitism argument were invalid, raising it within the community would have provided a chance to anticipate and defuse it. Radical multiculturalists are skeptical about whether anything like a fair marketplace of ideas exists in society at large, but they risk losing the benefits of free debate even among themselves, because conflicts about ideas inevitably risk degenerating into contests about group authenticity or relative victimization. When the message becomes inseparable from the messenger, intellectual disputes tend to turn into civil wars.

So far, we have considered how radical views of scholarship distort or defeat discourse among outsider scholars themselves. One distortion occurs because these scholars, relating their own stories to each other, may erroneously conclude that they fully understand societal structures when the stories in actuality are atypical. Another distortion occurs because storytelling and other forms of scholarship easily become struggles over who speaks for different groups and how those groups are defined. In the process, the substance of the discussion may be lost. The remainder of this chapter is devoted to ways that outsider scholars may fail to contribute to the larger societal debate over public policy.

Stories without Morals

Telling stories can sometimes be an effective way of communicating. It can misfire, however, in the context of public debate simply because of the difficulty of connecting the story to an issue of public policy. Some stories have an obscure connection with any issue of policy; others seem to point to so many different policy questions at once that the impact of the story is lost.

The first problem is illustrated by a much-cited law review article by Marie Ashe. It contains a "torrent of physical detail" about her own reproductive experiences (including graphic descriptions of the births of her children), with some brief and cryptic suggestions about law interspersed among the stories. Even Kathryn Abrams, an astute reader who praises storytelling in general and some aspects of Ashe's piece in particular, notes that "grasping the relation between her narratives and her prescriptions is . . . truly strenuous." In fact Abrams had to read the article three times before she even "began to suspect" that the point of the article was to urge the deregulation of reproduction. Clearly, these stories did little to advance the debate about the regulation of reproduction, since even the most sympathetic reader was hard-pressed to figure out the thesis which the stories were intended to support.[21]

The second problem is illustrated by what is now probably the paradigmatic exercise in legal storytelling, Patricia Williams's well-known Benetton story. (The story's fame may partly be due to the book jacket, where a blurb by Catharine MacKinnon proclaims, "See if you can ever shop at Benetton's again.") In this story, Williams describes how she was refused access to a Benetton store by a teenage clerk when she was trying to buy a sweater for her mother, and how she encountered difficulties in persuading a law review to publish a full account of this episode. Apart perhaps from encouraging readers to take their business to The Limited or The Gap, what is the point of the story?[22]

Radical multiculturalists seem quite confident about the meaning of the story, but their confident readings are at odds. In conversation, a radical feminist colleague of ours vehemently insisted that the Benetton story was a deep critique of the distinction many legal doctrines draw between the public and private spheres. Jerome Culp insists that the point is not the Benetton episode itself, but the difficulties Williams encountered with the law review: "This episode poses difficult question about how we create facts. . . . These and other stories point out how much the configuration of what counts as important, true, and real is a product of assumptions of power over the stories that people tell. We disempower people without power or people with stories that are discomforting to the majority."[23]

One could also see the story as an example of how badly blacks are treated in our society. Alex Johnson offers some readings along these lines. "First and foremost," he says, the story "juxtaposes the issue of formal equality, ostensibly provided by the law, against the practical reality of a society in which race is a powerful historical and currently viable social construct." He then suggests some other possibilities: that the story demonstrates the limits of current civil rights laws, or attacks the state-action doctrine, which limits constitutional protections to discrimination caused by government officials. He adds that the story also illustrates the privileging of white law review editors over authors of color; and, finally, the story "simply could mean that in this society one is never far from one's race, or blackness in this case, and that the law's failure to recognize that represents a travesty and failure of the legal system." Yet Richard Delgado insists that such readings miss the point; the story, he says, "is intended to prompt consideration of a new legal category, namely spirit-murder." Just what *is* the point of the Benetton story?[24]

The point of these stories remains obscure in part because of the paucity of explicit reasoning connecting them to a clear conclusion. Advocates of storytelling disagree about whether such an analytical framework is necessary at all. Mary Coombs and Kathryn Abrams, for example, reject the notion that scholarship must necessarily include some analysis or reasoned arguments. Although Abrams expresses a preference for the kind of "normative elaboration" that she says is rejected by many feminist storytellers, she views that preference as merely a debatable strategic choice. Alex Johnson regrets the traditional stress on reason and analysis in scholarship, which precludes result-oriented criteria for distinguishing good from bad stories. More recently, Richard Delgado has conceded that some kind of reasoned argument is necessary, but suggests that almost all storytellers provide analysis as well as narrative. While this may be true, our review of the storytelling literature indicates a lack of consistency in the strength of the analytical connections between narrative and conclusions. The weaker connections are typified by such well-known examples as Ashe's childbirth and Williams's Benetton stories.[25]

Another advocate of storytelling, Jane Baron, argues that any narrator inevitably uses a form of reasoning in structuring a story, so the distinction between narrative and analysis is false. Perhaps so, but whatever reasoning went into crafting these stories does not seem explicit enough to tell us what conclusion the narrator is asking us to draw, and what grounds we are being given for drawing that conclusion.[26]

The absence of a clear analytic framework can make it difficult for stories to contribute to public debate. If the story has no ascertainable point, it is impossible for anyone to know whether to agree or disagree. Instead, the story merely lies on the table, offering an aesthetic experience like a coffee-table ornament, but fails to move the discussion forward. If we wish as a society to have a conversation about issues of race and gender, unadorned stories may be too ambiguous in their implications to provide a basis for further dialogue. They can thus stall rather than expedite public discourse.

Different Voices, Different Rooms?

Radical multiculturalism further impedes dialogue with the mainstream when its adherents claim to be privy to special means of understanding the world, means that are unavailable to the dominant culture. This makes dialogue difficult. Mainstream criticisms can always be dismissed as demonstrations of the dominant culture's deafness to the special voice of outsiders; regardless of content, mainstream arguments can be dismissed on the basis of their form (too abstract, empiricist, and objectivist). Although not all radical multiculturalists go this far, many do reject conventional methods of reasoning as incurably white male.

Scholars in a variety of disciplines, including law, have suggested that women have a different way of understanding the world from that of men. For example, Lucinda Finley argues that law and legal reasoning reflect a male voice by emphasizing "rationality, abstraction, a preference for statistical and empirical proofs over experiential or anecdotal evidence," and "universal and objective thinking." The feminine voice is also portrayed as more caring and emotional. It is important to note the breadth of these claims. Feminist "different voice" scholars do not suggest simply that women might have a different perspective on issues directly involving gender relations, but rather that women's unique perspective casts a different light on virtually all legal issues.[27]

Similarly, minority scholars are said to have access to a "voice of color," which "rejects narrow evidentiary concepts of relevance and credibility." In the voice of color, Alex Johnson explains, scholars no longer study "facts, theories, heuristics, and paradigms." Instead, "insight is gleaned through doing rather than thinking," as legal issues are taken from books and classrooms and returned to the real world. This change is understandably "frightening to those people unable to live life as well as study it, or at the least, to learn from the life experiences of others." At the same time, the voice of color "puts to rest the notion that society is a meritocracy in which individual achievement is truly prized and awarded."[28]

Radical multiculturalists respond intolerantly to inquiries about the voice of color and its role in legal storytelling, illustrating how the "different voice" thesis impedes discussion. Alex Johnson, for example, sees critique as "destroying any worth of Critical Race Theory as

expressed through Narrative." Such mild suggestions as a requirement that narrative contain legal analysis would be devastating:
"Such claims, if true, have the effect of destroying any promotion,
tenure, or other benefit flowing from a determination of the worth of
such endeavors."[29]

Similarly, Derrick Bell considers mainstream commentary about
critical race theory "a pathetically poor effort to regain a position of
dominance." Echoing Johnson, he says that "many of these critics are
steeped in theory and deathly afraid of experience." They ask for definitions of the voice of color, rather than finding a sufficient proof of
its existence in "centuries of testimony by people of color regarding
their experiences." His hope is that "those doing critical race theory,
when reviewing these critiques, will consider the source. As to a response, a sad smile of sympathy may suffice." And if the critics don't
get the message that's too bad. Bell reminds his audience of Louis
Armstrong's response to the meaning of jazz—"Man, if you don't
know, don't mess with it." For those who might hope for a more substantive response, he says: "These are wonderful retorts precisely because they do not seek to justify."[30]

Responses like Bell's are unlikely to further communication between radical and mainstream scholars. First, of course, as one critic
of critical race theory points out, that kind of racially limited reasoning won't achieve its goal: in order to change current institutions,
"we don't need an argument . . . from a *black* perspective; we need an
argument that works from *all* reasonable perspectives, especially if
we want to convince people who are outside our race and ethnicity."
Moreover, statements like Bell's invite a hostile response. Two former women's studies professors who are critical of the radical feminist movement dismiss similar sentiments as based on a "disinclina-
tion to think hard and work diligently [because] a knowing and
dismissive sneer is obviously far more economical."[31]

The Dangers of Getting Personal

As we have seen, radical multiculturalism often fails in several ways
to contribute to constructive debate, either among the radicals themselves or between the radicals and the mainstream. It encourages reliance on atypical but striking examples, and discourages constructive
criticism by turning issues of substance into contests over commu-

nity definition and authenticity. It inhibits dialogue with the mainstream because stories may lack a clear moral that could be the basis for further discussion, and because mainstream criticisms may be dismissed as just more white male linear thinking, rather than receiving a response on the merits.

First-person stories can provide the greatest challenge in terms of integrating them into public debate. What can one say in response to such a story? "I have not had that experience" is not a counterargument, since the point of the story is to broaden the reader's horizons. "So what?" is essentially a request for analysis, asking the author to link the story to some broader, more readily debatable conclusion, which might then replace the story itself as the basis for further conversation. Worse yet are the questions of whether the story is atypical (which might suggest that the teller is an oddball) or factually incomplete or inaccurate (which might suggest that the teller is a liar).

Indeed, some advocates of storytelling come close to suggesting that silence is the only permissible response to stories. Whites who sympathetically analyze or even recount stories told by people of color are said to be guilty of misappropriating the storyteller's pain. For example, when a white woman at a CLS summer retreat referred to an Inuit woman's story as an example to defend the use of personal experiences, the original storyteller protested: "Did that woman intend to appropriate my pain for her own use, stealing my very existence, as so many other White, well-meaning, middle and upper class feminists have done?"[32]

The problem with personal stories is that, well, they're personal, so it's hard to say anything critical about the story without implicating the storyteller. Recently, Anne Coughlin wrote an article with the intriguing postmodern thesis that first-person storytelling, by using the format of autobiography, necessarily accepts the conventional individualism inherent in the autobiographical form. To demonstrate this thesis, she provided a detailed analysis of several narratives. Her readings are open to criticism—she may have had to stretch in order to classify all of these narratives as autobiographical, and her interpretations were uncharitable. Thus, the consternation of the subjects of her analysis is quite understandable and defensible.[33]

The rhetoric of their responses, however, does not bode well for further dialogue. Jerome Culp reacted by psychoanalyzing Coughlin and other storytelling critics, accusing them of having passed through denial into anger, as one of the standard stages of grief—here, he says, grief over the demise of white hegemony. Their views can be discounted, apparently, as merely one stage in some twelve-step program of recovery from their virulent racism. After rather convincingly critiquing Coughlin's analysis of his own story, Richard Delgado ends by dropping the rhetorical equivalent of a nuclear bomb. He quotes a feminist literary critic who worries that, by applying literary theory to texts by black writers, white feminists replicate a slave owner writing a "ruthlessly reductive" account of the behavior of his slaves. "Despite her professed intentions only to help," Delgado says, "Professor Coughlin strikes me as coming close to replicating the sin of the slave master described so starkly above in her mistaken analysis of the autobiographical efforts of critical race scholars."[34]

It's easy enough to blame this rhetorical explosion on insensitivity and aggressive over-reading on one side, or excessive personal sensitivity on the other. But the reality is that personal storytelling raises an inevitable risk of such confrontations. If there is any germ of truth at the heart of contemporary literary theory, it is that stories are inevitably viewed in ways that the authors did not originally intend. Neither in the academy nor in society at large can we always count on having friendly readers whose understanding will coincide with our own. When dealing with such personal matters, unfavorable interpretations at odds with the author's own perspective cannot be received as anything other than personal attacks, and only the saintly could refrain from responding with an outcry of pain and anger. The problem is that it is almost impossible for the conversation to move forward constructively from this point. Once again, radical multiculturalist scholarship seems to misfire as an element in public discourse, for it does not leave enough room for dialogue.[35]

A Cautionary Tale

Many of the dangers of radical multiculturalist discourse are exemplified by an exchange between two leading critical legal scholars, Mark Tushnet and Gary Peller. The exchange opened with an article by Tushnet discussing the relationship between narrative and the law, including some criticism of work by critical race theorists. In one relatively brief passage, he criticizes a story by Patricia Williams about anti-Semitism. The story recounts her experience as a customer in a store, overhearing anti-Semitic remarks by the clerks. She failed to speak up, feeling a sense of guilty complicity. Tushnet points out that, contrary to her usual practice, Williams does not identify the race of the clerks. Tushnet suggests that the reader might wonder whether they were also black, and if so whether Williams is avoiding a discussion of black anti-Semitism. If they were white, then the story becomes an account of how outsiders on one dimension (race) can be seduced into complicity by the promise of acceptance as insiders on another dimension (religion). In this case, a possible interpretation is that "Williams was and at some level wanted to be complicit in the expressed antisemitism of the salespeople." On this interpretation, the story then deals with "how a vicious community can sustain itself by at least fleetingly securing the affiliation of those who it demeans on other occasions." The problem, Tushnet says, is that as soon as the reader notices the ambiguity, attention to the ambiguity becomes the focal point rather than whatever point Williams actually was trying to make in the story.[36]

Tushnet's article sparked a vehement response by Peller. Admitting no possible ambiguity, Peller finds it clear that "there is simply no reason to conclude that the salespeople were black." Instead, he finds the point of the story obvious—what the story is "all about" is "how participation in the prejudices of the dominant group might serve as a substitute avenue of inclusion for those who are otherwise excluded." Peller then rebukes Tushnet for failing to reveal the fact that he is Jewish, "a social fact of some import in understanding why Tushnet might read her text in such an overreaching manner."[37]

At the end of his commentary, Peller returns to the question of Tushnet's perspective and motivation, seeking to explain what he views as the "sense of hostility and dismissiveness" in Tushnet's work. He offers two factors to explain this "undertone of hostility and disrespect" toward critical race theory and radical feminism. First, the critique of objectivity may cause anxiety because it challenges the hierarchies of intellectual life: "Now that the agenda has begun to consider the social construction of intellectual merit itself, many likely feel threatened." Second, the attack on the idea of a neutral public space is, Peller says, particularly disturbing for Jews because of the "basic cultural compromise that life in America has offered us." Under the terms of the compromise, "we would be permitted our Jewish identity in our private lives," but would accept a supposedly neutral public space (which he says in fact is specifically Protestant, middle class, and white). "Our cultural compromise requires that we suppress that perception of public space"; critical race theory threatens that delicate equilibrium.[38]

Whatever may be said of their applicability to Tushnet, some of Peller's remarks are insightful. It is true that the idea of a neutral public space has had particular importance to Jews, whose contributions to public debate might otherwise be dismissed by the overwhelmingly Christian majority. And as we have already seen, the radical critique of merit poses particularly threatening implications for Jews. But we view these explanations as significant for a different reason from that of Peller—not because they show that Tushnet is speaking in a "Jewish Voice," but because they show how important Enlightenment-based ideas are in creating a society that is open and tolerant toward minorities.

In reply to Peller, Tushnet offers his own explanations for what he views as Peller's unwarranted distortion of his positions. First, Peller's analysis is an example of a white male academic "colonizing" different voice scholarship by integrating it into his own theoretical discourse. Second, Peller's critique is "a contemporary version of a phenomenon common in the history of the white left in this country, having appeared under the heading 'white hipsters' or 'radical chic' at other times." In this syndrome, whites defend positions they attribute to the minority community and then "offer those defenses as evidence to show that the minority communities ought to welcome these white leftists as honorary members." Finally, Tushnet says, Peller's response reflects his own insecurity. Peller's remarks, Tushnet believes, are just what one expects from people "who know (at some level) that their contributions as scholars . . . are not as substantial as they believe (or fantasize) them to have been."[39]

The escalating incivility of this exchange is not the only reason why it deserves close examination. It is also noteworthy because of the identity of the scholars involved. Patricia Williams is one of the most engaging and consistently interesting of the legal storytellers. Mark Tushnet is not only a formative figure in CLS but also one of the leading constitutional scholars of any description. Peller (who has also been associated with CLS) is at the forefront of radical theorists. Their disagreements deserve serious attention.

Perhaps we should begin with the Williams story itself. Like Tushnet, we find the story somewhat ambiguous, though we tend toward Peller's interpretation that the clerks were white. (Interestingly enough, neither of them considers the possibility that the clerks might not all have been of the same race, or that they might have been something other than black or white—Asians and Hispanics seem quite invisible in this setting.) Like Peller, we also find Williams's stance of opposition to anti-Semitism quite unmistakable.

Most tellingly, the Tushnet/Peller exchange shows just how damaging radical multiculturalism is to constructive public discourse. The problem begins with Williams's story. Because it is ambiguous about the race of the clerks, and even more because it fails to provide a reasoned analysis connecting the narrative to a general conclusion, readers are left unclear about the point of the story. It is easy, then, for the debate to be sidetracked into a metadiscussion of what the story means, rather than a discussion of Williams's underlying point. Then, the "different voices" strand of radical multiculturalism rears its ugly head in Peller's attribution of Tushnet's comments to his specifically Jewish perspective. Tushnet then responds by accusing Peller of falsely assuming a black voice. Because the identity of the speakers becomes so inextricable from the content of their messages, a dispute about the reading of a text descends into fratricidal violence between fellow members of the intellectual Left.

Whatever contribution Williams might originally have hoped to make to understanding race and anti-Semitism is completely lost in this postmodern fiasco. Nothing could be better designed than this intellectual fracas to illustrate the way that radical multiculturalism threatens the possibility of useful debate of sensitive issues.

One reason this debate leads nowhere is that radical discourse is so focused on the speakers rather than on the outside world. If Williams's story is "about" anything, it is mostly about her own reaction to a situation, rather than about the situation itself. But Tushnet devotes himself to criticism of her storytelling technique, and he and Peller bludgeon each other with mutual accusations about this literary critique. When the dust has settled, one thing is clear: we have learned nothing about anti-Semitism, black or otherwise. The discussion is not about anti-Semitism, but about reactions to anti-Semitism, and reactions to the reactions, reactions to those reactions, and, in the final stage of the discussion, Tushnet's reaction to Peller's reaction to Tushnet's reaction to Williams's story about her reaction to anti-Semitism.

This difficulty in coming to grips with the outside world should be no surprise. As Peller reminds us, radical multiculturalism "takes as a starting point a rejection of the dominant vision of objectivity and neutrality"; only a formalist, he says, would believe that labeling a story a novel rather than a diary would make any fundamental difference. (Williams subtitled her book, *Diary of a Law Professor.*) In this setting, the whole idea of talking about reality—whether that reality is racism, anti-Semitism, or whatever—becomes problematic. This "problematicizing" of the concept of truth is the subject of our next chapter.[40]

5

The Assault on Truth and Memory

While the other gods feasted, Odin sat and pondered on what Thought and Memory had taught him. When they left him at dawn each morning, he often feared that they would not make their way back. He feared for both, but he admitted that it was for Memory that he feared most.

—GAIL HERIOT

Another chapter in Patricia Williams's *Alchemy of Race and Rights* highlights Peller's denial that there is any difference between a novel and a diary. Williams describes the case of Tawana Brawley, a fifteen-year-old black girl who claimed she was abducted, raped, tortured, and ultimately smeared with feces by a group of white men, including a state district attorney and two police officers. The case became a *cause célèbre* among certain black activists. Many of the facts eventually uncovered—including a total lack of any semen or plant matter on Brawley's body or clothing—suggested that she had made the whole thing up in order to fool her stepfather into forgiving her for running away from home. To fortify the illusion, she carved racial epithets into her clothing and wrote them across her chest with a burned cloth, then smeared dog excrement into her hair and on her body.

Although the incident sparked a great deal of racial and political rhetoric and mutual accusations, a grand jury ultimately concluded that no crime had occurred. Williams nevertheless writes that "Tawana Brawley has been the victim of some unspeakable crime. . . . No matter who did it to her—and even if she did it to herself. Her condition was clearly the expression of some crime against her, some tremendous violence, some great violation that challenges comprehension."[1] In other words, whether it was true or false, Tawana Brawley's story tells us something about the condition of black women.

Is Williams right? Does it matter whether Tawana Brawley was telling the truth about the white men or whether "she did it to herself"? In this chapter, we contend that it matters very much. And it matters most of all to those who are truly victimized. Leave aside the unfairness to the men Brawley accused. The radical multiculturalists seem unable or unwilling to differentiate between Brawley's fantasized rape and another woman's real one. Indifference to the distinction between fact and fiction minimizes real suffering by implying that it is no worse than imagined or self-inflicted suffering. As Anne Coughlin asked in her article critiquing some of the radical multiculturalists, "In what kind of legal system would it make no difference whether a woman who claimed that she had been raped was telling the truth?"[2] Had Tawana Brawley actually been subjected to the ordeal she described, what would we think of someone—however sympathetic to Brawley—who said she didn't care whether it had happened or not?

In this chapter, we follow the implications of this line of reasoning about truth. We mostly avoid any philosophical discussion of Truth with a capital T, or of whether there is an external reality. Instead, we focus on the position exemplified by Williams's discussion of the Tawana Brawley incident: that we need not attach much importance to whether a purportedly factual account mirrors external reality (if such a reality even exists). In a way, each of the two preceding chapters skirts this fundamental issue dividing us from the radical multiculturalists. Their views on merit and on modes of discourse ultimately depend on a particular picture of the world, and they seem not to care whether others would paint the same picture.

This focus is rather narrower than the question of whether Truth exists. When we are talking about perceptions or the recounting of a particular event, we can distinguish among three different statements:

1. "If you had been watching, this is what you would have seen."
2. "The situation might not have looked this way to you, but this is how it felt to me."
3. "The situation didn't feel this way to me at the time, but this is how it seems to me now."

The first statement represents the conventional view of a true or accurate account. To illustrate the differences, imagine three accounts of an unseen event:

1. "He slapped me."
2. "If you, a male observer, had been there, you probably would not have seen anything that looked like violence, but I felt exactly as if he had slapped me."
3. "Although I didn't feel like I had been slapped, I recognize now that the sort of event I am describing is a kind of slap in the face to women."

There is nothing wrong with any of these statements, and each has an important point to make. The problem is that the radical multiculturalists seemingly want to use all three statements interchangeably, with no warning to the reader. Thus Williams writes that Brawley was the "victim of an unspeakable crime," when a less radical Brawley defender might write that pervasive injustices against black women caused Brawley to act as she did out of desperation. Whether the latter statement reflects objective reality is not the point. We think readers are entitled to know which type of statement is being made, and the radicals' casual attitude toward truth eliminates the distinction.

This casualness about truth stems from their basic social constructionism. If objective reality does not exist, as they suggest, then there is no need to be concerned about truth. Thus the radical multiculturalists want no truck with "facts" and have no patience with those who want to search for truth. "Facts must be constructed and interpreted," one radical feminist tells us, and when "facts are presented as natural and interpreted as truth, . . . much misogynistic work is done in the construction of 'reality.'"[3] If there are no solid facts, then it makes no sense to ask whether any particular narrative is "true." We might as well give up searching for truth, because the pretense of its existence only strengthens the particular truths of those in power, masking both competing truths and the power relationship itself.

Thus, in addition to Williams's comments about the Tawana Brawley incident, consider the views of Kathryn Abrams, one of the most thoughtful defenders of the storytelling movement. She says that she "would not be particularly disturbed" if a narrative purporting to be nonfiction turned out not to "track the life experiences of [its] narrator in all particulars," or to be a composite. Alex Johnson suggests that "it is perfectly acceptable . . . if that which is presented as the truth turns out not to be objectively true in the way in which that standard typically is viewed and used." Jane Baron, another defender of storytelling, suggests that not all stories "aim to tell what is 'true,'" but instead "seem meant to cast doubt on the idea of truth." Other radical multiculturalists attack truth more indirectly by arguing that legal scholarship should serve goals other than truth, even if truth is sacrificed in the process. All these sentiments echo—although possibly also misread—Foucault, who says that power and knowledge are inextricably intertwined: "There is no power relation without the correlative constitution of a field of knowledge, nor any knowledge that does not presuppose and constitute at the same time power relations." The greatest delusion of all, it would seem, is the injunction, "Ye shall know the truth, and the truth shall make you free." When we think we know truth, we are merely giving voice to power.[4]

Continuing our approach in earlier chapters, we do not intend to engage in a philosophical debate about the existence or meaning of truth. Instead, we want to examine where the radical view of truth leads. What kind of a society would we live in if we all agreed not to search for objective truth because it could never be found? What consequences might follow from a recognition that all truths are the subjective creatures of those who hold them? What beliefs might become credible if we abandoned the current standards for separating truth from fiction?

But Do They Really Mean It?

At this point, we expect many readers to be somewhat skeptical. Despite the quotations we provide above, it's hard to believe that the radical multiculturalists really mean it when they say they don't care whether a particular account is "true." After all, the radicals, too, tell stories and make factual claims, and presumably believe in the truth of what they are saying. Indeed, Patricia Williams was infuriated when law review editors and some readers did not believe her Benetton story. Richard Delgado was incensed when Anne Coughlin questioned one of his autobiographical snippets. It "happened just as I said it did," he tells us, and he resents the implication that he is a "fabricator and a liar." And the assumption of truth extends beyond facts to interpretation: as we pointed out in the previous chapter, Culp, Delgado, Johnson, and others are all quite certain of their own "true" interpretations of Williams's Benetton story.[5]

We cannot know for sure whether the radical multiculturalists mean what they say, but we can try to assuage doubts. When we first wrote about the storytelling movement in 1993, we published what we thought was mild and constructive criticism. We endorsed the place of stories in legal literature, and suggested that we had much to learn from the storytellers. Indeed, one of our critics "commended" us for our "attempt to rehabilitate the use of Narrative and Critical Race Theory." We cautioned, however, that the movement should be especially wary of two pitfalls: the possibility of distortion, and the severing of the story from any legal anchor. We thus suggested that storytellers should be careful about the veracity and verifiability of their stories, and that they should tie those stories to legal doctrine or analysis. Perhaps we were naive, but we thought we were strengthening the storytelling movement by pushing it away from a course fraught with danger.[6]

We certainly did not expect the torrent of criticism our article unleashed. For the most part, the critiques were thoughtful and civil— sometimes even friendly—but they were also eye-opening. It became clear that we had mistaken the depth of disagreement between the storytelling radical multiculturalists and more mainstream scholars. What we thought was a shift in form was in fact a major substantive rupture. In no uncertain terms, our critics told us that our fundamental premises were mistaken.

At the heart of our appraisal of legal storytelling was a vision of legal scholarship as an effort to discover and communicate truths about the legal system. That vision rested in turn on several key assumptions, and it was those assumptions that the radical multiculturalists attacked. We assumed, first and foremost, that the truth to which scholars aspire is objective in the sense that it is independent of both our heartfelt desires or political commitments and of our racial, sexual, religious, or class-based identities. The responses to our article belied our easy reliance on what we thought was an un-contested assumption. Jerome Culp argued that truth is socially con-structed rather than objective, and both Alex Johnson and Jane Baron suggested that truth might not be separable from personal identity and group membership. Johnson also accused us of "defeating the purpose" of narratives by "attempt[ing] to interject objectivity and universality." William Eskridge pointed out our failure to recognize the social constructivist foundation of the storytelling movement, and labeled us "conservative pragmatists." (In the law school world, "conservative" is generally not a compliment.) Similarly, Gary Peller's response to Mark Tushnet's criticism of the new radicals ac-cused him of missing the point: Tushnet, said Peller, viewed assump-tions about objectivity as "unproblematic," overlooking the fact that the purpose of much radical scholarship is to "oppose and contest" those very assumptions. Whether these radical multiculturalists truly believe, deep down, that truth and reality are socially constructed, they certainly appear to take the claim very seriously.[7]

And, as one would expect from committed social constructivists, their own accounts sometimes exhibit a nonchalance about verifiable facts. For example, the stories they tell about law school hiring are at odds with actual data on hiring, as we detailed in the previous chap-ter. Perhaps they are trying to say something along the lines of "Even though we are hired more often than whites, there is something about the system that troubles us, and here is what it is." But they are much blunter than that in accusing law schools of blatant hiring dis-crimination; this again fails to distinguish between the different types of accounts of events.

Their casualness about truth extends to legal doctrine and the his-torical record as well. Patricia Williams, for example, states that "through the first part of the century" the U.S. Supreme Court had upheld "a state's right to forbid blacks to testify against whites." This is a rather shocking assertion, but the typical reader would probably feel safe in relying on this legal claim by a Columbia professor spe-cializing in race law. But Williams's claim is false. Since 1866, federal law has entitled blacks to testify in court on the same terms as whites. The only case Williams cites to support her assertion was decided in 1871, not in "the first part of the century." And, more important, that case did not uphold any state law, but merely resolved a technical jurisdictional question about which court a criminal defendant ought to be tried in.[8]

History is treated with similar negligence. Mari Matsuda, a prominent critical race theorist, misdescribes Civil War hero Robert Gould Shaw as a "Negro colonel," thus assuring him the status of a victim. In fact, as any Civil War history—or even the movie *Glory*—will tell you, Shaw was white. The story of how he came to lead a black regiment—and to die and be buried with his men—might be much more interesting than the stereotypical vision conjured up by mischaracterizing his race. Ann Scales, a radical feminist, propounds a theory about how the use of the solar calendar rather than the lunar calendar is a method of consolidating male power. One of her illustrative examples involves the computation of the date of Easter. She seems either unaware or uncaring that the computation of Easter depends in part on the *lunar* calendar: Easter falls on the first Sunday after the first full moon after the vernal equinox. Patricia Williams implies that only racism could account for incredulity at the assertion that Beethoven was a mulatto. But the assertion is almost certainly false: A black scholar concluded in 1990 after a thorough examination that the claim has no factual basis. Williams's attribution of racism betrays a similar indifference to probabilities. She implies that the student who doubted the claim necessarily rejected the possibility that blacks might have produced great music. But as Judge Richard Posner points out, the doubter "may simply have been incredulous that *Beethoven* had a black ancestor, just as I would be incredulous to discover that my cat was Siamese, though I know that some cats are."[9]

Although these historical errors are not central to the arguments of the radical multiculturalists, they are illustrative of their careless treatment of factual issues. And the radicals' inattention to facts is not limited to the arcana of law and history. For example, it is almost an article of faith among radical multiculturalists that single-parent families—whether the result of unwed births or divorce—should not be discouraged, penalized, or stigmatized, because such families are every bit as beneficial for children as two-parent families. But there is overwhelming evidence that single parenthood is one of the primary causes of family poverty, and can have a devastating effect on the life chances of the children. "As compared with children of two-parent families, children from one-parent families have lower scores on standardized tests of IQ and educational achievement, lower educational attainment, lower occupational status and income, and higher rates of early marriage, births to unmarried women, and marital dissolution." Many of these effects are present in children whose parents divorce as well as in children whose parents have never married. The radical multiculturalist indifference to reality can have tragic consequences.[10]

We all make mistakes. (No prizes to readers who discover factual errors in this book!) But the radicals' attitude toward truth makes them more prone to such mistakes and less mortified—even nonchalant—when they are discovered. This attitude also tends to skew the mistakes in a less-than-random direction: No unpleasant fact would be allowed to stand without extensive and careful checking, while mistakes favoring their arguments escape scrutiny.

We thus have good reason to take seriously the radicals' views on truth. Moreover, not doing so risks distorting and domesticating a truly radical doctrine, which fails to accord it and its authors the respect they deserve. One radical feminist has criticized this form of domestication as "inoculation": "In inoculation, a tamed virus—a weakened, distorted, or dead variant—is introduced to the body. As the body fights off this impotent impostor, it develops antibodies that enable it to resist a future assault by the true virus."[11] The impulse may be charitable, but the result is destructive to the very heart of the radical critique. If the radical multiculturalists take the socially constructed nature of truth seriously, so shall we. Where might their approach take us?

The Specter of Authoritarianism

What should we seek and what should we speak if not the truth? The unhappy answers are politics, and political power. Delgado, for example, suggests that legal scholarship should sometimes be judged by its ability to change the world rather than as an attempt simply to understand it. Robert Chang, a proponent of the emerging critical Asian scholarship movement, admits that he views scholarship as nothing but "a question of power." The danger in this approach lies in its potential for diminishing rather than increasing human freedom.[12]

Two events from history may serve to illustrate the point. The first involves the affair of Alfred Dreyfus, a Jewish military officer convicted of treason against France in 1894 but later exonerated and freed. At the very end of the 1890s, while Dreyfus languished in jail and Emile Zola stirred up emotions about the case with his *J'Accuse!* the French were still divided on the matter of Dreyfus's guilt. One argument put forward at the time stands out for its unacceptability. According to historian Albert Lindemann, some "right-wing" opponents of Dreyfus argued "that to rehabilitate Dreyfus, *whether or not he was innocent*, would deeply undermine the army—and implicitly the principles of authority—and could not be allowed because the survival of the nation was at stake."[13] It is not only progressive causes that can be served by substituting politics for truth.

Conversely, searching for objective truth can be liberating. Our second illustration involves a Soviet General turned historian. General Dmitri Antonovich Volkogonov was assigned the task of supervising the official Soviet history of World War II. Although he had previously shown mild resistance to pressures toward ideological conformity, he had not achieved his distinguished position by leading a life of heroic dissent—on the contrary, he was very much a man of the system. As director of the military's main historical institute, he had access to the major archives of the Communist Party, the KGB, and the military. What he found in those archives could not be squared with the party's version of history. In late 1990, he submitted a manuscript that candidly assessed Stalin's wartime failings, thereby depriving the regime of its only remaining claim to honor, that of defeating Hitler. Volkogonov was then shunted aside by some of the same men who would later attempt a right-wing coup. Volkogonov was not a heroic rebel against the system, but merely a scholar of ordinary integrity in a society where that had become unusual. He remained unrepentant even when later dying of cancer: "The generals in the army . . . say I am a traitor or a renegade. But personally I think it is a more courageous stance to abandon honestly something which has been devalued by history instead of carrying it to the end in your soul."[14] Confusing scholarship with politics is not always transformative; sometimes it can be merely tragic.

For the radical multiculturalists, however, truth must sometimes take second place to political effectiveness. If political effectiveness (or, as some prefer, community building) is the test of good scholarship, then politically counter-productive scholarship is bad—even when it is true. The case of black Harvard law professor Randall

Kennedy, who was pressured against publishing a critique of critical race theory and ostracized when he published it anyway, offers one example of this dangerous tendency. The vilification of Julius Lester, drummed out of the Afro-American Studies Department at the University of Massachusetts for essentially refusing to stand silent while other blacks made anti-Semitic remarks, is another.[15]

A further example comes from litigation testimony by historians, who have had their own battles over objectivity. (We'll discuss them a little later.) But when they testify in court, they do so as experts: they purport to be giving an accurate and objective account of historical facts. What happens when that role intersects the radical multiculturalist critique of objectivity and truth?

EEOC v. Sears, Roebuck & Co. was a massive sex discrimination case. The federal government argued that a deficiency in the number of women Sears employed to sell big-ticket, big-commission items was due to discrimination. After a ten-month trial, discrimination charges against Sears were dismissed. The historical evidence related to a small but significant part of the dispute. The government had relied entirely on statistical evidence to demonstrate widespread intentional discrimination against women. There was a huge gap in the data about how many women had applied for (or were interested in) these particular jobs. Sears argued that because these specific positions involved job stress and financial risk, women would have been less likely to apply, so any statistical disparity in hiring would have to be adjusted to take this difference into account. After all, Sears argued, an employer cannot be blamed for intentional discrimination if some category of work is simply unappealing to female applicants.[16]

In support of this theory, Sears called historian Rosalind Rosenberg to testify about the history of women's attitudes toward the workplace. Rosenberg has been called the author of the most original and sophisticated historical work on women's culture. She testified that historically women have been socialized not to seek risky or stressful employment such as that involved in the case. The government responded with the testimony of another historian, Alice Kessler-Harris. She testified that any disparity in hiring was probably due to discrimination by Sears rather than any gender difference in job interests; her testimony seemed somewhat at odds, however, with some of her previous writings about women in the workplace. In her rebuttal testimony, Rosenberg pointed out discrepancies in Kessler-

Harris's positions. Kessler-Harris was infuriated. As she reported later, she was particularly offended when Rosenberg attacked her credibility "by suggesting that my testimony was infused with a particular political perspective and by citing selective examples from my work that purported to demonstrate contradictions between the two bodies of material." Seemingly sharing Kessler-Harris's reaction, the leading American academic journal of feminism published a purported "archive" on the case that deleted Rosenberg's rebuttal.[17]

Although the judge credited Rosenberg's testimony, professional reaction against her was swift and devastating. At a meeting of 150 feminist scholars at Columbia, no one defended her against charges of attacking working women and undermining sexual equality. A committee of female historians passed a resolution declaring that "as feminist scholars we have a responsibility not to allow our scholarship to be used against the interests of women struggling for equity in our society." The entire controversy seemed designed, according to two liberal commentators, "to insure that no other historian, especially one without tenure, ever will dare to express similar views in court or in any other forum."[18]

The shameful cases of Kennedy and Rosenberg illustrate the dangerous paradox of the radical multiculturalist critique of truth. In the name of empowering the disenfranchised, radical multiculturalism takes away objective truth as a standard for judging speakers and their speech. What creeps into the resulting vacuum is a political standard that uses the interests of the group to censure—if not actually to censor—individual speakers. Our dictionary defines "totalitarian" as describing "a political regime based on subordination of the individual to the state." Does it become any less totalitarian when the individual is subordinated to the group?[19]

And the insidious undermining of human freedom goes well beyond freedom of speech. As law professor Eric Blumenson has argued in a thoughtful article about the radical multiculturalists, their "perspectivist" critique of objectivity necessarily leads them into moral relativism. "The perspectivist critique," he writes, "deconstructs the ethical claim no less than [other claims], and reduces ethics to a heavily mystified form of politics." Richard Rorty observes that although this insight is "hard to live with," it means that moral relativism ultimately has no defenses against totalitarianism and other dehumanizing regimes. It means, he claims, "that when the secret police come, when the torturers violate the innocent, there is nothing to be said to them of the form 'There is something within you which you are betraying.'"[20]

The world is unfortunately full of culturally contingent oddities that threaten human freedom. As Blumenson asks, do the radicals really "believe that the universal human rights claim is false, and that clitoridectomy and caste *do* constitute equality in the cultures that accept them?" Even if they do not, their theory will not allow them to condemn such culturally induced beliefs. And how would the radical multiculturalists deal with such tragedies as a Japanese American mother who kills her two children and unsuccessfully tries to kill herself, then raises as a defense the time-honored Japanese tradition of mother-child suicide? Or a Laotian Hmong man, living in America, who kidnaps and rapes a woman and defends himself by pointing to the ancient Hmong practice of marriage-by-capture? The problem here is that "someone who rejects the idea of an impartial standpoint as transcendental nonsense can describe the difference between a Jim Crow law and a civil rights law only in terms of whose ox is gored, not in terms of legitimate and illegitimate power, or justice and injustice, because these claims purport to be nonperspectival." It is not easy to give a philosophically coherent account of just what it means to say something is really wrong (not just "wrong from my personal point of view"). But it is a distinction we cannot afford to abandon.[21]

It is no surprise that the end product of radical multiculturalism has affinities with totalitarianism. As part of the attack on the Enlightenment, the critique of truth suffers from a tendency to reinforce pre-Enlightenment despotism. The Enlightenment replaced individual and institutional power with more objective measures of validity, and it is no surprise that the rejection of objectivity collapses back into power as the means for defining absolute truth. Indeed, Foucault himself may have recognized this tendency, apparently implicitly applauding (as the kind of transformative politics engendered by his theoretical approach) two of the most totalitarian regimes of the late twentieth century. Although his meaning is often opaque, he gives indications of supporting both the Chinese Cultural Revolution of the early 1970s and the Iranian fundamentalist revolution of the late 1970s.[22]

More important, the aspiration toward truth and objective methods of seeking it are integral to democratic constitutionalism. The two progeny of the Enlightenment, democracy and the scientific method so disparaged by the radical multiculturalists, are indeed siblings. Both democracy and the scientific method—empirical experimentation designed to approach objective truth—are closely related in their preference for intellectual authority over institutional authority, their insistence on universalism and objectivity, and their intellectual skepticism. In science as in democracy, what matters is not who says it but whether it is right. We are all free to reject another's beliefs, and no dogma is too sacred to challenge.

John Dewey was not the first to recognize the connection between democracy and science—he had a wonderfully inclusive vision of both—but he is probably the best known. Dewey explicitly linked the disinterestedness and objectivity of science and the "future of democracy." Democracy, as one modern Deweyan has pointed out, "is unalterably opposed to ignorance. It trusts that knowledge and understanding have the power to set people free." American scholars were never more aware of this connection than in the 1930s and 1940s. In 1938, in the shadow of Nazism, American sociologist Robert K. Merton published *Science and The Social Order.* In it, he contrasted the objective values of science, maligned today by the radical multiculturalists, with the Nazi misuse of science in the name of the needs of the regime. "The sentiments embodied in the ethos of science," he wrote, "characterized by such terms as intellectual honesty, integrity, organized skepticism, disinterestedness, impersonality—are outraged by the set of new sentiments which the State would impose in the sphere of scientific research."[23]

Regardless of the method, a willingness to search for truth—rather than to dismiss it as an impossible dream—is central to democracy. In an insightful article on the search for truth as a justification for freedom of speech, law professor William Marshall argues that the search for truth is essential to democracy in a number of ways. He suggests that "the personal qualities that a search for truth reflects— such as open-mindedness, humility, tolerance, and an awareness of obligations beyond self-interest—are important attributes of the democratic citizen." Moreover, "the premise of humanity engaged in a common search suggests a politics of dialogue and mutual persuasion—attributes essential to a political democracy." Thus because we are all engaged in a common search for truth, "political decisions [must] be made through persuasion by shared language rather than through authoritarian pronouncement." Finally, commitment to a search for truth "provides a check on the state's attempts to impose its own orthodoxy."[24] To condemn scientific objectivity and the aspiration toward universal truth, then, is to place democracy at risk.

Remembering the Past: Some History and a Story

"Legal scholars," Kathryn Abrams has pointed out, "are natural scavengers." The questions of truth and objectivity that so captivate the radical multiculturalists have been explored for decades by historians. Historians, too, sometimes intentionally blur fact and fiction—and sometimes their peers castigate them for doing so. If the radical multiculturalists are reiterating questions raised earlier in another discipline, then perhaps we can learn something from that discipline's experiences.[25]

While a general review of the historians' confrontation with social constructionist ideas is beyond the scope of this book, one response is particularly intriguing. Hayden White is one of the most prominent of the anti-objectivists. In a 1982 article, he bluntly cautioned his fellow historians against objectivity: "One must face the fact that when it comes to apprehending the historical record, there are no grounds to be found in the historical record itself for preferring one way of construing its meaning over another." History, in other words, is no more factual or objective than any other discipline. Ten years later, in response to numerous attacks on his position, he published what one historian called a "compromise" position, "a way of escaping the most extreme corollaries or implications of his relativism." In "Historical Emplotment and the Problem of Truth," White argued that while historical facts are objectively real, interpretation of those facts is inevitably socially constructed. He thus attempted to avoid some of the most potent challenges to social constructionism.[26]

White's compromise position was a response to charges that social constructionism diminishes our ability to condemn such horrors as the Holocaust. His essay appears in a volume dedicated to exploring the problems posed by the intersection of postmodernist historiography and the history of Hitler's "Final Solution." As the volume's editor notes, social constructionism creates a dilemma for those who believe that with regard to the Holocaust, "some claim to 'truth' appears particularly imperative": "postmodern thought's rejection of the possibility of identifying some stable reality or truth beyond the constant

. . . self-referentiality of linguistic constructs challenges the need to establish the realities and the truths of the Holocaust."[27]

Scholars like White can only respond with horror to the co-optation of their ideas in this setting. Indeed, the legal radical multiculturalists themselves have clearly recognized Holocaust denial as dangerous nonsense. Mari Matsuda condemns it in no uncertain terms: "To call the holocaust a myth is to defame the dead, as Elie Wiesel has so eloquently put it. It is a deep harm to the living. In a range of different contexts, the common law has recognized the likelihood of emotional harm to the living from carelessness in treatment of the dead."[28]

Horrified or not, the radical multiculturalists cannot limit the use of their theories by others. Deborah Lipstadt notes that radical multiculturalism has allowed Holocaust denial to flourish and to be treated as "the other side," another "point of view," or a "different perspective":

> [Radical multiculturalism] fostered an atmosphere in which it became harder to say that an idea was beyond the pale of rational thought. At its most radical it contended that there was no bedrock thing such as experience. . . . [B]ecause deconstructionism argued that experience was relative and nothing was fixed, it created an atmosphere of permissiveness toward questioning the meaning of historical events and made it hard for its proponents to assert that there was anything "off limits" for this skeptical approach.[29]

This misuse of anti-objectivism is not merely theoretical: When Holocaust deniers submitted ads to major college newspapers across the country, some of the newspaper editors defended their decision to run the ads by pointing to the values served by protecting freedom of speech. (Many of them had not noticed those values when they rejected ads that were offensive to women or people of color; some had even refused cigarette advertising.) Some newspapers refused to run the ads, exercising their own freedom not to speak. But the editor of the Duke University newspaper defended her decision in radical multiculturalist language: "The deniers are simply revisionists who are 'reinterpreting history, a practice that occurs constantly, especially on a college campus.'"[30]

White's approach avoids insanities such as Holocaust denial while still sharply limiting the idea of objective historical truth. What if our legal radicals take this approach, as indeed they might? It seems to avoid all the silliness about whether airplanes or people can fly, and still retains the critical punch of the rejection of objectivity. Some of their truth claims might then be recast as a combination of presenting factual reality and questioning the conventional interpretation. Unfortunately, that approach has two problems: it is still subject to co-optation, and it still will not get the radicals where they want to go. Even if facts are objectively real, the subjectivity of "interpretation" remains troublesome.

Eric Muller, a young law professor at the University of Wyoming, tells a story that illustrates the consequences of viewing all interpretations as equally valid:

> On my very first day of teaching, in my very first class . . . I spent a while giving a thumbnail sketch of constitutional history, focusing for a while on the Civil War and the work of the Reconstruction Congress. In doing so, I talked about slavery.
>
> After class, as I was gathering my notes and generally heaving a huge sigh of relief, a student approached me. She told me that I had said some things that had so deeply offended her that she'd been unable to concentrate for the rest of the class, and warned me that I was going to have to be a lot more careful about what I said. Naturally I was mortified that I'd blundered so badly on my very first day, and so apologized profusely. I told her that I'd appreciate knowing what it was I'd said, so that I could be more careful the next time. She told me, and I am essentially quoting, "Slavery was not bad. There were a lot of individual slaveholders who mistreated their slaves, and that gave slavery a bad name. My family were slaveholders, and our slaves loved us. What you gave us was the Union version of the War, but the victors always get to write the history."
>
> I was speechless. I know we live in a relativist world, but I thought it safe to work from the premise that a couple of things, say slavery and the Holocaust, were evil. I guess I was wrong.[31]

As this story indicates, even if the "facts" are objective, we lose a great deal if we concede that their "interpretation" is purely subjective.

Although Muller's story is unusual, it relates to an issue of significant concern to radical multiculturalists. For the last few decades, there have been sporadic legal battles over the display of the Confederate flag. Should its display by individuals be banned as hate speech? At the very least, shouldn't it be removed from southern capitols or public schools? The case for regulating its display rests, of course, on its genesis in southern resistance to the abolition of slavery and its consequent racist message. But the Civil War did more than end slavery, and the fall of the Confederacy can be seen as a cultural tragedy as well as a victory for equality. Marxist historian Eugene Genovese, whose earlier work includes a moving study of slave culture, has recently written a laudatory book on the southern conservative tradition. Unlike Muller's student, he did not of course seek to defend slavery, but he did make it clear that there were other aspects of southern culture. So when southerners proudly display the Confederate flag, are they celebrating their independently valuable traditions or expressing approval of slavery? If the radical multiculturalists remain true to their theoretical commitments, they cannot condemn those who would memorialize the loss of the southern tradition: the display of the flag is merely an alternative interpretation of the events of the Civil War. Although critical race theorists have indeed taken a strong stand against the display of the Confederate flag, this seems inconsistent with their theory. Trying to limit the implications of social constructionism by reducing it to "interpretation" rather than facts does not lessen its nihilistic potential.[32]

In the end, conventional scholars want to be able to argue what the radical multiculturalists deny: that some interpretations are simply wrong. With Henry Louis Gates, they lament that "to speak of the social construction of reality is already to give up the very idea of 'getting it right.'"[33] The past should not be viewed as infinitely malleable. Whether or not we can ever actually achieve objective truth, some stories come closer than others.

In one way, this leads back to some of the problems with storytelling as a discourse. Stories have tremendous manipulative potential, even when the "facts" are objectively true. Despite an author's best intentions, first-person storytelling is fraught with exactly the kind of dangers that scholarship is designed to avoid: creating, through interpretation, a biased, misleading, and nonverifiable account of the world. Even telling stories about others carries that potential, both because the teller may be relying on similarly biased first-person stories, and because the teller may have some of the same conscious and unconscious motivations to shade otherwise nonverifiable facts. If we suggest that a judicial decision or historical fact should be interpreted in a particular way, a reader can consult other sources to confirm that the decision or the historical fact is as we describe it and then use her own judgment about our interpretation. If we tell stories, however, whether our own or someone else's, the reader must rely solely on our presentation of the facts as we interpret them. Especially in cases where the point we are trying to make creates incentives for us to shade those facts, denying that we need to be concerned about the veracity of stories puts us at moral hazard and our readers at our mercy.

The "story" in the subtitle of this section is meant to offer an illustration of these dangers. Here we tell, and then deconstruct, a personal story about one of the authors, factually accurate in all its details but terribly misleading in its overall interpretation:

The Story

I grew up in a single-parent family in New York City public housing. My mother was an alcoholic and a compulsive gambler who abused me physically and emotionally. Drunk, she would make me stand in front of her for hours at a time, berating me and cataloguing my many faults, sometimes until two or three in the morning. She once threw a pan of newly scrambled eggs at me, burning the side of my face. We had very little money, of course; I began working for pocket money when I was eleven, and by thirteen I was buying all my own clothes and saving for college.

In addition to the problems at home, I suffered my share of ethnic and gender discrimination. There were many parts of town I didn't dare enter because of my race, and even on home turf my brother and sister and I were beaten for being the wrong race. I couldn't go to the magnet high school nearest my home because it did not accept girls. The only magnet school that did was an hour and a half subway ride in each direction, so I did not attend. I couldn't go to the college of my choice because it did not want "too many" students of my ethnic background.

At the college I did attend, there were almost no female faculty members. I recall taking only a single class from a woman. Male teachers considered female students fair game for sexual conquest, and could be verbally abusive to women who were either unattractive or noncompliant. My law school experience was even worse: my class was only about 15 percent women, and there were no women on the faculty at all. Few women made law review, and none made the editorial board.

The law firm I eventually worked for was no better: there were no female partners, and I was one of only three female associates. Not surprisingly, during the time I was there, one of the other female associates and I were the two lowest paid lawyers at the firm.

The Story behind the Story

Now we deconstruct the story, adding detail and interpretation. By doing so, we show how stories can mislead through what Patricia Williams calls "calculated disjunctures, rhetorical rearrangements, and surgical revisionism."[34] (She is talking about the stories of Justice Clarence Thomas, and seems unaware that she might be describing all stories, even her own.)

Every fact in the story is technically true, to the best of my knowledge. Where I can have no knowledge—such as in imputing intentions to others—I have drawn conclusions that are not inconsistent with the facts as I know them. However, the story as a whole, as well as many of its details, presents an extremely misleading portrait of my life.

I grew up in a single-parent family in New York City public housing. *My parents were divorced when I was nine. Until then I lived in a "traditional" family, with a father who worked and a mother who stayed at home and took care of the children. Even afterward, my father sent regular child-support payments and kept in touch with us. The "public housing" was Mitchell-Lama middle income housing, which, although it was not a five-bedroom house in the suburbs, was not what most people think of as "the projects."*

My mother was an alcoholic and a compulsive gambler . . . *Her alcoholism was confined to drinking several cocktails every evening. It never interfered with her job or her general ability to function. She never left us alone in order to buy or drink alcohol, and was never so drunk that she could not respond to an emergency. Her gambling began as innocuous weekly home poker games—in which $10 was a big win or loss—and did not become a problem until long after I had left home. I never felt its effects, and indeed gave her legal advice when casinos began pressing her to repay her debts.*

. . . who abused me physically and emotionally. Drunk, she would make me stand in front of her for hours at a time, berating me and cataloguing my many faults, sometimes until two or three in the morning. She once threw a pan of newly scrambled eggs at me, burning the side of my face. *Although these instances sound like merely examples, they are instead almost the sum total of her "abuse." The late-night sessions occurred perhaps two or three times a year, and did me very little actual harm although they were unpleasant. The scrambled eggs were thrown in a fit of pique, and my mother was horrified at the very minor burns she caused. She was not a perfect mother, but she was far from abusive. Moreover, she was a responsible person who both set a good example and made sure that we always had whatever we needed.*

We had very little money, of course; I began working for pocket money when I was eleven, and by thirteen I was buying all my own clothes and saving for college. *We were not wealthy, but neither were we below the poverty level. My mother worked full time in a clerical job on Wall Street, and my father also helped support us. We lacked some things that seem important to children and adolescents: no color television, no vacations, no fancy clothes or expensive bicycles, not even an allowance. But my mother made sure that we always had plenty of nourishing food, and she sacrificed to give us private schools (mostly on scholarship) and summers at the beach. I always knew I would have to pay for college myself, and I was aware that my mother worried about our finances, but otherwise I didn't feel particularly deprived. The "work" in this case was babysitting, hardly an unusual or taxing enterprise even at that age. As to clothing, I think I went through two pairs of blue jeans and a few turtlenecks and T-shirts every year; for a teenager in the 1960s, clothing was not a major expense.*

In addition to the problems at home, I suffered my share of ethnic and gender discrimination. There were many parts of town I didn't dare enter because of my race, and even on home turf my brother and sister and I were beaten for being the wrong race. *I am white, and the parts of town I couldn't enter included Harlem and the South Bronx, places I had little interest in going anyway. To the extent the story (deliberately) gives the impression that I suffered from "racism," it is at least partially misleading, since some readers might well conclude that it was racism against a person of color. The beating incident did happen, exactly once, and we were more shaken up than physically hurt. Although the three girls who attacked us were indeed black, I have no evidence that the motive for the attack was in fact race. They might have attacked us because we appeared rich and happy (we were carrying shopping bags of wrapped Hanukkah presents at the time), or to take our belongings (which they did) or just because we were there. Only in the story am I confident that I was attacked because of my race.*

I couldn't go to the magnet high school nearest my home because it did not accept girls. The only magnet school that did was an hour and a half subway ride in each direction, so I did not attend. *Instead, I attended a prestigious private school, mostly on scholarship. There was never any question that I would not attend the local public high school.*

I couldn't go to the college of my choice because it did not want "too many" students of my ethnic background. *It was well known that even in the early 1970s, when I applied to college, many of the Ivies set limits on the number of New York City Jews who would be admitted. The motive was only partly straightforward discrimination against Jews—too many Jews would have been admitted under the ordinary admission standards, changing the character of the schools. It was also partly the effect of racial, geographic, and "legacy" preferences. While the effects may be the same, and some of the preferences may have originally been implemented to exclude Jews, it would be misleading to attribute them solely to ethnic prejudice.*

At the college I did attend, there were almost no female faculty members. I recall taking only a single class from a woman. Male teachers considered female students fair game for sexual conquest, and could be verbally abusive to women who were either unattractive or noncompliant. *Some sexual liaisons between faculty and students probably occurred everywhere in the early 1970s, before sexual harassment was recognized as such. Indeed, the women who were sexually involved with their professors—and it was only a handful of professors who engaged in such conduct, even then—were generally boastful, envied, and at least outwardly pleased with the state of affairs. I recall only one professor who was verbally abusive, and he was that way toward both male and female students, especially those who paid him insufficient respect. Selective powers of observation coupled with an assumption of sexism could have led one to conclude, however, that his behavior was discriminatory as opposed to immature.*

My law school experience was even worse: my class was only about 15 percent women, and there were no women on the faculty at all. Few women made law review, and none made the editorial board. *The three years I attended law school were something of a fluke; there was at least one woman on the faculty for most of the years before and after that time. Law review membership was based almost entirely on grades, and thus the number of women on law review reflected only the differential grades achieved by men and women. Even if the blind grading process somehow favored "male thinking"—a proposition for which I have no evidence—that is not the same as accusing the law review of bias. There were indeed no women on the editorial board my third year, but there were in other years. I doubt that discrimination had anything to do with it.*

The law firm I eventually worked for was no better: there were no female partners, and I was one of only three female associates. Not surprisingly, during the time I was there, one of the other female associates and I were the two lowest paid lawyers at the firm. *The firm had only sixteen lawyers altogether, so almost 20 percent were women. One associate made partner the year after I left, right on schedule. The reason the other female associate and I were at the bottom of the salary scale was because we were the two most junior associates.*

Why should we prefer the deconstructed version of the story to the misleading one? The radical multiculturalists have no answer. If one judges the value of stories by their efficacy, the first one wins hands down. It is both politically and therapeutically valuable insofar as it makes the narrator not only a victim but one who has faced great obstacles and has nevertheless succeeded. So why should it matter that it didn't happen that way, any more than it matters to Patricia Williams that it didn't happen the way Tawana Brawley told it?

It matters for the reasons we have already explored in earlier chapters. It is not equally fair to everyone: while it may be good for the narrator, it is unfair to others, including especially her mother. (Even the dead have a claim to justice.) It also distorts discourse both within and without the narrator's immediate community. Her brother and sister were witnesses to many of these events, and if she insists on creating her own reality, her relationship with them might well suffer. The same observation holds true with regard to relationships with teachers, classmates, and former colleagues. And by putting forth to others a self that isn't accurate, the storyteller lets dishonesty poison any dialogue she might have with the larger community. In telling this kind of story, one's integrity as a person is at stake. Even if no other consequences follow, letting ourselves be comforted by false or distorted memories, or refusing to take responsibility for our own past and present, is contrary to "our best vision of what it is to be a human being."[35]

Finally, it matters simply because truth matters. To quote a great French philosopher, "again and again there comes a time in history when the man who dares to say that two and two make four is punished with death."[36] The radical multiculturalists would scoff at Camus: "Perhaps your addition is culturally contingent, perhaps it is politically inexpedient, and besides, why should men risk death for truth?" The answer: Because the alternative is too horrible to contemplate.

The radical multiculturalist dismissal of the possibility of objective truth is fraught with peril. With no possibility of appeal to a standard of truth independent of politics, there is no way to mediate among truth claims except by recourse to authoritarian fiat. This resort to power risks silencing not only dissenters from the radical multiculturalist party line. It also hurts innocent bystanders, such as the men Tawana Brawley falsely accused, children whose parents are encouraged to divorce or not to marry in the first place—and one author's mother, whose character was much more complex and admirable than the stilted story would have the reader believe.

6

Anatomy of an Ideology

I spent twenty years of my life in a country whose official ideology, when confronted with any human problem, was always to reduce it to a political phenomenon. (This ideological passion for the reduction of man is the evil that those coming from "back there" have learned to despise the most.)

—MILAN KUNDERA

If there is any central message of radical multiculturalism, that message is, "It's all politics." Merit, law, and truth are exercises of power by one group over another. This is supposed to be a slogan of liberation—all the apparent barriers to our heart's desire can be overturned, for what lives by power can die by revolution.

We have seen, however, that this form of politicization has some unhappy consequences. If merit is an exercise of power, a certain kind of racism—that directed against successful minorities like Jews and Asians—becomes excusable. Discourse becomes a political battle over the authority to speak as a group representative and an effort to silence opposition. And truth is defined by political utility. Despite its promise of liberation, the ideology of radical multiculturalism contains menacing shadows.

At this point, there are still some loose ends to our analysis. First, although we've looked at and evaluated aspects of radical multiculturalism, we haven't really considered how they fit together. For an ideology to be viable, its premises need to be mutually reinforcing. Having explored each of the central premises in some depth, we are now in a position to flesh out the relationships between the various tenets of radical multiculturalism.

A second loose end is to explain the survival of this ideology. Besides being thoroughly unattractive in its implications, radical multiculturalism defies common sense. What is one to make of the idea that merit is purely a dominance game? This claim is hard to square with the fact that some despised, downtrodden groups have won the game at the expense of the supposedly dominant culture (our argument in chapter 3). The attack on merit is also implausible in its own right if taken as a general rule—the difference between a good heart surgeon and a bad one seems to be something more than opinion. The supposed social construction of truth is equally hard to swallow as a generality; Holocaust denial is merely the clearest example of how reality is not so easily negated.

Perhaps the acceptability of these ideas in the humanities is not quite so surprising—fanciful readings of Hamlet, unlike unfounded methods of cardiac surgery, do not result in dead patients and malpractice lawsuits. Law, of course, does involve the reading of texts, but it also involves flesh and blood, and we might expect that such implausible ideas would face tough sledding. In particular, we might expect that people who view their mission as attacking critical social problems would take a hardheaded approach to identifying those problems. Given a world view that is superficially implausible and that has ugly implications, how do we explain its continued viability?

Part of the answer, as we saw in chapter 4, is that radical multiculturalists have adopted a form of discourse that makes it more difficult for them to engage collectively in critical thinking. Preconceptions are readily reaffirmed by the exchange of stories, and disagreements over substance are easily diverted into arguments about authenticity and voice. Another part of the answer is that the tenets are mutually reinforcing, so that a challenge to any one tenet has to overcome the defense of all the tenets. But this is not the full answer, and it behooves us to look more carefully at how radical multiculturalism protects itself from challenge.

How Multiculturalist Tenets Fit Together

In our discussion so far, we have treated the radical critiques of merit and truth separately. The two are actually closely related, and both are tied to the indeterminacy thesis about law.

The critique of merit holds that the rules for distributing social goods, such as good jobs or educational slots, have no inherent validity and are merely means by which the elite maintains its dominance. For many important positions, however, the key to "merit" is supposed to be some kind of knowledge: expertise in cardiac physiology, or in the functioning of securities markets, or in nineteenth-century history. So to challenge the concept of merit is also to challenge expertise, and this in turn puts in question the "truths" of which the expert claims to have special knowledge.

Specifically, consider a history professor who specializes in modern European history. A prerequisite for possessing "merit" in this field is an expert knowledge of the history of Europe. But to say that someone has expert knowledge is necessarily to say that various beliefs about the subject are not all equally meritorious—some are better than others, which is to say, truer. If there is no intrinsic difference between a terrible historian and a competent one, it must follow that there is also no intrinsic reason why one set of beliefs about the past (those held by the terrible historian) are worse than another (those held by the competent historian). Of course, "merit" with respect to a historian also includes more intangible factors such as originality, but the radical critique of merit claims that even the core concept of merit (knowledge of history) is only a social construct. If the idea of a good historian is entirely a social construct, then history must also be a social construct. For example, a history book denying the Holocaust is intrinsically no worse than another that details the Final Solution—it's all a matter of which group the rules of the game favor. The argument also works in reverse: if there's no historical truth, there's no difference between a bad historian and a competent one.

Similarly, merit and truth are tied to law. A trial is a battle over the history of some event, and if historical judgments lack any objective validity, we know at the outset that legal judgments can do no better. The critique of merit clearly implies that one law review article is intrinsically as good as another, the distinction again resting only on how the power rules are defined. But conventional law review articles mostly argue for or against particular legal results, and if all the articles are intrinsically equal, then so must be all the arguments.

The indeterminacy thesis also reinforces the radical critiques of merit and truth. Legal reasoning often purports to rest on historical analysis—regarding, for example, the original intent of the framers of the Constitution. If history were determinate, then law would have the capacity to be determinate as well. So, if we believe law is hopelessly indeterminate, we can conclude that history must be indeterminate as well—otherwise, historical investigations might be able to rescue law. So historical truth also must be culturally contingent or socially constructed. The indeterminacy thesis also implies that certain kinds of merit have no intrinsic validity. The difference between a good lawyer or judge and a bad one cannot rest on the ability to make valid judgments about legal issues since, according to the indeterminacy thesis, such judgments do not exist.

The strength of these links varies. The critique of truth seems to require acceptance of the other two critiques, so it may be the most fundamental of the tenets. But it is possible to view the indeterminacy thesis as relating to some special failings of the legal system, which leave the core concepts of truth and merit intact. This seems to be Mark Tushnet's position (which is why Gary Peller accused him of deserting the Left). Duncan Kennedy seems to embrace legal indeterminacy and a modified form of the merit critique (recognizing some minimal components of merit as valid but viewing the bulk of merit standards as arbitrary). It's less clear whether he believes that all truth is socially constructed. It is also possible to accept the merit thesis but not to accept the others fully. Catharine MacKinnon seems to hold the merit thesis and perhaps the indeterminacy thesis, but only a modified form of the truth thesis—there actually is an objective reality, but all of the conventional methods for learning about that reality are fatally infected by racism and sexism.[1]

On the other hand, Richard Delgado embraces all three tenets enthusiastically. In some respects, his position (apparently shared by others such as Gary Peller and Patricia Williams) is stronger because he is able to take full advantage of the mutual reinforcement that these tenets can provide each other. Although "mix and match" is not necessarily an invalid strategy, consistency provides a certain rhetorical power that is lost in more nuanced approaches.

Thus, radical multiculturalism has a conceptual core of beliefs about the social construction of law, truth, and merit. This conceptual core provides strong support for other positions held by radical multiculturalists. If merit is just a dominance game, there can be no "objective" argument against changing the rules, through affirmative action or otherwise, to obtain immediate proportional representation of all groups. If law is indeterminate, we need not worry about the first amendment in crafting rules against hate speech or pornography— once we decide where we want to go, constitutional law will dutifully follow along, like a well-trained dog. Artistic or other merit being purely socially constructed, we need not worry that antipornography or hate speech rules will impinge on valuable expression. And since truth is also socially constructed, we don't have to worry that these regulations of speech will impede the search for truth.

The argument so far is that the core tenets of radical multiculturalism support its proposals for legal change. As is often the case, the "core/periphery" metaphor is somewhat misleading, because the core can just as well be seen as the product of the supposedly less fundamental periphery. We suspect that many people who believe in the core tenets got to this view by first embracing the periphery. Someone who is really enthusiastic about broadscale affirmative action or pornography regulation or hate speech rules may find herself drawn to the social construction idea because it makes the case so much easier. For instance, one basic rationale for affirmative action is that it brings a diversity of viewpoints. If someone wants to give affirmative action the greatest possible scope, she is led pretty naturally to the "different voices" thesis, which in turn takes her to seeing conventional views of merit and truth as merely white male perspectives. It all hangs together quite nicely.

Another way to see how the pieces fit together is to begin with the form of discourse rather than with its substance. In chapter 4, we saw how radical multiculturalists embrace storytelling. Suppose for the moment that someone were really to accept storytelling as the main road to knowledge about social problems (not just as a useful complement to analytic reasoning, which we think it is). There are two different ways such a person might proceed. She might decide, along with Catharine MacKinnon, that certain stories are privileged (the kind that emerge from feminist consciousness-raising sessions). She would then follow along with MacKinnon's view that, although an objective reality exists, our society's view of the truth and merit have nothing to do with that objective reality and everything to do with oppression. She would also be likely to agree with MacKinnon's arguments for suppressing hate speech and pornography. Or she might view all stories as equally valid, so that her criticism is that society has listened selectively to some stories but not others; only to men, when it should have listened to both men and women, or only to whites, when it should have listened to both blacks and whites. If all stories are equally valid, she is then led to the critique of truth and merit, demands for immediate proportional representation, legal rules to prevent the "silencing" of oppressed groups, and so forth. In other words, once one embraces the practice of radical multiculturalist discourse, both the theoretical apparatus and the specific legal demands follow naturally.[2]

Radical multiculturalism is also coherent in another way, because it relies consistently on metaphors of concealment and disguise. For the radical multiculturalist, what appears civilized and normal is at heart violent, self-serving, and oppressive. The indeterminacy thesis says that what passes for principled legal reasoning is nothing but a thin veil, hiding the real bases for judicial decisions. Merit, we learn, isn't objective; it's just an affirmative action program designed by white males to favor themselves. And truth is the story told by the victors.

A similar metaphor underlies the arguments for specific legal changes. For MacKinnon, violent pornography reveals the way in which society has constructed "normal" sexuality as an exercise in sadism—strip away the veil and you learn from pornography what men really think about sex and about women. Academic institutions pose as fonts of tolerance and understanding, but critical race theorists tell us that the reality is quite the opposite: a hostile atmosphere in which hate speech is rampant and blacks are rightfully fearful of associating with whites. Indeed, according to Richard Delgado, universities are actually the most white supremacist of institutions, not (as they portray themselves) the least. Government actions that do not refer to race, and that were not taken with any conscious intention to discriminate, conceal unconscious racial hatred and stereotyping, and under the veneer of government neutrality, transmit these evils to the public. Everywhere, behind the mask of health are the sicknesses of racism and sexism, which must be rooted out. This passion to penetrate the mask of innocence structures radical multiculturalist discourse, which easily descends into a hunt for hidden signs of racism and sexism even among the most avowedly radical, who must always fear the presence of hidden pockets of the disease. And so we find people carefully compiling lists of all the times in the day when being white works to their benefit, lest they commit the sin of unknowing complicity in racism.[3]

As we saw in chapter 2, many radical multiculturalists view thought and behavior as the products of "mindsets." Radical multiculturalism itself is a powerful and coherent mindset. It provides a philosophical outlook (social constructionism), a legal reform program, and a set of governing metaphors, all in one convenient package. This package has the added benefit of resonating with ideas that are popular in other parts of the academy. If one has doubts about the social construction of truth or merit, one can rest assured that the matter has been settled in the impenetrable prose of some esteemed French philosopher.

To gain a foothold, an ideology should not only be consistent and supported by prestigious sources, but it must also resonate with the life experiences of its adherents. In our conceptual taxonomy of radical multiculturalism, the issue of affirmative action plays only a small part. Radical multiculturalism makes affirmative action unproblematic, but affirmative action can be defended under a traditional meritocratic vision as well.

But the psychological role played by affirmative action programs may be more central to the ideology. Affirmative action, as we and most legal scholars—including the radical multiculturalists—use the term, means taking into account the racial or ethnic background of a candidate for admission or employment. Thus, a law school might admit a black or Hispanic applicant with lower college grades and LSATs than a white applicant, despite the school's ordinary reliance on those numeric factors. Indeed, the ordinary reliance on these criteria is shown by the fact that within any racial or ethnic group the school puts great weight on them. But for any number of reasons, including a desire to enroll a racially diverse student body or a belief that the school ought to compensate for societal discrimination or disadvantage, most law schools do in fact deviate substantially from reliance on numeric predictors of performance. When they do so on the basis of racial or ethnic criteria (or, less frequently, gender), that is affirmative action.

The problem comes because the conventional indicators, like college grades and LSAT scores, are designed to predict performance in law school. And they do predict that performance reasonably well. The indicators, by and large, have some statistical validity, which means that on average they connect with some conventional measure of performance. People with lower LSATs tend on average to have lower first-year grades in law schools. But this means that if, for some other good reason, a school decides to admit one group with lower LSATs than a second group, the first group will probably end up with lower grades. (This assumes that tests predict performance equally well for both groups, and this assumption turns out to be empirically valid for blacks and whites.) The same is true of many other employment and admissions decisions—the price of deviation from the standard criteria is usually a lower average success rate as measured by other standard criteria. There may be excellent, even compelling reasons for taking this course, but it does have this almost inevitable consequence.[4]

Of course, the more aggressively we pursue affirmative action, the more we will face this consequence. But even for the mildest forms of affirmative action—where an institution "casts the net more broadly" by interviewing people or encouraging applications from people who otherwise would not be considered equally good risks—has the same kind of consequence. If a school is looking for faculty members who are good at writing conventional articles and teaching conventional classes, the conventional standards (prestigious law school, good grades, law review, and so on) are probably good indicators. When the school interviews people who lack these indicators, the odds are increased that it won't find the conventional qualities that it is looking for. The result is that more affirmative action candidates will be turned down after interviews, as in the story by Richard Delgado discussed in chapter 4.

Conservatives are fond of using this problem as an argument against affirmative action. The standard liberal response is to agree that this is a price of affirmative action, but to say it is a price well worth paying. This is a debatable proposition, however, and two other responses may be psychologically more appealing. It is that psychological comfort that may lead some radicals to their extreme position.

The first response is to re-examine the idea of merit. Note that the result of lowering conventional criteria (like test scores) is a statistically lower outcome as measured by other conventional standards (like grades). But why accept those other conventional standards or the conventional concept of performance they are designed to measure? For instance, LSATs may successfully predict lower first-year grades for blacks, but that only raises the question of the validity of the grading system. (If you don't trust test scores, why trust exam grades?) After all, those standards were adopted before women and minorities were part of the system, so there's no reason to think that the standards represent their perspectives and interests. Thus, one is led toward the critique of merit.[5]

An alternative response to the standards problem is to question whether the new admittees actually have had a fair chance to meet the conventional standard. Here, one might look for more subtle barriers to achievement, such as a hostile environment within the school or workplace. This line of argument leads to an endorsement of hate speech regulation. Because these subtle forms of discrimination are difficult to document statistically and depend for their effectiveness on psychological impact, narratives by the victims seem like the natural way to obtain information. So unqualified support for affirmative action can make hate speech regulation and legal storytelling both seem attractive.

Again, the more aggressively affirmative action is pursued—the more it moves in the direction of quotas—the greater the need to rely on these arguments. Hence, if you begin by believing that affirmative action should be greatly expanded, you are likely to find yourself sharply questioning the way in which conventional merit standards are applied and looking intently for subtle forms of discrimination in the environment. Social constructionism is a psychologically comforting response to the discomfort caused by affirmative action.

These responses are not irrational, and indeed to some extent they may be well founded. But taken to the extreme, they lead to radical multiculturalism. Thus, in practice, one tenet of multiculturalism—such as strong support for proportional hiring or admission—is easily tied to other tenets to make an appealing package. This coherence makes radical multiculturalism a viable mindset.

Defense Mechanisms

The internal coherence of radical multiculturalism is all well and good, but it must also face external challenges. Given their implausibility by conventional standards, radical multiculturalist views are likely to be confronted by sharp criticism from outsiders. If nothing else, these criticisms will have the weight of established society behind them. How does radical multiculturalism repel these attacks? There are several such defense mechanisms.

Making Falsification Impossible

The first defense mechanism derives from the internal logic of multiculturalism, which can defeat challenges by depriving critics of any ground from which to mount a challenge. We saw in chapter 4 that concerns about storytelling can be rebuffed this way. Defenders of storytelling need only point out that the challengers necessarily assume the very concepts of objectivity and truth that the storytellers are attacking. The critique of truth is peculiarly immune from attack—after all, by what standard could one judge a critique of truth itself to be "false"?

Multiculturalist tenets repel by discrediting in advance any evidence against them. Consider an effort to use empirical information, such as survey results, to rebuff a radical multiculturalist claim. Such a stratagem is subject to a whole string of objections. The basic concepts used in surveys, such as random sampling and statistical tests of significance, reek of objectification. In deciding whether to trust the results of the survey, we must rely on the competence of the surveyors—which is a merit determination, and so inherently suspect. Given the rejection of the concept of objectivity, it's impossible to retain the idea of an unbiased survey question. The interaction between the surveyors and the interviewees, like any other social interaction, is drenched in sexism and racism, which are guaranteed to warp the results. Interviewees may have acquired so much of the dominant mindset that they don't recognize their own oppression.

For example, Catharine MacKinnon is unfazed by the fact that pornography-tolerant Denmark and Japan have very low rates of rape. She insists that Denmark, like Sweden and Germany, has had an unreported "explosion in sexual abuse." The reason it's unreported is simple: "If your government supports pornography, reporting sexual abuse seems totally pointless to women." In Japan, on the other hand, women don't report rape because "sexual abuse is just part of the way women are normally treated. If you're still essentially chattel, what is it to rape you?" No need, apparently, to worry about the empirical data.[6]

Besides being impervious to formal empirical evidence, multiculturalist views also resist counter-stories. Any story that is inconsistent with multiculturalist views can be knocked out—either the storyteller is not an authentic member of the group, or his perceptions have been warped by the dominant culture. So it doesn't matter, for example, what Yale law professor Stephen Carter may have to say about the effects of affirmative action in his own life, or what Justice Clarence Thomas may have to say about his experiences. They are merely, in Jerome Culp's terms, black men in white face. And besides, as Derrick Bell points out, their views must be taken for what they are: pandering to white interests. After all, Bell says, the selection of Thomas as a Justice "replicates the slave masters' practice of elevating to overseer . . . those slaves willing to mimic the masters' views."[7]

At a more abstract level, an attack on any one doctrine can be defeated by invoking others. As we saw earlier, the critiques of truth, merit, and legal reasoning are all tightly intertwined. It is difficult to defend merit if the concept of truth is open-ended. Similarly, it is difficult to defend truth if the merit of an analysis or argument is wholly subjective. And without either merit or truth, how could judicial reasoning hope to stand?

The critiques also defy attack by eliminating in advance the simplest and most powerful counter-arguments. The most powerful attack on the radicals' premises relies on common sense: statements that we know to be objectively true, assessments of merit that we find incontestable, or judicial decisions that seem inescapable. But the more intuitively clear a statement may be, the more we are reduced, when questioned, to relying on its obviousness. The whole point of the radical critique is that obviousness, too, is only a socially constructed quality. So there's no foothold with which a challenge can get started, once you accept the system as a whole. Thus, radical multiculturalism has a marvelous self-sealing quality, which automatically repairs ruptures before they can spread.

Using Stock Stories

Like any mindset, radical multiculturalism comes complete with stock stories about how the world works, stories that reinforce its own viewpoint. As it happens, some of the crucial stock stories are not borne out by the facts, but (not unlike Ronald Reagan's anecdotes) they seem to survive this handicap without embarrassment. Here are some sample stock stories, which seem to be articles of faith among radical multiculturalists, together with a brief description of their flaws. All of these stock stories uphold the world view of the multiculturalists about dominance and victimization.

The rapidly deteriorating black situation embodies the plight of people of color in America. There are two problems with this particular stock story. First, the U.S. minority population is almost evenly split between African Americans and others (Hispanics, Native Americans, and Asians). The assumption that one-half of a population can be taken as representative of the whole population is a mistake—as feminists have not hesitated to point out in other contexts. In reality, the situations of other groups differ significantly from that of blacks. We saw in chapter 3 that in many ways the situation of some Asian groups is more like that of Jews than like that of blacks. That of Hispanics is also different from that of blacks in crucial respects. For example, they are subject to much less residential segregation and, unlike blacks, often marry outside of their own group.[8]

Second, it is not at all clear that the position of blacks has worsened in the past several decades. The picture is quite complicated, with a mixture of progress and defeat. The rapid emergence of the black middle class clearly demonstrates substantial progress on the part of an important group of blacks. Overall, despite the existence of some extremely worrisome trends, in important respects life has improved for the majority of blacks.[9]

Because race and gender are both grounds for oppression, black women must be the most oppressed group of all. Actually, in many respects black women are much better off than black men. They have a much lower incarceration rate and are far less likely to be victims of homicides. In contrast to black men, who do more poorly than comparable white men in the job market, black women seem less disadvantaged by race than by gender. Black women who have jobs now earn as much on average as white women with jobs, and black women with college degrees actually earn more than white female college graduates. A recent study showed that black women were heavily over-represented among law teachers compared to their percentage of the lawyer population, more so than black men or white women.[10]

If it were not for job discrimination (including white-oriented hiring standards), blacks—and other minorities—would do as well as whites. This is the heart of the merit critique. It's not true, unfortunately. (We say "unfortunately" because, if the radical multiculturalists were right about this, it would be easier to know how to cure the problem.) The disturbing reality is that society has simply failed to give a disproportionate number of blacks the skills needed in today's economy. Quite apart from formal education or test scores, disparity in skill levels has also been found in tests of such fundamental skills as writing a letter, balancing a checkbook, or reading a map. These basic skills have obvious relevance to a whole range of jobs. The shift toward a more skilled labor market has been especially devastating for younger black men without a college education. Between 1973 and 1986, employment for black high school dropouts fell dramatically, and even high school graduates without a college education suffered substantially increased unemployment. Moreover, "the sharp rise in the income returns to schooling . . . favored the more highly educated white worker" over the average black worker in terms of wages.[11]

Academic hiring, especially in the sciences, provides an even clearer contrast to the stock story. Subjective evaluations of quality or debatable hiring standards simply aren't the major barriers to blacks in the sciences. In 1992, only 1 percent of the nation's scientists, and 2 percent of the Ph.D. pool, were black. In some fields, the situation was even worse: for example, in 1987 there were no new black Ph.D.s at all in astronomy, botany, ecology, or immunology. Thus, the primary factor excluding blacks from the sciences is a lack of the minimum educational requirement, rather than any contestable judgments about merit.[12]

The pool of stock stories reinforces the central premise of radical multiculturalism that racism and sexism permeate our society and are the direct causes of all our social ills; only a radical restructuring of our culture can solve the problem. The real world is more complex, but the whole point of stock stories is to protect against the distraction of messy realities.

Ignoring the Mainstream

The standard radical multiculturalist complaint about the legal system is that judges are formalists who avidly believe in color blindness and ignore the historical and social contexts of legal issues. This is a fairly apt characterization of Justices Thomas and Scalia, a few prominent federal court of appeals judges, and a handful of conservative academics. Thus, it can't be said that the radical multiculturalists are attacking straw men. But the conservative formalists regard themselves, and are regarded by their colleagues, as insurgents rebelling against the mainstream. The mainstream legal view is antiformalist, sensitive to factual context, and not necessarily opposed to race consciousness.

On the color blindness point, the Supreme Court contains four strong supporters of affirmative action, and at most only three Justices who unswervingly support color blindness. (Admittedly, those three have tended to pick up the support of a few moderates in recent cases.) Even a cursory examination of the law reviews reveals an overwhelming academic sentiment against color blindness. On this issue, Laurence Tribe (a stronger advocate of affirmative action) is much closer to the median than Robert Bork, who received notably little academic support in his Supreme Court bid.[13]

The issues of formalism and context-sensitivity take us back to the history of modern legal thought in chapter 1. The realists, later followed by critical legal scholars, posed a major challenge to the legitimacy of the legal system. They demonstrated unequivocally that judicial decisions cannot be straightforwardly dictated by mechanical application of formal legal rules. CLS writers seemed to be under the impression that they had proved the bankruptcy of legal reasoning. It was only a matter of time, however, until mainstream scholars detected the hole in this argument: it assumed that legal reasoning should consist of the mechanical application of formal legal rules.

Recent jurisprudential thought is now characterized by a widespread rejection of this formalist view.

This new perspective, sometimes known as legal pragmatism, commands the allegiance of legal thinkers ranging from Judge Richard Posner on the Right to Harvard's Frank Michelman on the Left. These thinkers reject the formalist picture of reasoning, in which both the acceptable methods of reasoning and permissible raw materials are rigidly specified in advance. Rather, they believe that reasoning cannot be reduced to an algorithm or predetermined methodology. In the legal context, pragmatism implies a certain degree of eclecticism. Pragmatists are notorious believers in sensitivity to context, history, and openness to empirical information.[14]

A recent book by University of Chicago law professor Cass Sunstein provides a good overview of legal pragmatism. Arguing against the view that legal decisions should be based on mechanical rules or ambitious grand theories, he stresses the role of analogy in legal reasoning. He rejects "a familiar and exceedingly unfortunate kind of formalism in law—the effort to decide cases in law solely by reference to decisions made by someone else, when one's own judgments are inevitably at work." Instead, he is quite open to the idea that legal reasoning involves a variety of cognitive tools and often requires value judgments. Although clearcut rules may sometimes be useful, he agrees that law may often "rely on a complex set of judgments and understandings not reducible to any simple verbal formulation."[15]

Sunstein's work is also notable because he has been at the forefront of efforts to reconcile the defense of individual rights with the importance of community. Radical multiculturalists often criticize the dominant culture for exalting isolated, atomistic individuals while forgetting that peoples' identities are rooted in particular cultures and communities. Sunstein, among others, has struggled to rescue the idea of individual rights from this kind of atomism.[16]

Although pragmatism has been newly rediscovered as a jurisprudential position, it is well rooted in American legal history. Justice Oliver Wendell Holmes developed his highly influential theories of law under the influence of pragmatist philosophers. His close friend Louis Brandeis put pragmatism into practice, first as a champion of legal reform and then as a Supreme Court Justice. Brandeis had not only a fervent belief in individual rights but also a strong vision of community and civic responsibility. So, modern-day pragmatists can invoke some powerful links with our legal tradition.[17]

Our purpose here is not to argue on behalf of the positions taken by today's legal pragmatists (although we tend to agree with them). Those positions are, however, much closer to the current intellectual center of gravity than those of Justice Scalia and other formalists whom radical multiculturalists target. But ignoring the mainstream in favor of those atypical conservatives is a useful strategy. It suggests that Scalia and his followers are typical of mainstream legal thought, which makes the mainstream an easy target. It also suggests that, even if radical multiculturalism is flawed, the only available alternative is wholly unacceptable. Better the radical multiculturalist frying pan than the conservative formalist fire.

Thus, by creating a false dichotomy between themselves and conservative formalists, in which the mainstream is essentially ignored, radical multiculturalists can convince themselves that any bending of their views can only lead to intellectual disaster. This might be considered a specific application of the Warsaw Palace of Culture principle—if a favorite position is hard to defend, concentrate on the fundamental flaws of the opposition. This tactic is all the more effective if one can pick opponents who themselves are considered suspect by the audience.

The flaw here is not in the attack on formalism. The radical multiculturalist critique of formalism is basically sound. What is wrong instead is the implicit conclusion: "If they are wrong, we must be right, because there is no other alternative." Pragmatist philosopher Martha Nussbaum paraphrases this all-or-nothing reasoning as: "if not the heavens, then the abyss." Interestingly, she attributes this view to both Bork the formalist and Fish the radical multiculturalist.[18]

The Paranoid Mode of Thought in American Legal Theory

So far, we have investigated how the radical multiculturalist mindset insulates itself from challenge. But although these explanations are true as far as they go, they miss a key aspect of the dynamics. What we have explained so far is how challenges can be dismissed as invalid because of the self-sealing nature of radical multiculturalism. But these explanations only show how seemingly plausible challenges might be rejected as incorrect. What we have not explained is why the challenges are often rejected as not merely incorrect but illegitimate, symptomatic of racism and sexism and therefore not worthy of serious intellectual engagement.

Examples of this response are not hard to find. Several are given in earlier chapters, such as Derrick Bell's assertion that critiques of critical race theory should not be dignified with a response and Jerome Culp's view that criticisms of storytelling are merely the anger stage in the process of grieving for the death of white supremacy. Several authors have recently denounced all critiques of critical race theory as "backlash scholarship," designed to "preempt debate on the difficult questions raised by such subjects as multiculturalism and race." Legitimate criticism is apparently not possible, in the view of these radicals. Or consider Alex Johnson's view about what he admits is a *seemingly* complimentary article about legal storytelling: "Make no bones about it, though, this is a not-so-thinly veiled attack" on the ability of critical race theorists to get promotion, tenure, and other benefits. Rather than a good-faith questioning of storytelling, Johnson sees a covert defense of white supremacy by "staunch defenders who will not go down without a fight." Thus, he sees criticism as only the first stage in a long war between minority and white scholars with "many skirmishes and many heated battles" ahead. Even more dramatically, Catharine MacKinnon accuses her feminist opponents of selling out to funders such as the Playboy Foundation: "What I really want to know is how much of the women's movement the pornographers own."[19]

It's easy to dismiss these remarks as the result of oversensitivity or defensiveness, but we think that something deeper is at work. Radical multiculturalism has a built-in tendency toward just this kind of reaction because of its obsession with power. This theme runs all through the tenets of radical multiculturalism and is reflected in its concrete legal program as well, so it's little wonder that the pieces hang together so well. Radical multiculturalism provides adherents with a vision of the world in which they are inevitably victims of white male power.

As we saw earlier, however, this power is not apparent on the surface of things. The metaphors of concealment and deception, which are so characteristic of radical multiculturalism, tell how the iron hand of power is hidden within the velvet glove of "neutral principles." As critical race theorist Mari Matsuda approvingly explains, "The work of feminists, critical legal scholars, critical race theorists, and other progressive scholars has been the work of unmasking: unmasking a grab for power disguised as science, unmasking a justification for tyranny disguised as history, unmasking an assault on the poor disguised as law." Everywhere on the surface we see claims of truth, logic, and objectivity; everywhere underneath we find sexism, racism, and domination. As feminist legal theorist Katharine Bartlett disapprovingly observes, increased sophistication in the ways of radical theory is signified by "heightened awareness of residual, unconscious as well as conscious forms of discrimination." Those who can spot these subtler forms of discrimination become "an increasingly narrow elite vanguard." She points out that this is a self-reinforcing process: "To those who 'get it,' the enemy grows."[20]

Encountered in everyday life, this kind of world view would be cause for concern. Imagine you were to meet someone who, after some initial small talk, revealed to you his fundamental view of the world. The courts are rigged against him: although the judges purport to apply neutral principles, the principles are only used as a way of making sure that he never gets ahead. Employment standards and school admission tests are also designed, not to measure true job performance, but to make sure other people—not him—get into the good schools and get all the good jobs. Moreover, everywhere he goes, others create a "hostile environment" in which he always feels threatened and victimized. Most significantly, even seemingly innocent statements by other people (even those who purport to be sympathetic), when carefully analyzed, turn out to embody a world view that excludes him and keeps him from succeeding. It does not take psychiatric training to make a diagnosis of paranoia.[21]

This analogy risks being seriously misleading in three respects. First, our hypothetical paranoid is presumably wrong—the world is not rigged against him. In contrast, believing that the world is rigged against certain groups isn't necessarily wrong. Women and members of racial or religious minorities are often subject to mistreatment, overt or otherwise, and it isn't crazy for them to be worried about the possibility. But the presumption that *everything* is a concealed form of discrimination transforms a reasonable concern into an obsession.

Second, we don't mean to imply that radical multiculturalism reflects some kind of personality flaw or neurosis. (Far be it from *us* to accuse other people of being neurotic!) But just as racism, like anti-Semitism, can be institutional rather than personal, paranoia can be a matter of intellectual style rather than psychological disturbance. The heart of the radical multiculturalist position is that, below the deceptive surface of things, social institutions are universally designed to keep the oppressed at the bottom and the powerful on top. Only the elite know how to penetrate the deceptively innocent surface to see the hidden malevolence of the system. This is a paranoid mode of thought. (Again, however, we note that being paranoid doesn't necessarily mean they're not out to get you.)

A final difference is that paranoia is a constant condition for the individual sufferer but only an intermittent risk for radical multiculturalists. Surely, unlike the feminist conference we considered in chapter 4, many disagreements between radical multiculturalists do not dissolve into mutual charges of victimization and silencing. Criticism can sometimes, but not always, be interpreted as disguised attack. Personality differences can operate to exacerbate or lessen the tendency toward paranoid reactions, just as in any other group. But the potential for paranoia is always present, embedded in the centrality of the concept of concealment. Given the ideological premise that naked power is constantly concealed behind claims of neutrality and normality, it is not pathological to be on the look-out for hidden threats.

Although this paranoid mode of thought does not necessarily signify either falsity or abnormality, it does isolate radical multiculturalists from the kind of dialogue that might lead them to modify their views. For paranoids can be difficult patients to treat—any overtures are interpreted as hostile, and their ideas are impossible to refute. Radical multiculturalists tend to take a similar posture with respect to outsiders. Either the criticism is another effort by members of the dominant group to maintain their status and power, or it is pandering by members of the oppressed group to the power structure. Even outsiders who purport to be sympathetic to the radical multiculturalist position may be viewed with suspicion—they may be co-opting the radical potential of the movement. Indeed, once you take the position that truth and merit are masks for the exercise of power, there really isn't any way to consider an argument except as an attempted exercise of power. So the natural response is not to ask whether the argument is valid, but instead to look for the right tactical response to the hostile move. In addition, it becomes almost impossible to conceive of friendly criticism; to admit that the critic is honestly motivated by a concern about the truth of your own position would be to concede that "truth" is something other than a mask for power. If truth and merit do not exist, concerns about the truth or merit of work by multiculturalists can only be yet another power play.[22]

Moreover, as we have already discussed, radical multiculturalists, like paranoids, can explain away any seemingly adverse evidence, because they know in advance that it cannot be valid. The paranoid knows that there is a conspiracy against him, and if there is evidence to the contrary, that only proves the power and deviousness of the conspiracy. Similarly, the radical multiculturalist can always deconstruct any apparently contrary evidence. The research agenda, after all, is not to test whether society is irredeemably racist and sexist but to uncover precisely *how* society is shaped by racism and sexism. Counter-evidence only increases the challenge.

The paranoid mode of thought is a threat to efforts at dialogue between radical multiculturalists and others. Combined with the self-sealing nature of social constructionism and its reliance on stock stories of oppression, it makes genuine intellectual engagement with outsiders difficult. Nevertheless, as we discuss in our "Conclusion," prospects are not utterly hopeless. Something constructive may yet emerge from the clash between the radical multiculturalists and the mainstream.

Conclusion

The ignorant cannot be free. Or so the philosophers of the Enlightenment believed.

—ALAIN FINKIELKRAUT

This book has been an attempt to show how the basic tenets of what we have called radical multiculturalism imply an unattractive vision of politics—a vision in which some kinds of racism are not only exempt from criticism but even implicitly endorsed, in which public discourse threatens to dissolve into a series of dead ends and mutual recriminations, and in which truth is rightfully established by fiat and even the greatest crimes against humanity may become merely matters of opinion. This is not a world in which we wish to live; and it is not, we believe, a world in which the radical multiculturalists themselves would want to live.

It's time to step back for an overall appraisal of our dispute with the radical multiculturalists. Just how seriously concerned should one be about the flaws in their viewpoint? To what extent do these flaws discredit such forms of scholarship as radical feminism, critical race theory, and CLS? Is there any room for a constructive debate between these scholars and the mainstream about the nature of law, truth, and merit?

Assume, just for purposes of discussion, that our charges against radical multiculturalism are valid. So what? How much should the radicals or anyone else worry about these particular flaws in their viewpoint? After all—to take probably the most serious of our charges—even if radical multiculturalism does have certain anti-Semitic implications, these implications aren't really intended and don't seem to pose any immediate risk of causing anti-Semitic acts. In the meantime, maybe radical multiculturalism will do some good in addressing racial and gender issues. We believe, however, that the flaws are very serious indeed.

To begin with, we do not regard anti-Semitic implications, even unintended ones, as trivial flaws. A scientific theory that was otherwise appealing but that implied that the earth is flat would have to be rejected. For the same reason, we believe, a political theory that might be otherwise appealing, but that implies that Jews have unjustly taken more than their fairly earned share, also should be rejected. In addition, even though these implications are unintended and don't pose any immediate risk of harm, the long history of anti-Semitism makes it difficult to be completely sanguine about the lack of any danger. In particular, given the prevalence of anti-Semitism in some minority communities and its endorsement by some minority leaders, it may well occur to someone sooner or later that radical multiculturalism provides the perfect rationale for anti-Semitic beliefs.

Anti-Semitism is also just the most clear-cut symptom of broader problems with radical multiculturalism. As we discussed in chapter 3, the same implications apply to some groups of Asian Americans. These groups are supposedly among the intended beneficiaries of radical multiculturalism, and the fact that the theory has some threatening implications for them is significant.

But the problem is broader still. In the radical multiculturalist scheme of things, *anyone* who succeeds is suspect, regardless of group membership. White male success is, of course, understandable. As Harlon Dalton, a critical race theorist at Yale, puts it, the term white male means "more than simply pigment and chromosomal structure." It invokes "the social meaning that attaches to being part of the master race, and that flows from being one of those for whose benefit patriarchy exists and the memory of the goddess has been expunged."[1] It goes without saying that success by white males is merely a result of "white privilege" rather than something fairly earned.

But what about success by women or by minorities? From the perspective of radical multiculturalism, successful women and minorities are also suspect. If merit is a white male construct, then a black who succeeds can only have done so at the cost of some sacrifice of her authentic culture in favor of the oppressor's. We view this as a profoundly unfair judgment. It is also socially destructive to the extent that it reinforces a subculture in which education and other conventional signs of merit are rejected as signs of "whiteness."[2]

Thus, though the anti-Semitic implications of radical multiculturalism may pose no immediate threat, they are symptomatic of other, more immediate problems that are also serious. The critique of truth does not lead the radical multiculturalists themselves to Holocaust denial—although logically it could just as well do so—because they have no inclination in that direction. But radical scholars do have an inclination to deny some important facts about race and gender in favor of poorly supported stock stories, and the critique of truth helps license them to do so.

The distortions in discourse that radical multiculturalism causes are also significant. It may be no more than an academic spat when radicals accuse each other of silencing, or accuse the scholarship of outsiders of being designed to suppress feminist and minority scholars. But these same radicals want to expand the power of the law to control speech that harms women and minorities. Their internal battles, and their charges against other scholars, do not augur well for speech regulations, which may receive an alarmingly broad interpretation in the hands of their radical multiculturalist advocates. An intellectual style tinged by paranoia is the last thing we want when restrictions on speech are being imposed.

In short, we regard the flaws in radical multiculturalism as being far more than peripheral. This does not mean that all of critical race theory, critical legal studies, or radical feminist legal theory must be discarded. Derrick Bell points out that there has always been a tension between two strands of critical race theory. The deconstructive strand takes the form of radical critique, while the reconstructive strand contains a commitment toward transformation and emancipation. Our attack is aimed at the deconstructive strand, and even there only at the most radical forms of deconstruction. There are many scholars whose work we have not mentioned in this book because they focus on reconstruction rather than deconstruction. Examples that come quickly to mind include Lani Guinier and Gerald Torres in critical race theory, Margaret Radin and Martha Minow in feminist legal theory, Dan Ortiz and Janet Hailley in gaylegal studies, and Robert Gordon and Morton Horwitz in CLS—but there are many others. Their presence creates the potential for a dialogue that transcends the battle between radical multiculturalism and the Enlightenment tradition.[3]

Such a dialogue is urgently needed. The radical multiculturalists are terribly wrong on several scores, but they are right about two key points: our society does face urgent problems relating to race and gender, and we do need new ideas and fresh criticisms of the conventional wisdom. For example, although we find unacceptable their idea that "merit" is a bankrupt concept, we believe they are right to call for reappraisal of the specific contours of the concept of merit.

We see some reason to hope that a dialogue will occur. In the past, one barrier to dialogue has been the radicals' view that the Enlightenment tradition is frozen and closed to transformative ideas. As Stanley Fish has pointed out, however, a tradition is a living thing rather than something carved in stone: "Tradition does not preserve itself by pushing away novelty and difference but by accommodating them, by conscripting them for its project; and since accommodation cannot occur unless that project stretches its shape, the result will be a tradition that is always being maintained and is always being altered."[4] There seems to be a growing realization among progressive scholars of the potential for redeeming the Enlightenment tradition rather than abandoning it.

In an important essay, Katharine Bartlett has explored the possibility of a reconstructive feminist theory that would transform rather than seeking to erase existing traditions. Notably, she rejects theorists who "appear to have given up the tools of reason as well as tradition." She proposes "an interactive view of tradition and change" that seeks "the right linkage between feminist insight and matters of collective and individual identity—of which tradition and reason are both important components." Another hopeful sign is Margaret Radin's effort to link pragmatism and feminist theory.[5]

Even some writers who have on occasion seemingly espoused radical multiculturalism have at times also sought a more constructive interaction with the tradition. William Eskridge's recent work on legal interpretation explores the role of tradition and the ways in which apparent "ruptures" can revitalize a tradition and maintain its legitimacy. Mari Matsuda celebrates American culture as the meeting place of diverse cultures—the land of the "kosher burrito"—and she invokes "the Enlightenment ideals of liberalism that attended our national birth" as well as the antisubordination principle. In the struggle against subordination, she continues to see "claims of logic, legality, and justice as both useful and true." "I can claim as my own," Matsuda says, "the Constitution my father fought for at Anzio, the Constitution that I swore to uphold and defend when I was admitted to the bar. It was not written for me, but I can make it my own."[6]

We can only hope that these voices will prove to be the wave of the future, leading to a vigorous and vibrant dialogue between progressive scholars and the mainstream. The alternative is a conversation that is constantly threatened by outbreaks of a paranoid mode of thought that sees behind every social institution nothing but the tracks of white supremacy and male oppression.[7]

For ourselves, we find sustenance in the pragmatic tradition represented historically by Brandeis and Holmes, a tradition that contains lessons for all sides. It was Brandeis who taught that the problems facing our society cannot be solved until "the logic of words" has yielded to the "logic of realities." For, as Holmes said, "the life of the law has not been logic but experience." Too many radical multiculturalists have been content to play word games rather than facing facts. As Henry Louis Gates has pointed out, they have focused on ever more refined analyses of racism and sexism at the expense of scholars "who, whatever their differences, are attempting to discover how things work in the real world, never confusing the empirical with the merely anecdotal." But pragmatism also has lessons for traditionalists. Brandeis made a point that must be remembered by traditionalists today: "If we would guide by the light of reason, we must let our minds be bold." Those of us in the mainstream must remain open-minded; we must not be afraid to learn from others.[8]

In the end, we hope that progressive and mainstream scholars will, despite inevitable quarrels, work together to address the problems facing our society. Whatever the shape of future legal scholarship, we also hope that progressives will shed the paranoid style and rigidity currently characterizing radical multiculturalism. We agree with Stanley Fish on the need to combine an open, improvisational style with a willingness to make commitments. Or, as philosophers Amy Gutmann and Dennis Thompson have put it, we must all "seek a balance" between "holding firm convictions" and being responsive to "objections that, on reflection, one cannot answer."[9]

In short, we must always be open to dialogue. But even pragmatists, we believe, must sometimes stand on principle.

Acknowledgments

Timing, they say, is everything. The perfect time to begin a joint project is not always obvious. After a decade of close collegiality and one coauthored book, one of us made the mistake of spending a summer at home nursing a newborn son and assuaging the jealousy of his two-year-old sister. The other—perhaps overwhelmed by new-found freedom—decided that then would be the perfect time for us to write a joint article on the newly emerging storytelling movement in legal scholarship. Frazzled and sleepless, his colleague couldn't figure out how to say no. Thus began a five-year collaboration that has culminated in this book.

We began with storytelling, but soon we realized that it was inex-tricably related to other new movements. Our focus expanded. And with each new article, we drew more, and sharper, responses. We gradually realized that the storytelling movement was more than a new form of scholarship; it was an attack on the reigning vision of law, academics, and politics. As more and more radical ideas ap-peared in the law reviews, we became convinced that our critique needed a wider audience. Academics in search of a wide audience—unless they become television commentators for notorious trials—have only one choice: write a book. And so we did.

Given the gradual genesis of this book, it should come as no sur-prise that some of the ideas, and a bit of the prose, have appeared in print before. Readers might want to consult the following articles for our earlier attempts to grapple with the questions addressed in this book. Those coauthored by us include: "Telling Stories Out of School: An Essay on Legal Narratives," 45 *Stan. L. Rev.* 807 (1993); "The 200,000 Cards of Dimitri Yurasov: Further Reflections on Scholarship and Truth," 46 *Stan. L. Rev.* 647 (1994); "Is the Radical Critique of Merit Anti-Semitic?," 83 *Cal. L. Rev.* 853 (1995); and "Legal Storytelling and Constitutional Law: The Medium and the Message," in *Law's Stories: Narrative and Rhetoric in the Law*, ed. Peter Brooks and Paul Gewirtz (New Haven: Yale University Press, 1996). Those written by Daniel A. Farber are: "The Outmoded Debate Over Affirmative Action, 82 *Cal. L. Rev.* 893 (1994); and "Reinventing Brandeis: Legal Pragmatism for the Twenty-First Century," 1995 *U. Ill. L. Rev.* 163. Suzanna Sherry's are: "Responsible Republicanism: Educating for Citizenship," 62 *U. Chi. L. Rev.* 131 (1995); and "The Sleep of Reason," 84 *Geo. L.J.* 453 (1996).

We are grateful for the help of many people in writing this book. Two successive deans at the University of Minnesota Law School, Robert A. Stein and E. Thomas Sullivan, generously supported our scholarship. We are also grateful to Joan Howland, the Director of the University of Minnesota Law Library, and her staff, for their extraordinary attention to our sometimes unusual research requests. Our editor at Oxford University Press, Helen McInnis, had (a perhaps unwarranted) faith in us from the very beginning and made excellent suggestions for improving the manuscript. Laurie Newbauer spent countless hours at her computer, making revisions and adding and deleting the same paragraphs again and again as we kept changing our minds about what to include. Marti Blake also provided excellent secretarial help. Kaitlin Hallet (Minnesota J.D. 1998) provided invaluable research assistance, finding sources, checking cites, and generally keeping us honest. She also read the manuscript in draft and provided many helpful editorial suggestions. Kaitlin was ably assisted in her cite-checking efforts by Mindy Fredrikson (Minnesota J.D. 1998) and Brian Manson (Minnesota J.D. 1998). An impressive group of people took time from their own work to read and comment on earlier drafts of the manuscript: Jim Chen, Murray Dry, Frank Edelman, Rick Eldridge, Bill Eskridge, Bob Hudec, Jeff Kahn, Laura Kalman, Roger Park, Richard Posner, Susan Sullivan, Tom Sullivan, and Jessica Young.

Finally, there are two people who have read every draft of every one of our jointly authored works, and who have also provided countless other forms of support. Although this book is not dedicated to either of them, perhaps it should have been: it could not have been written without Dianne Farber and Paul Edelman.

Notes

Introduction

1. Testimony of Professor George Priest, in 2 *Hearing Before the Committee on the Judiciary of the United States Senate on the Nomination of Robert H. Bork to be Associate Justice of the Supreme Court of the U.S.*, 100th Cong., 1st Sess. 2437 (1989).

2. Catharine A. MacKinnon, *Feminism Unmodified: Discourses on Life and Law* at 54 (Cambridge: Harvard University Press, 1987). For excellent overviews of the critical race theory part of this movement, see Jeffrey Rosen, "The Bloods and the Crits," *The New Republic*, Dec. 9, 1996, at 27; Douglas E. Litowitz, "Some Critical Thoughts on Critical Race Theory," 72 *Notre Dame L. Rev.* 515 (1996).

3. J. Peter Byrne, "Academic Freedom: A 'Special Concern of the First Amendment,'" 99 *Yale L.J.* 251, 269–71 (1989); G. Edward White, "Felix Frankfurter, the Old Boy Network, and the New Deal: The Placement of Elite Lawyers in Public Service in the 1930's" in *Intervention and Detachment: Essays in Legal History and Jurisprudence* 149, 155 (1994); Rodney Smolla, "Academic Freedom, Hate Speech, and the Idea of A University," in *Freedom and Tenure in the Academy* 195, 216, William van Alstyne, ed. (Durham, NC: Duke University Press, 1993) ("island of intellectual inquiry"); Robert C. Post, "Racist Speech, Democracy, and the First Amendment," 32 *Wm. & Mary L. Rev.* 267, 324 (1991); see also J. Peter Byrne, "Racial Insults and Free Speech Within the University," 79 *Geo. L.J.* 399, 419 (1991) ("the commitment to forms of thought and expression conducive to truth and coherence lies at the core of academic values"); Edward L. Rubin, "The Practice and Discourse of Legal Scholarship," 86 *Mich. L. Rev.* 1835, 1846 (1988);

Byrne, supra, at 258 ("basis of reason"). See also id. at 261 ("The structures of academic discourse can be justified because they facilitate the rational pursuit of truth").

4. Camille Paglia, *Sex, Art, and American Culture* at 231 (New York: Vintage, 1992); Alan Sokal, "A Physicist Experiments With Cultural Studies," *Lingua Franca*, May/June 1996, at 62.

5. Paul Brest, "The Fundamental Rights Controversy: The Essential Contradictions of Normative Constitutional Scholarship," 90 *Yale L.J.* 1063, 1096 and n.189 (1981).

6. Daniel A. Farber, "The Outmoded Debate Over Affirmative Action," 82 *Cal. L. Rev.* 893 (1994).

7. And some would rebuke her for exhibiting an unseemly obsession with intellectual coherence. See Harlon L. Dalton, "Storytelling on Its Own Terms," in *Law's Stories: Narrative and Rhetoric in the Law* 59, Peter Brooks and Paul Gewirtz, eds. (New Haven: Yale University Press, 1996).

8. For a discussion of traditional and modern anti-Semitism, see Albert S. Lindemann, *The Jew Accused: Three Anti-Semitic Affairs (Dreyfus, Beilis, Frank) 1894–1915* (Cambridge: Cambridge University Press, 1991).

9. Mary I. Coombs, "Outsider Scholarship: The Law Review Stories," 63 *U. Colo. L. Rev.* 683, 708 n.5 (1992). She also includes Martha Fineman and Mari Matsuda on this list.

Chapter 1

1. Charles Taylor, Amy Gutmann, Michael Walzer, Steven Rockefeller, and Susan Wolf, *Multiculturalism: Examining the Politics of Recognition* 66, 68 (Princeton: Princeton University Press, 1994); Diane Ravitch, "Multiculturalism: E Pluribus Plures," 59 *Am. Scholar* 337, 340–41 (1990); Stephan Fuchs and Steven Ward, "What Is Deconstruction, and Where and When Does It Take Place? Making Facts in Science, Building Cases in Law," 59 *Am. Sociological Rev.* 481, 484 (1994); William N. Eskridge Jr., "Gaylegal Narratives," 46 *Stan. L. Rev.* 607, 643 (1994). For an overview of critical race theory by a sympathetic observer (whose description is nevertheless quite similar to ours), see Victor F. Caldwell, "Book Review," 96 *Colum. L. Rev.* 1363 (1996).

2. Edward L. Rubin, "The New Legal Process, The Synthesis of Discourse, and the Microanalysis of Institutions," 109 *Harv. L. Rev.* 1393, 1395 (1996).

3. Laura Kalman, *The Strange Career of Legal Liberalism* at 15–16 (New Haven: Yale University Press, 1996) ("each legal rule"); Walter Wheeler Cook, "Book Review," 38 *Yale L.J.* 405, 406 (1929); Karl N. Llewellyn, "Remarks on the Theory of Appellate Decision and the Rules or Canons About How Statutes Are to be Construed," 3 *Vand. L. Rev.* 395, 401, 405 (1950).

The best history and overview of the legal realist movement is Laura Kalman, *Legal Realism at Yale 1927–1960* (Chapel Hill: University of North Carolina Press, 1986).

4. G. Edward White, *Patterns of American Legal Thought* at 125 (Indianapolis, New York, Charlottesville: Bobbs-Merrill, 1978) ("artificial logical concepts"); Robert Maynard Hutchins, *Report of the School of Law to the President and Fellows of Yale University, 1926–27,* at 118–19 (New Haven: Yale University Press, 1928), quoted in John Henry Schlegel, *American Legal Realism and Empirical Social Science* 84 (Chapel Hill: University of North Carolina Press, 1995). Schlegel's book is a break with tradition in that it suggests that "realism is best understood as something that the Realists did" rather than their beliefs. Schlegel, *American Legal Realism* at 2.

5. The standard case for the legal realist influence on the New Deal is put forth in G. Edward White, *Patterns of American Legal Thought* at 99–163 (Indianapolis, New York, Charlottesville: Bobbs-Merrill, 1978), and questioned in Neil Duxbury, *Patterns of American Jurisprudence* (Oxford: Clarendon Press, 1995). For descriptions of the realists' emphasis on efficiency rather than social change, see Laura Kalman, *Legal Realism at Yale 1927–1960* at 21 (Chapel Hill: University of North Carolina Press, 1986); G. Edward White, *Patterns of American Legal Thought* at 130.

6. Herbert Wechsler, "Toward Neutral Principles of Constitutional Law," 73 *Harv. L. Rev.* 1, 17, 19 (1959). See also Henry Hart and Albert Sacks, *The Legal Process: Basic Problems in the Making and Application of Law,* William N. Eskridge Jr. and Philip P. Frickey, eds. (Westbury: Foundation Press, 1994).

7. Herbert Wechsler, "Toward Neutral Principles of Constitutional Law," 73 *Harv. L. Rev.* 1, 26, 31–35 (1959); id. at 26, 31–35.

8. G. Edward White, "From Realism to Critical Legal Studies: A Truncated Intellectual History," 40 *Sw. L.J.* 819, 823 (1986). For further discussion of the differences between legal realism and CLS, see Neil Duxbury, *Patterns of American Jurisprudence* at 421–91 (Oxford: Clarendon Press, 1995); G. Edward White, "The Inevitability of Critical Legal Studies," 36 *Stan. L. Rev.* 649 (1984).

9. Mark Tushnet, *Red, White, and Blue: A Critical Analysis of Constitutional Law* at 318 (Cambridge: Harvard University Press, 1988); Lawrence B. Solum, "On the Indeterminacy Crisis: Critiquing Critical Dogma," 54 *U. Chi. L. Rev.* 462, 462 (1987) (definition of indeterminacy thesis).

10. Mark Tushnet, "An Essay on Rights," 62 *Tex. L. Rev.* 1363, 1371 (1984); Peter Gabel and Duncan Kennedy, "Roll Over Beethoven," 36 *Stan. L. Rev.* 1, 26 (1984).

11. Patricia J. Williams, "Alchemical Notes: Reconstructing Ideals from Deconstructed Rights," 22 *Harv. C.R.-C.L. L. Rev.* 401, 431 (1987); Kimberlé

Williams Crenshaw, "Race, Reform, and Retrenchment: Transformation and Legitimation in Antidiscrimination Law," 101 *Harv. L. Rev.* 1331, 1357–58 (1988). For other critiques of CLS from women and people of color, see S. Benhabib and D. Cornell, eds., *Feminism as Critique: On the Politics of Gender* (Minneapolis: University of Minnesota Press, 1987); "Minority Critiques of the Critical Legal Studies Movement" (Symposium), 22 *Harv. C.R.-C.L.L. Rev.* 297 (1987); Kimberlé Williams Crenshaw, "Race, Reform, and Retrenchment," Carrie Menkel-Meadow, "Feminist Legal Theory, Critical Legal Studies, and Legal Education or 'The Fem-Crits Go to Law School,'" 38 *J. Legal Educ.* 61 (1988); Robin West, "Deconstructing the CLS-FEM Split," 2 *Wisc. Women's L.J.* 85 (1986).

12. Gary Peller, "The Discourse of Constitutional Degradation," 81 *Geo. L.J.* 313, 315, 336 (1992); Mark Tushnet, "Reply," 81 *Geo. L.J.* 343, 349, 350 (1992); Kimberlé Williams Crenshaw, "Race, Reform, and Retrenchment: Transformation and Legitimation in Antidiscrimination Law," 101 *Harv. L. Rev.* 1331, 1356 (1988) ("proclivities of mainstream"). We consider the Peller/Tushnet exchange in more detail in chapter 4.

13. The two famous CLS articles we refer to are Duncan Kennedy, "The Structure of Blackstone's Commentaries," 28 *Buffalo L. Rev.* 205 (1979); and Clare Dalton, "An Essay in the Deconstruction of Contract Doctrine," 94 *Yale L.J.* 999 (1985).

14. Kimberlé Crenshaw, "A Black Feminist Critique of Antidiscrimination Law and Politics," in *The Politics of Law: A Progressive Critique* 195, 213 n.7, David Kairys, ed. (New York: Pantheon, rev. ed., 1990); Richard Delgado, "When a Story Is Just a Story: Does Voice Really Matter?" 76 *Va. L. Rev.* 95, 95 n.1 (1990) (eight themes of critical race theory); Robin West, "Jurisprudence and Gender," 55 *U. Chi. L. Rev.* 1, 61 (1988) ("patriarchal jurisprudence"); Francisco Valdes, "Queers, Sissies, Dykes, and Tomboys: Deconstructing the Conflation of 'Sex,' 'Gender,' and 'Sexual Orientation' in Euro-American Law and Society," 83 *Calif. L. Rev.* 1, 9 (1995) ("pervasive phenomenon"). See also Francisco Valdes, "Unpacking Hetero-Patriarchy: Tracing the Conflation of Sex, Gender & Sexual Orientation to Its Origins," 8 *Yale J.L. & Human.* 161, 211 (1996) (one purpose of gaylegal studies is "to galvanize a comprehensive sex/gender reformation that addresses both the androsexism and heterosexism of the law, and their joint operation in the form of conflationary hetero-patriarchy").

15. Gary Peller, "The Discourse of Constitutional Degradation," 81 *Geo. L.J.* 313, 339 (1992).

16. Lawrence B. Solum, "On the Indeterminacy Crisis: Critiquing Critical Dogma," 54 *U. Chi. L. Rev.* 462, 463 (1987) ("relations of domination") (describing but not espousing the CLS position); Alan Freeman, "Legitimizing Racial Discrimination Through Antidiscrimination Law: A Critical Re-

view of Supreme Court Doctrine," 62 *Minn. L. Rev.* 1049 (1978). Perhaps ironically, one of us now inhabits Freeman's former office at the University of Minnesota.

17. Derrick Bell, "*Brown v. Board of Education* and the Interest-Convergence Dilemma," 93 *Harv. L. Rev.* 518, 523 (1980); Robin West, *Progressive Constitutionalism: Reconstructing the Fourteenth Amendment* at 45 (Durham, NC: Duke University Press, 1994); see also id. at 261.

18. Ann Scales, "The Emergence of Feminist Jurisprudence," 95 *Yale L.J.* 1373, 1378 (1986) ("myth"). For Searle's views, see John R. Searle, *The Construction of Social Reality* (New York: Free Press, 1995).

19. Stanley Fish, "Not of An Age, But for All Time: Canons and Postmodernism," 43 *J. Leg. Educ.* 11, 20 (1993).

20. Derrick Bell, "Racial Realism," 24 *Conn. L. Rev.* 363, 364 (1992). On Foucault's view of knowledge, see, e.g., *The Foucault Reader* at 7–9, Paul Rainbow, ed. (New York: Pantheon, 1984); Michel Foucault, *Madness & Civilization: A History of Insanity in the Age of Reason*, Richard Howard, trans. (New York: Pantheon, 1965).

21. Jerome M. Culp Jr., "Telling a Black Legal Story: Privilege, Authenticity, "Blunders," and Transformation in Outsider Narratives," 82 *Va. L. Rev.* 69, 90–91 (1996) ("white male establishment"); Richard Delgado, "Zero-Based Racial Politics and an Infinity-Based Response: Will Endless Talking Cure America's Racial Ills?" 80 *Geo. L.J.* 1879, 1880 (1992); Jerome M. Culp Jr., "Telling Tales In School: Black Legal Scholarship, Race, and Authenticity," unpub. ms., at 20 ("Cabrini Green"). (Cabrini Green, by the way, is a notorious Chicago housing project.) Interestingly enough, Culp's definition of the "white male establishment" appears to include *both* the authors of this book, as well as our Taiwan-born colleague Jim Chen. See Culp, "Telling a Black Legal Story," at 91–92.

22. Susan H. Williams, "Feminist Legal Epistemology," 8 *Berkeley Women's L.J.* 63, 75 (1993) ("deep connections").

23. Alex M. Johnson Jr., "Defending the Use of Narrative and Giving Content to the Voice of Color: Rejecting the Imposition of Process Theory in Legal Scholarship," 79 *Iowa L. Rev.* 803, 833–34 (1994); Stanley Fish, *There's No Such Thing as Free Speech And It's a Good Thing, Too"* at 18, 19 (New York: Oxford University Press, 1994); Eric Blumenson, "Mapping the Limits of Skepticism in Law and Morals," 74 *Tex. L. Rev.* 523, 541 (1996) ("demand for capitulation"—describing but not espousing radical position).

24. Derrick Bell, "Space Traders," *Faces at the Bottom of the Well: The Permanence of Racism* at 186–187 (New York: Basic Books, 1992).

25. Ann C. Scales, "The Emergence of Feminist Jurisprudence: An Essay," 95 *Yale L.J.* 1373, 1378 (1986); A. W. Phinney III, "Feminism, Epistemology and the Rhetoric of Law: Reading *Bowen v. Gilliard*," 12 *Harv.*

Women's L.J. 151, 176 (1989) (objectivity as "cover"); Gary Peller, "Reason and The Mob: The Politics of Representation," in *Tikkun: To Heal, Repair, and Transform the World: An Anthology* at 163, 164, Michael Lerner, ed. (Oakland, CA: Tikkun Books, 1992) ("no objective reference point"); Amy Gutmann, "Introduction," in Charles Taylor, Amy Gutmann, Michael Walzer, Steven Rockefeller, and Susan Wolf, *Multiculturalism: Examining the Politics of Recognition* 3, 18 (Princeton: Princeton University Press, 1994) (describing but not endorsing view that standards are "mask"); Richard Delgado, "Norms and Normal Science: Toward a Critique of Normativity in Legal Thought," 139 *U. Pa. L. Rev.* 933, 951 (1991) ("normative orderings"); Patricia J. Williams, *The Alchemy of Race and Rights: Diary of a Law Professor* at 103 (Cambridge: Harvard University Press, 1991) ("structured preferences"); Neil W. Hamilton, *Zealotry and Academic Freedom: A Legal and Historical Perspective* at 249 (New Brunswick: Transaction Publishers, 1995) (describing but not endorsing view of "masks of oppression").

26. Catharine A. MacKinnon, *Feminism Unmodified: Discourses on Life and Law* at 50, 54 (Cambridge: Harvard University Press, 1987).

27. Deborah Rhode, "Missing Questions: Feminist Perspectives on Legal Education," 45 *Stan. L. Rev.* 1547, 1555 (1993) ("knowledge is socially constructed"); Gary Peller, "Race Consciousness," 1990 *Duke L.J.* 758, 806; Frederick M. Gedicks, "Public Life and Hostility to Religion," 78 *Va. L. Rev.* 671, 686 (1992) ("creationism"); Gary Peller, "Reason and The Mob: The Politics of Interpretation," in *Tikkun: To Heal, Repair, and Transform the World: An Anthology* at 163, 165, Michael Lerner ed. (Oakland, CA: Tikkun Books, 1992).

28. Catharine A. MacKinnon, *Feminism Unmodified: Discourses on Life and Law* at 54 (Cambridge: Harvard University Press, 1987); Richard Delgado, "Rodrigo's Tenth Chronicle: Merit and Affirmative Action," 83 *Geo. L.J.* 1711, 1721 (1995); Lucinda M. Finley, "Breaking Women's Silence in Law: The Dilemma of the Gendered Nature of Legal Reasoning," 64 *Notre Dame L. Rev.* 886, 893 (1989) ("statistical proofs"); Mari J. Matsuda, "When the First Quail Calls: Multiple Consciousness as Jurisprudential Method," 11 *Women's Rts. L. Rep.* 7, 8 (1989) ("narrow evidentiary concepts"); Susan H. Williams, "Feminist Legal Epistemology," 8 *Berkeley Women's L.J.* 63, 73 (1993) ("Cartesian knower"); Nomi Maya Stolzenberg, "'He Drew a Circle That Shut Me Out': Assimilation, Indoctrination, and the Paradox of a Liberal Education," 106 *Harv. L. Rev.* 581, 611 (1993) ("indoctrination"); Jane B. Baron, "Resistance to Stories," 67 *S. Cal. L. Rev.* 255, 273 (1994) ("background assumptions"). For similar assertions, see Genevieve Lloyd, *The Man of Reason: "Male" and "Female" in Western Philosophy* (Minneapolis: University of Minnesota Press, 1984); Patricia Cain, "Feminist Legal Scholarship," 77 *Iowa L. Rev.* 19, 27 (1991); Linda R. Hirshman, "Foreword: The Waning of the Middle Ages," 69 *Chi.-Kent L. Rev.* 293, 297–98 (1993).

29. Richard Delgado and Jean Stefancic, "Why Do We Tell the Same Stories? Law Reform, Critical Librarianship, and the Triple Helix Dilemma," 42 *Stan. L. Rev.* 207, 218–19, 222, 224–25 (1989). As far as we can tell, Delgado and Stefancic are entirely serious about this argument.

30. Richard Delgado, "Rodrigo's Seventh Chronicle: Race, Democracy, and the State," 41 *U.C.L.A. L. Rev.* 720, 729, 734, 735 (1994); Alan Ryan, "Foucault's Life and Hard Times," *New York Review of Books*, April 8, 1993, at 12.

31. Sanford Levinson, "Religious Language and the Public Square," 105 *Harv. L. Rev.* 2061, 2076 (1992).

32. Alex M. Johnson Jr., "Defending the Use of Narrative and Giving Content to the Voice of Color: Rejecting the Imposition of Process Theory in Legal Scholarship," 79 *Iowa L. Rev.* 803, 819 (1994).

33. Richard Delgado, "Storytelling for Oppositionists and Others: A Plea for Narrative," 87 *Mich. L. Rev.* 2411, 2413 (1989).

34. Carol Gilligan, *In a Different Voice: Psychological Theory and Women's Development* (Cambridge: Harvard University Press, 1982). For her later softening of the thesis, see Carol Gilligan, Annie Rogers, and Lyn Mikel Brown, "Epilogue: Soundings into Development," in *Making Connections: The Relational Worlds of Adolescent Girls at Emma Willard School* at 314, 317–18, Carol Gilligan, Nona P. Lyons, and Trudy J. Hanmer, eds. (Cambridge: Harvard University Press, 1989); Carol Gilligan and Jane Attanucci, "Two Moral Orientations," in *Mapping the Moral Domain: A Contribution of Women's Thinking to Psychological Theory and Education* at 73, 82–85, Carol Gilligan, Janie Victoria Ward, and Jill McLean Taylor, eds. (Cambridge: Harvard University Press, 1988). For criticism of Gilligan, see, e.g., John M. Broughton, "Women's Rationality and Men's Virtues: A Critique of Gender Dualism in Gilligan's Theory of Moral Development," 50 *Soc. Res.* 597 (1983); Owen J. Flanagan Jr. and Jonathan E. Adler, "Impartiality and Particularity," 50 *Soc. Res.* 576, 584–88 (1983); Linda K. Kerber, Catherine G. Greeno, and Eleanor B. Maccoby, Zella Luria, Carol B. Stack, and Carol Gilligan, "On *In A Different Voice:* An Interdisciplinary Forum," 11 *Signs* 304, 310–21 (1986); Joan G. Miller and David M. Bersoff, "Culture and Moral Judgment: How Are Conflicts Between Justice and Interpersonal Responsibilities Resolved?" 62 J. Personality & Soc. Psychol. 541, 552 (1992); Debra Nalis, "Social-Scientific Sexism: Gilligan's Mismeasure of Man," 50 *Soc. Res.* 643 (1983); Lawrence J. Walker, Brian de Vries, and Shelley D. Trevethan, "Moral Stages and Moral Orientations in Real-Life and Hypothetical Dilemmas," 58 *Child Dev.* 842, 844–45 (1987); Lawrence J. Walker, "Sex Difference in the Development of Moral Reasoning: A Critical View," 55 *Child Dev.* 677, 688 (1984).

35. Stephen L. Carter, "Loving the Messenger," 1 *Yale J.L. & Humanities* 317, 325 (1989); Richard Delgado, "The Imperial Scholar: Reflections on a

Review of Civil Rights Literature," 132 *U. Pa. L. Rev.* 561, 564 n.15 (1984); Peter Halewood, "White Men Can't Jump: Critical Epistemologies, Embodiment, and the Praxis of Legal Scholarship," 7 *Yale J.L. & Feminism* 1, 25 (1995) (males should reconsider). The previous work by one of the authors is Suzanna Sherry, "Civic Virtue and the Feminine Voice in Constitutional Adjudication," 72 *Va. L. Rev.* 543 (1986).

36. Mary I. Coombs, "Outsider Scholarship: The Law Review Stories," 63 *U. Colo. L. Rev.* 683, 713 (1992) ("advance interests"); Richard Delgado, "On Telling Stories in School: A Reply to Farber and Sherry," 46 *Vand. L. Rev.* 665, 673–74 (1993) ("not at understanding the law"); William N. Eskridge Jr., "Gaylegal Narratives," 46 *Stan. L. Rev.* 607, 625 (1994).

37. Richard Delgado, "Storytelling for Oppositionists and Others: A Plea for Narrative," 87 *Mich. L. Rev.* 2411, 2413 (1989) ("destroying mindset"); Mary I. Coombs, "Outsider Scholarship: The Law Review Stories," 63 *U. Colo. L. Rev.* 683, 695 (1992) ("explode"); Lynne N. Henderson, "Legality and Empathy," 85 *Mich. L. Rev.* 1574, 1576 (1987) ("received wisdom"); Jane B. Baron, "Intention, Interpretation, and Stories," 42 *Duke L.J.* 630, 631 (1992) ("disrupt"); Richard Delgado, "Storytelling for Oppositionists and Others: A Plea for Narrative, 87 *Mich. L. Rev.* 2411, 2414 (1989) ("shatter"); Coombs, *supra*, at 697 ("seduce"); Kathryn Abrams, "Hearing the Call of Stories, 79 *Cal. L. Rev.* 971, 1002–3 (1991) ("flash of recognition," "resonates"); Thomas Ross, "The Rhetorical Tapestry of Race: White Innocence and Black Abstraction," 32 *Wm. & Mary L. Rev.* 1, 2 (1990) ("magical thing"). On "transformation" and "construction" see, e.g., Mari J. Matsuda, "Looking to the Bottom: Critical Legal Studies and Reparations," 22 *Harv. C.R.-C.L. L. Rev.* 323, 335 (1987); Mary I. Coombs, "Outsider Scholarship: The Law Review Stories," 63 *U. Colo. L. Rev.* 683, 715 (1992); Thomas Ross, "The Rhetorical Tapestry of Race: White Innocence and Black Abstraction," 32 *Wm. & Mary L. Rev.* 1, 2 (1990); Steven L. Winter, "The Cognitive Dimension of the Agon Between Legal Power and Narrative Meaning," 87 *Mich. L. Rev.* 2225, 2228 (1989); Jerome McCristal Culp Jr., "Autobiography and Legal Scholarship and Teaching: Finding the Me in the Legal Academy," 77 *Va. L. Rev.* 539, 543 (1991); Jane B. Baron, "Resistance to Stories," 67 *S. Cal. L. Rev.* 255, 261 (1994); Richard Delgado, "Shadowboxing: An Essay on Power," 77 *Cornell L. Rev.* 813, 818 (1992); William N. Eskridge Jr., "Gaylegal Narratives," 46 *Stan. L. Rev.* 607, 607 (1994).

38. Robert L. Hayman Jr. and Nancy Levit, "The Tales of White Folk: Doctrine, Narrative, and the Reconstruction of Racial Reality," 84 *Cal. L. Rev.* 377, 403 (1996).

39. Duncan Kennedy, "A Cultural Pluralist Case for Affirmative Action in Legal Academia," 1990 *Duke L.J.* 705, 708, 733; Stanley Fish, *Doing What Comes Naturally: Change, Rhetoric, and the Practice of Theory in Literary and*

Legal Studies at 164 (Durham, NC: Duke University Press, 1989). For similar views by other radical multiculturalists, see Alan Freeman, "Racism, Rights and the Quest for Equality of Opportunity: A Critical Legal Essay," 23 *Harv. C.R.-C.L. L. Rev.* 295, 324, 382–85 (1988); Gary Peller, "Race Consciousness," 1990 *Duke L.J.* 758, 803, 806–7.

40. Richard Delgado, "Rodrigo's Tenth Chronicle: Merit and Affirmative Action," 83 *Geo. L.J.* 1711, 1718, 1719 (1995) ("elite class"); Catharine A. MacKinnon, "Reflections on Sex Equality Under Law," 100 *Yale L.J.* 1281, 1291 (1991); Diana M. Poole, "On Merit," 1 *J. Law & Ineq. J.* 155, 157 (1983) ("reward white men"); Richard Delgado, "Brewer's Plea: Critical Thoughts on Common Cause," 44 *Vand. L. Rev.* 1, 9 (1991) (merit as judging "Other"); Richard Delgado, "Rodrigo's Chronicle," 101 *Yale L.J.* 1357, 1364 (1992) ("white people's affirmative action"); Delgado, "Rodrigo's Tenth Chronicle," 1719 ("neutral laws as racism").

41. Alex M. Johnson Jr., "The New Voice of Color," 100 *Yale L.J.* 2007, 2052 (1991) ("gate built by white men"); John O. Calmore, "Critical Race Theory, Archie Shepp, and Fire Music: Securing an Authentic Intellectual Life in a Multicultural World," 65 *S. Cal. L. Rev.* 2129, 2219 (1992) ("cultural bias"); Jerome M. Culp Jr., "Posner on Duncan Kennedy and Racial Difference: White Authority in the Legal Academy," 41 *Duke L.J.* 1095, 1097 (1992); Patricia J. Williams, *The Alchemy of Race and Rights: Diary of a Law Professor* at 103 (Cambridge: Harvard University Press, 1991). See also Catharine A. MacKinnon, *Feminism Unmodified: Discourses on Life and Law* at 36 (Cambridge: Harvard University Press, 1987) (merit standards are "an affirmative action plan" for men); Robert L. Hyman Jr. and Nancy Levit, "The Tales of White Folk: Doctrine, Narrative, and the Reconstruction of Racial Reality," 84 *Cal. L. Rev.* 377, 402–3 (1996) ("processes of meritocratic assessment and reward do not cleanse or even escape the taint of racial bias: indeed, they embody it").

42. Richard Delgado, "The Imperial Scholar: Reflections on a Review of Civil Rights Literature," 132 *U. Pa. L. Rev.* 561, 572 (1984); Patricia J. Williams, *The Alchemy of Race and Rights: Diary of a Law Professor* at 103 (Cambridge: Harvard University Press, 1991). Kennedy's unpublished proposal is described in G. Edward White, "The Inevitability of Critical Legal Studies," 36 *Stan. L. Rev.* 649, 658 (1984).

43. Jerome M. Culp Jr., "Posner on Duncan Kennedy and Racial Difference: White Authority in the Legal Academy," 41 *Duke L.J.* 1059, 1101, 1113 (1992); Richard Delgado, "Rodrigo's Tenth Chronicle: Merit and Affirmative Action," 83 *Geo. L.J.* 1711, 1741 (1995); Stanley Fish, *There's No Such Thing as Free Speech And It's a Good Thing, Too* at 68 (New York: Oxford University Press, 1994). See also id. at 12–13: "What I find is a straight line between contemporary hostility to black studies, ethnic studies, gay and lesbian studies,

and so on and the anti-immigration, anti-Catholic, frankly racist writings of the late nineteenth and twentieth century—by and large the same fears, the same scapegoats, the same rhetoric."

Chapter 2

1. David Kairys, "Law and Politics," 52 *Geo. Wash. L. Rev.* 243, 244, 247 (1984) (footnote omitted). For a sampling of recent scholarship on indeterminacy and references to earlier work, see Jules Coleman and Brian Leiter, "Determinacy, Objectivity, and Authority," 142 *U. Pa. L. Rev.* 549 (1993); J.M. Balkin, "Review Essay: Ideology as Constraint," 43 *Stan. L. Rev.* 1133 (1991); Ken Kress, "Legal Indeterminacy," 77 *Cal. L. Rev.* 283 (1989). It would be a massive task simply to sort through the various versions of the indeterminacy thesis and the supporting arguments offered in its behalf. Rather than undertake that task here, we refer the reader to the useful synthesis presented by Larry Solum in an article several years ago, in which he catalogues the following reasons why legal reasoning might be indeterminate. First, individual legal rules may be ambiguous or indeterminate, thereby providing no foothold for argument. Second, legal rules taken as a group may be circular or contradictory, or they may embody contradictory policies. Third, metarules may provide the continual option of over-riding existing legal rules. The indeterminacy thesis holds that these factors combine to deprive legal reasoning of its power to constrain outcomes in significant cases. Lawrence B. Solum, "On the Indeterminacy Crisis: Critiquing Critical Dogma," 54 *U. Chi. L. Rev.* 462, 465–66 (1987). (We are making use of Solum's description of the indeterminacy thesis, rather than his critique. Based on our own review of the critical literature, we believe that he has provided a fair summary of the CLS position.)

2. On easy cases, see Ronald Dworkin, *Taking Rights Seriously* at 31–39 (London: Duckworth & Co., 1977); Mark V. Tushnet, "Following the Rules Laid Down: A Critique of Interpretivism and Neutral Principles," 96 *Harv. L. Rev.* 781, 806–18 (1983). One possibility is that the missing determinacy is supplied by a political or moral theory, which guides judges to their decisions. Possible candidates might include Richard Posner's economic theory of law or the political philosophies of Robert Nozick or John Rawls. Critical legal scholars generally have been skeptical of this possibility. They view such theories as suffering from much the same indeterminacy as the legal system. More recently, Richard Delgado and Pierre Schlag have claimed that all normative argument suffers from inherent flaws like those that earlier critical scholars attributed to the legal system. In their view, with or without an articulated theory, arguments based on moral claims simply lead nowhere.

If morality is also indeterminate, it cannot supply determinacy to the legal system. See Duncan Kennedy, "Cost-Benefit Analysis of Entitlement Problems: A Critique," 33 *Stan. L. Rev.* 387 (1981); Jay M. Feinman, "Critical Approaches to Contract Law," 30 *U.C.L.A. L. Rev.* 829, 847 (1983); Richard Delgado, "Norms and Normal Science: Toward a Critique of Normativity in Legal Thought," 139 *U. Pa. L. Rev.* 933, 960–62 (1991); Pierre Schlag, "Values," 6 *Yale J.L. & Humanities* 219, 277 (1994).

3. Joseph William Singer, "The Player and the Cards: Nihilism and Legal Theory," 94 *Yale L.J.* 1, 21 (1984). See also Robert W. Gordon, "Critical Legal Histories," 36 *Stan. L. Rev.* 57, 125 (1984); Clare Dalton, "An Essay in the Deconstruction of Contract Doctrine," 94 *Yale L.J.* 997, 1009–10 (1985). Similarly, Mark Tushnet speaks of the judge's image of the judicial role as the deciding factor, while Steve Winter refers to gestalts. Mark V. Tushnet, "Following the Rules Laid Down: A Critique of Interpretivism and Neutral Principles," 96 *Harv. L. Rev.* 781, 823 (1983); Steven L. Winter, "Indeterminacy and Incommensurability in Constitutional Law," 78 *Calif. L. Rev.* 1443, 1463 (1990); see also id. at 1473 (discussing "cultural constructs and stabilized matrices").

4. Derrick Bell, "Who's Afraid of Critical Race Theory?" 1995 *U. Ill. L. Rev.* 893, 899–900 ("not a formal mechanism") (Bell attributes this view to Stanley Fish, but says it is shared by critical race theorists); Derrick Bell, "*Brown v. Board of Education* and the Interest-Convergence Dilemma," 93 *Harv. L. Rev.* 518, 523–26 (1980) (white self-interest); Patricia J. Williams, "*Metro Broadcasting, Inc. v. FCC:* Regrouping in Singular Times," 104 *Harv. L. Rev.* 525, 544 (1990). See also Catharine A. MacKinnon, *Feminism Unmodified: Discourses on Life and Law* at 153–54 (Cambridge: Harvard University Press, 1987) (discussion of how judge's sexual attitudes affect rulings in pornography cases).

5. Joseph William Singer, "Persuasion," 87 *Mich. L. Rev.* 2442, 2455 (1989).

6. For an introduction to this trend, see *Law's Stories: Narrative and Rhetoric in the Law*, Peter Brooks and Paul Gewirtz, eds. (New Haven: Yale University Press, 1996). On a similar trend in the humanities, see Adam Begeley, "The I's Have It: Dukes "Moi" Critics Expose Themselves," *Lingua Franca*, March/April 1994, at 54.

7. Critiques of storytelling include Anne M. Coughlin, "Regulating the Self: Autobiographical Performances in Outsider Scholarship," 81 *Va. L. Rev.* 1229 (1995); Daniel A. Farber and Suzanna Sherry, "Telling Stories Out of School: An Essay on Legal Narratives," 45 *Stan. L. Rev.* 807 (1993); Mark Tushnet, "The Degradation of Constitutional Discourse," 81 *Geo. L.J.* 251 (1992).

8. Lucinda M. Finley, "Breaking Women's Silence in Law: The Dilemma of the Gendered Nature of Legal Reasoning," 64 *Notre Dame L. Rev.* 886, 903 (1989) ("legal voice"); Mari J. Matsuda, "Looking to the Bottom: Critical Legal Studies and Reparations," 22 *Harv. C.R.-C.L. L. Rev.* 323, 324 (1987) ("liberal promise"); Richard Delgado, "Storytelling for Oppositionists and Others: A Plea for Narrative," 87 *Mich. L. Rev.* 2411, 2437 (1988) (psychic therapy).

9. Gerald P. Lopez, "Lay Lawyering," 32 *U.C.L.A. L. Rev.* 1, 10 (1984); Kathryn Abrams, "Hearing the Call of Stories," 79 *Cal. L. Rev.* 971, 976 (1991); see also id. at 1028–44; Robin West, "Jurisprudence and Gender," 55 *U. Chi. L. Rev.* 1, 64 (1988). Other authors question the very distinction between reason and emotion. Mirroring the critical view of how judges really decide cases, Steven Winter suggests that "the cognitive process" proceeds by imposing narratives on experience, rather than through top-down reasoning. If so, then traditional legal scholarship, with its linear, rational arguments, fundamentally fails to capture the essence of human reasoning. The cure, of course, is storytelling. According to Jane Baron, storytelling is designed to question the received definitions of such things as "reason" and "analysis," and to deny the distinction between "reason and analysis" and "emotive appeal." Steven L. Winter, "The Cognitive Dimension of the Agon Between Legal Power and Narrative Meaning," 87 *Mich. L. Rev.* 2225, 2228 (1989); Jane B. Baron, "Resistance to Stories," 67 *S. Cal. L. Rev.* 255, 255–57, 277–85 (1994); see also Mari J. Matsuda, "When the First Quail Calls: Multiple Consciousness as Jurisprudential Method," 11 *Wom. Rts. L. Rep.* 7, 8 (1989) (outsider scholars "reject the artificial bifurcation of thought and feeling"); Martha L. Minow and Elizabeth V. Spelman, "Passion for Justice," 10 *Cardozo L. Rev.* 37, 47–48 (1988) (criticizing distinction between reason and emotion). For a thoughtful discussion of the role of emotions in law see Susan Bandes, "Empathy, Narrative, and Victim Impact Statements," 63 *U. Chi. L. Rev.* 361 (1996).

10. For some recent contributions to the pornography debate, see Carlin Meyer, "Sex, Sin, and Women's Liberation: Against Porn-Suppression," 72 *Tex. L. Rev.* 1097 (1994); Marianne Wesson, "Girls Should Bring Lawsuits Everywhere . . . Nothing Will Be Corrupted: Pornography as Speech and Product," 60 *U. Chi. L. Rev.* 845 (1993). For background on the ordinance, see Paul Brest and Ann Vandenberg, "Politics, Feminism, and the Constitution: The Anti-Pornography Movement in Minneapolis," 39 *Stan. L. Rev.* 607 (1987); David P. Bryden, "Between Two Constitutions: Feminism and Pornography," 2 *Const. Comm.* 147 (1985). We will utilize MacKinnon's latest book, *Only Words,* as a succinct synthesis of her views. MacKinnon's views on the role of language in constructing reality—and specifically, the role of

pornography in constructing sexuality and gender—are explored in Jeanne L. Schroeder, "The Taming of the Shrew: The Liberal Attempt to Mainstream Radical Feminist Theory," 5 *Yale J. L. & Fem.* 123 (1992).

11. Catharine A. MacKinnon, *Only Words* at 13, 30–31, 106 (Cambridge: Harvard University Press, 1993).

12. Id. at 108, 16–17, 62. Pornography results in rape because of a conditioning process, not because rapists are persuaded by ideas or even inflamed by its emotions. Id. at 16. Because of MacKinnon's reliance on conditioning as the cause of behavior, the term "mindset" might be more accurately replaced with "culturally conditioned propensities toward behavioral responses." We do not regard the distinction as significant for present purposes, though her behaviorist leanings do raise interesting philosophical issues.

13. Id. at 99, 104.

14. Mari J. Matsuda, Charles Lawrence III, Richard Delgado, and Kimberlé Crenshaw, *Words that Wound: Critical Race Theory, Assaultive Speech, and the First Amendment* at 136 (Boulder, CO: Westview Press, 1993) ("cross burning"); id. at 62 ("construct the social reality"); id. at 129 (distorts behavior).

15. Id. at 68–74 (rational persuuasion); id. at 91–93 (physiological shock); id. at 77 ("computer virus" and "epidemic").

16. On law formation, see id. at 49. On "all deliberate speed," see Charles B. Lawrence III, "The Id, the Ego, and Equal Protection: Reckoning with Unconscious Racism," 39 *Stan. L. Rev.* 317, 342–43 (1987). Compare Delgado's recent efforts to explain the warped mindsets of civil libertarians: Richard Delgado, "Hate Speech, Loving Communities: Why Our Nation of "A Just Balance" Changes So Slowly," 82 *Cal. L. Rev.* 851 (1994). See also John E. Morrison, "Colorblindness, Individuality, and Merit: An Analysis of the Rhetoric Against Affirmative Action," 79 *Iowa L. Rev.* 313 (1994).

The arguments for controlling pornography and hate speech quite clearly parallel the claims made for the curative powers of storytelling. What pornography and hate speech do, legal storytelling seeks to undo. Thus, within the storytelling literature itself, there are references to counterstories designed to combat the dominant stories. See, e.g., Richard Delgado, "On Telling Stories in School: A Reply to Farber and Sherry," 46 *Vand. L. Rev.* 665, 670 (1993). Not surprisingly, the theories of language employed to support both the substantive and the methodological positions are the same.

17. Catharine A. MacKinnon, *Feminism Unmodified: Discourses on Life and Law* at 175 (Cambridge: Harvard University Press, 1987).

18. Stanley Fish, *There's No Such Thing as Free Speech And It's a Good Thing, Too* at 110 (New York: Oxford University Press, 1994); see also Mari J. Matsuda, "Public Response to Racist Speech: Considering the Victim's Story," 87 *Mich. L. Rev.* 2320 (1989) (on non-neutrality).

19. Stanley Fish, *There's No Such Thing as Free Speech And It's a Good Thing, Too* at 75–76 (New York: Oxford University Press, 1994).

20. Derrick Bell, *Faces at the Bottom of the Well: The Permanence of Racism* at 121, 124–25 (New York: Basic Books, 1992).

21. See Catharine A. MacKinnon, *Only Words* at 22 (Cambridge: Harvard University Press, 1993); Catharine MacKinnon and Andrea Dworkin "proposed a law against pornography that defines it as graphic sexually explicit materials that subordinate women through pictures or words."

22. Robert C. Post, "Racist Speech, Democracy, and the First Amendment," 32 *Wm. & Mary L. Rev.* 267, 282; Carlin Meyer, "Sex, Sin, and Women's Liberation: Against Porn-Suppression," 72 *Tex. L. Rev.* 1097, 1197 (1994) (also observing that at least some of the advocates of suppressing pornography have a "one-dimensional view of representation," which holds that "what an image *depicts*, it *urges*," id. at 1142); Burt Neuborne, "Ghosts in the Attic: Idealized Pluralism, Community and Hate Speech," 27 *Harv. C.R.-C.L. L. Rev.* 371, 394 (1992) ("bruised emotions"); id. at 399 ("demonstrable").

23. Henry Louis Gates Jr., makes this point, noting in opposition that "things like reason, argument and moral suasion did play a significant role in changing attitudes toward 'race relations.'" Henry Louis Gates Jr., "Let Them Talk: Why Civil Liberties Pose No Threat to Civil Rights," *The New Republic*, Sept. 20 & 27, 1993, at 48. On the connection between economic views of rationality and the first amendment, see Daniel A. Farber, "Free Speech Without Romance: Public Choice and the First Amendment," 105 *Harv. L. Rev.* 554 (1991). Justice Holmes first proposed the idea of a marketplace of ideas in his dissent in *Abrams v. United States*, 250 U.S. 616 (1919).

24. Charles R. Lawrence III, "The Id, the Ego, and Equal Protection: Reckoning with Unconscious Racism," 39 *Stan. L. Rev.* 317, 322, 331–39 (1987).

25. Id. at 362–63 (1987). For Lawrence's views on hate speech, see Mari J. Matsuda, Charles Lawrence III, Richard Delgado, and Kimberlé Crenshaw, *Words That Wound: Critical Race Theory, Assaultive Speech, and the First Amendment* at 68 (Boulder, CO: Westview Press, 1993).

26. The existing rule was established in *Washington v. Davis*, 426 U.S. 229 (1976). Lawrence's approach is explained in Charles R. Lawrence III, "The Id, the Ego, and Equal Protection: Reckoning with Unconscious Racism," 39 *Stan. L. Rev.* 317, 356 (1987) (the quote is at 358). For criticism of the rule, see, e.g., Robin West, *Progressive Constitutionalism: Reconstructing the Fourteenth Amendment* at 34, 37, 58 (Durham, NC: Duke University Press, 1994).

27. Richard Delgado, "Brewer's Plea: Critical Thoughts on Common Cause," 44 *Vand. L. Rev.* 1, 12 n.58 (1991) ("racial justice"); Richard Delgado,

"The Imperial Scholar: Reflections on a Review of Civil Rights Literature," 132 *U. Pa. L. Rev.* 516, 572 (1984) ("overhaul"); Derrick Bell, "Xerces and the Affirmative Action Mystique," 57 *Geo. Wash. L. Rev.* 1595, 1605 (1989).

28. Larry Alexander, "What We Do, and Why We Do It," 45 *Stan. L. Rev.* 1885, 1890–96 (1993); Henry Louis Gates Jr., "Let Them Talk: Why Civil Liberties Pose No Threat to Civil Rights," *The New Republic*, Sept. 20 & 27, 1993, at 37, 47. For other rationalist criticisms of radical multiculturalism, see Daniel A. Farber and Suzanna Sherry, "Telling Stories Out of School: An Essay on Legal Narratives," 45 *Stan. L. Rev.* 807 (1993); Mark V. Tushnet, "The Degradation of Constitutional Discourse," 81 *Geo. L.J.* 251 (1992); Toni M. Massaro, "Empathy, Legal Storytelling, and the Rule of Law: New Words, Old Wounds?" 87 *Mich. L. Rev.* 2099 (1989); Suzanna Sherry, "The Sleep of Reason," 84 *Geo. L.J.* 453 (1996).

Chapter 3

1. Richard Delgado, "Rodrigo's Tenth Chronicle: Merit and Affirmative Action," 83 *Geo. L.J.* 1711, 1744 (1995).

2. John Rawls, *A Theory of Justice* at 66 (Cambridge: Harvard University Press, 1971).

3. Duncan Kennedy, "A Cultural Pluralist Case for Affirmative Action in Legal Academia," 1990 *Duke L.J.* 705, 710 (describing but opposing this position). See also Daniel Bell, "On Meritocracy and Equality," 29 *The Public Interest* 29, 37 (1972).

4. Randall L. Kennedy, "Racial Critiques of Legal Academia," 102 *Harv. L. Rev.* 1745, 1807 (1989). Another notable recent defense of merit is Stephen L. Carter, "Academic Tenure and 'White Male' Standards: Some Lessons from the Patent Law," 100 *Yale L.J.* 2065 (1991). For Kennedy's defense of affirmative action, see Randall L. Kennedy, "Persuasion and Distrust: A Comment on the Affirmative Action Debate," 99 *Harv. L. Rev.* 1327 (1986). For a good critique of existing standards of merit that does not adopt the radical rejection of the whole concept of merit, see Yxta Maya Murray, "Merit-Teaching," 23 *Hastings Constit. L.Q.* 1073 (1996).

5. On the radicals' concentration on university professors, see, e.g., Daniel A. Farber, "The Outmoded Debate Over Affirmative Action," 82 *Cal. L. Rev.* 893, 919 (1994); Richard Delgado, "The Imperial Scholar: Reflections on a Review of Civil Rights Literature," 132 *U. Pa. L. Rev.* 561 (1984); Richard Delgado, "The Imperial Scholar Revisited: How to Marginalize Outsider Writing, Ten Years Later," 140 *U. Pa. L. Rev.* 1349 (1992); Charles Lawrence, "Minority Hiring in AALS Law Schools: The Need for Voluntary Quotas," 20 *U.S.F. L. Rev.* 429 (1986). For data on law professor hirings,

see Richard A. White, "Statistical Report on the Gender and Minority Composition of New Law Teachers and AALS Faculty Appointments Register Candidates," 44 *J. Legal Educ.* 424, 429–30 (1994). For salary data, see Richard Bernstein, *Dictatorship of Virtue: Multiculturalism and the Battle for America's Future* at 135 (New York: Alfred A. Knopf, 1994).

6. On the black middle class and the black underclass, see, e.g., *A Common Destiny: Blacks and American Society* at 274–77, Gerald D. Jaynes and Robin M. Williams Jr., eds. (Washington, DC: National Academy Press, 1989); Laurence E. Harrison, *Who Prospers: How Cultural Values Shape Economic and Political Success* at 202–4; Charles Murray, *Losing Ground: American Social Policy 1950–1980* at 140–41 (New York: Basic Books, 1984) (presenting graphs of income and employment); Andrew Hacker, "Goodbye to Affirmative Action?" *New York Review of Books,* July 11, 1996, at 21, 29 ("Since 1970, black families who are upper middle class . . . have grown from 11.6 percent to 21.2 percent, a sharper rise than for whites"). Harrison notes that, by 1973, black college graduates were earning more than white college graduates. The "course that Thurgood Marshall proposed" refers to the policy of integration commanded by the U.S. Supreme Court in *Brown v. Board of Education,* 347 U.S. 483 (1954). Thurgood Marshall masterminded the case and argued it before the Supreme Court.

7. The figures in this paragraph are taken from the following sources: Thomas Sowell, *Ethnic America: A History* at 5 (New York: Basic Books, 1981) (original figures on Jewish income derived from 1970 census data; tables in *Essays and Data on American Ethnic Groups* at 257–58, Thomas Sowell, ed. [New York: Basic Books, 1978]); Seymour Martin Lipset and Earl Raab, *Jews and the New American Scene* at 26 (Cambridge: Harvard University Press, 1995) (statistics on richest Americans); U.S. Commission on Civil Rights, *The Economic Status of Americans of Asian Descent: An Exploratory Investigation* at 29, 71 (Washington, DC: U.S. Commission on Civil Rights, 1988); U.S. General Accounting Office, *Asian Americans: A Status Report* at 23 (Washington, DC: U.S. General Accounting Office, 1990); Charles E. Silberman, *A Certain People: American Jews and Their Lives Today* at 118, 148–44 (New York: Summit Books, 1985) (noting that in 1984, percentage of Jewish households with incomes above $50,000 was four times the percentage of non-Hispanic white households in the same income level); Seymour Martin Lipset and Earl Raab, *Jews and the New American Scene* at 26 (Cambridge: Harvard University Press, 1995) (in 1988, per capita Jewish income almost doubled that of non-Jews); see also Gerald Krefetz, *Jews and Money: The Myths and the Reality* (New Haven: Ticknor & Fields, 1982); Sidney Goldstein, "American Jewry, 1970: A Demographic Profile," in 72 *American Jewish Yearbook* at 3, 80–85 (Philadelphia: The Jewish Publication

Society of America, 1971) (more Jews in high-income categories; fewer in low-income categories). Even including foreign-born Asian Americans (who typically earn less than their native-born counterparts) does not eliminate the disparity between whites and Asians. U.S. Commission on Civil Rights, *The Economic Status of Americans of Asian Descent* at 29. Moreover, the disparity is not solely the result of more family members working: these groups of native-born Asian American men and women also have higher *individual* annual and hourly earnings than non-Hispanic whites. See id. at 68, 90.

8. The data in this paragraph are taken from: Gerald Krefetz, *Jews and Money: The Myths and the Reality* at 31, 35–36 (New Haven: Ticknor & Fields, 1982); Sidney Goldstein, "Profile of American Jewry: Insights from the 1990 Jewish Population Survey," in 92 *American Jewish Yearbook* at 77, 110–11, David Singer and Ruth R. Seldin, eds. (Philadelphia: The Jewish Publication Society of America, 1992); U.S. General Accounting Office, *Asian Americans: A Status Report* 26 (Washington, DC: U.S. General Accounting Office, 1990); Henry Rosovsky, *The University: An Owner's Manual* at 67–68 n.12 (New York: W.W. Norton, 1990); Deborah Woo, "The 'Overrepresentation' of Asian Americans: Red Herrings and Yellow Perils," in *Race and Ethnic Conflict: Contending Views on Prejudice, Discrimination, and Ethnoviolence* at 314, 316, Fred L. Pincus and Howard J. Ehrlich, eds. (Boulder, CO: Westview Press, 1994); Nathan Belth, *A Promise to Keep: A Narrative of the American Encounter with Anti-Semitism* at 96–110 (New York: Times Books, 1979); Leonard Dinnerstein, *Antisemitism in America* at 84–86 (New York: Oxford University Press, 1994); Alan Dershowitz, *Chutzpah* at 64–71 (Boston: Little, Brown, 1991); Charles E. Silberman, *A Certain People: Jews and Their Lives Today* at 144 (New York: Summit Books, 1985); David A. Hollinger, *Science, Jews, and Secular Culture: Studies in Mid-Twentieth Century American Intellectual History* at 8 (Princeton: Princeton University Press, 1996); Seymour Martin Lipset and Earl Raab, *Jews and the New American Scene* at 26–27 (Cambridge: Harvard University Press, 1995). See also U.S. Commission on Civil Rights, *The Economic Status of Americans of Asian Descent: An Exploratory Investigation* at 55–56 (Washington, DC: U.S. Commission on Civil Rights, 1988) (many groups of Asian Americans have more years of schooling than non-Hispanic whites)

9. Richard A. Posner, "Duncan Kennedy on Affirmative Action," 1990 *Duke L.J.* 1157, 1158; Duncan Kennedy, "A Cultural Pluralist Case for Affirmative Action in Legal Academia," 1990 *Duke L.J.* 705, 732 (jobs as political resources); Richard Delgado, "Rodrigo's Chronicle," 101 *Yale L.J.* 1357, 1364 (1992) (affirmative action). For general population figures on Jews, see Barry Kosmin and Jeff Scheckner, "Jewish Population in the United States, 1989," in 90 *American Jewish Yearbook* at 278, 280–81, David Singer and Ruth

R. Seldin eds. (Philadelphia: The Jewish Publication Society of America, 1990). For 1970 data on law faculties, see Robert Burt, *Two Jewish Justices: Outcasts in the Promised Land* at 64 (Berkeley: University of California Press, 1988); Charles E. Silberman, *A Certain People: American Jews and Their Lives Today* at 99 (New York: Summit Books, 1985). A recent unpublished study concluded that 26 percent of American law faculty are Jewish. James Lindgren, "Measuring Diversity," unpublished manuscript.

10. Derrick Bell, *Confronting Authority: Reflections of an Ardent Protester* at 76–77 (Boston: Beacon, 1994). Some readers might be inclined to read Bell as attacking credentialism rather than "real" merit. We disagree with this reading, based on Bell's many broad statements about the racist qualities of merit. In any event, this reading would not eliminate the anti-Semitic implications of Bell's positions. In considering the implications of his position, it may be helpful to compare merit determinations with medical testing. Suppose some medical condition were equally prevalent among Jews and gentiles. When we test people, however, a disproportionately high number of the "positive" test results turn out to be Jewish. Logically, there are only two possibilities. First, Jews may have a higher rate of "false positives" (positive test results for people who don't have the condition). Second, gentiles may have a higher rate of "false negatives" (negative test results for people who really do have the condition). By analogy, if true merit is equally distributed across the population, but Jews turn out disproportionately to have high credentials, then there are the same two possibilities: (1) Jews are more likely than gentiles to have high credentials even if they lack true merit, or (2) gentiles with low credentials are more likely than Jews with similar credentials to possess true merit. (Unless one of these statements were true, the percentage of Jews with true merit and the percentage with high credentials would have to be identical, which would mean that merit is not in fact distributed equally among all societal groups.) In either event, for some part of the population, given a Jew and a gentile with identical (high or low) credentials, we can deduce that the Jew is less likely to have true merit. This conclusion seems undeniably anti-Semitic.

11. G. Edward White, *Intervention and Detachment: Essays in Legal History and Jurisprudence* at 167 (New York: Oxford University Press, 1994). For a history of Frankfurter's activities, see Peter H. Irons, *The New Deal Lawyers* at 60 (Princeton: Princeton University Press, 1982).

12. Catharine A. MacKinnon, "Reflections on Sex Equality Under Law," 100 *Yale L.J.* 1281, 1291 (1991). For a more conventional view of cultural differences, see Thomas Sowell, *Migrations and Cultures: A World View* at 379 (New York: Basic Books, 1996) ("Cultures are particular ways of accomplishing the things that make life possible").

13. Alex M. Johnson Jr., "The New Voice of Color," 100 *Yale L.J.* 2007, 2052 (1991) ("white male hegemony"); Patricia J. Williams, *The Alchemy of Race and Rights: Diary of a Law Professor* at 103 (Cambridge: Harvard University Press, 1991) (structured to "like or to dislike" groups). We should note that Williams has made clear her disapproval of anti-Semitism, see *Alchemy* at 125–28.

14. On the changing admissions standards of universities, see Deborah Woo, "The 'Overrepresentation' of Asian American: Red Herrings and Yellow Perils," in *Race and Ethnic Conflict: Contending Views on Prejudice, Discrimination, and Ethnoviolence* at 314, 319–23, Fred L. Pincus and Howard J. Ehrlich, eds. (Boulder, CO: Westview Press, 1994).

15. Blaming Jews for violence on television is an outgrowth of the belief that Jews dominate Hollywood. See Arnold Forster and Benjamin R. Epstein, *The New Anti-Semitism* at 109–11, 210 (New York: McGraw Hill, 1974); Bernard Weinraub, "Stereotype of Jews is Revived," *New York Times*, Nov. 7, 1994, at C11. The myth that Jewish doctors are deliberately spreading AIDS, especially to black children, is popular in many black communities. See Leonard Dinnerstein, *Antisemitism in America* at 221 (New York: Oxford University Press, 1994); Arthur Hertzberg, "Is Anti-Semitism Dying Out?" *New York Review of Books*, June 24, 1993, at 51, 52.

16. Heiko Oberman, *The Roots of Antisemitism in the Age of Renaissance and Reformation* at 117 (Philadelphia: Fortuss Press, 1984) ("storm troops"); Martin Luther, *On the Jews and Their Lies* (1543), republished in translation in 47 *Luther's Works* at 137, 268–69, Helmut Lehmann, ed. (St. Louis: Concordia Publishing House, 1971). Luther's angry diatribe goes on, finally concluding that the best course is simply to banish Jews altogether. Id. at 272. For a history of premodern anti-Semitism, see Robert S. Wistrich, *Antisemitism: The Longest Hatred* at 29–30 (New York: Pantheon, 1991); Joel Carmichael, *The Satanizing of the Jews: Origin and Development of Mystical Anti-Semitism* at 44–78 (New York: Fromm International, 1992). One occasionally finds hints of anti-Semitism even among modern American jurists. See Steven Lubet, "That's Funny, You Don't Look Like You Control the Government: The Sixth Circuit's Narrative on Jewish Power," 45 *Hastings L.J.* 1527 (1994).

17. On the myths about Passover, see Robert S. Wistrich, *Antisemitism: The Longest Hatred* at 30–31, 207, 310–11 (New York: Pantheon, 1991); Leonard Dinnerstein, *Antisemitism in America* at xxii–xxiii, 28, 101 (New York: Oxford University Press, 1994); Robert Chazan, "Medieval Anti-Semitism," in *History and Hate: The Dimensions of Anti-Semitism* at 49, 61, David Berger, ed. (Philadelphia: Jewish Publication Society, 1986). On Jews and poison, see e.g., Joel Carmichael, *The Satanizing of the Jews: Origin and Development of Mystical Anti-Semitism* at 74 (New York: Fromm International,

1992); Robert S. Wistrich, *Antisemitism: The Longest Hatred* at 29, 32–33 (New York: Pantheon, 1991); Leonard Dinnerstein, *Antisemitism in America* at xxv (New York, Oxford University Press, 1994); see also David Berger, "Anti-Semitism: An Overview," in *History and Hate: The Dimensions of Anti-Semitism* at 3, 7, David Berger, ed. (Philadelphia: Jewish Publication Society, 1986) (noting belief that Jewish doctors poisoned their patients); David Remnick, *Lenin's Tomb: The Last Days of the Soviet Empire* at 91–92, 96–97 (New York: Random House, 1993) (describing "Doctor's Plot," which charged Jewish doctors with poisoning Party officials). On the "Protocols" and their history, see, e.g., Norman Cohn, *Warrant for Genocide: The Myth of the Jewish World-Conspiracy and the Protocols of the Elders of Zion* (New York: Harper & Row, 1966); Carmichael, *The Satanizing of the Jews* at 138–40; Dinnerstein, *Antisemitism in America* at 80–83; Wistrich, *Antisemitism: The Longest Hatred* at 107, 253–54; Gerald Krefetz, *Jews and Money: The Myths and the Reality* at 47–48 (New Haven: Ticknor & Fields, 1982); Nathan C. Belth, *A Promise to Keep: A Narrative of the American Encounter With Anti-Semitism* at 75–84 (New York: Times Books, 1979). The information about the Wellesley college course, as well as quotes from "The Secret Relationship Between Blacks and Jews," are from Richard Bernstein, *Dictatorship of Virtue: Multiculturalism and the Battle for America's Future* at 116–17 (New York: A. A. Knopf, 1994). Needless to say, Bernstein does not share the sentiments and uses the quotations as illustrations of the hatefulness of the literature.

18. See John W. Dower, *War Without Mercy: Race and Power in the Pacific War* at 20–21, 83–84, 156–64, 172–73, 313–14 (New York: Pantheon, 1986); John J. Stephan, "The Tanaka Memorial (1927): Authentic or Spurious?" 7 *Mod. Asian Stud.* 733, 739–43 (1973).

19. For discussions of university quotas against Jews, see, e.g., Leonard Dinnerstein, *Antisemitism in America* at 84–87 (New York: Oxford University Press, 1994); David A. Hollinger, *Science, Jews, and Secular Culture: Studies in Mid-Twentieth Century American Intellectual History* at 9 (Princeton: Princeton University Press, 1996); Dan A. Oren, *Joining the Club: A History of Jews and Yale* (New Haven: Yale University Press, 1985); Charles E. Silberman, *A Certain People: American Jews and Their Lives Today* at 52–55 (New York: Summit Books, 1985); Marcia G. Synnott, *The Half-Opened Door: Discrimination and Admissions at Harvard, Yale, and Princeton 1900–1970* at 20, 112 (Westport, Connecticut: Greenwood Press, 1979). For discussions of the growing use of quotas against Asian Americans, see, e.g., Jayjia Hsia, *Asian Americans in Higher Education and at Work* at 1, 92–119 (Hillsdale, NJ: Lawrence Erlbaum Associates, 1988); Pat K. Chew, "Asian Americans: The 'Reticent' Minority and Their Paradoxes," 36 *Wm. & Mary L. Rev.* 1, 61–64 (1994); Deborah Woo, "The 'Overrepresentation' of Asian Americans: Red Herrings and Yellow Perils," in *Race and Ethnic Conflict: Contending Views on Prejudice, Discrim-*

ination, and Ethnoviolence at 314, 321–22, Fred L. Pincus and Howard J. Ehrlich, eds. (Boulder, CO: Westview Press, 1994). On conspiracy theories and the Holocaust, see, e.g., Joel Carmichael, *The Satanizing of the Jews: Origin and Development of Mystical Anti-Semitism* at 152–80 (New York: Fromm International, 1992); Norman Cohn, *Warrant for Genocide: The Myth of the Jewish World-Conspiracy and the Protocols of the Elders of Zion* at 194–215 (New York: Harper & Row, 1966). On conspiracy theories and Japanese relocation and internment, see, e.g., John W. Dower, *War Without Mercy: Race and Power in the Pacific War* at 79–81 (New York: Pantheon, 1986); Ronald Takaki, *Strangers from a Different Shore: A History of Asian Americans* at 388–405 (New York: Little, Brown, 1989). On conspiracy theories and the treatment of black slaves, see, e.g., Michael K. Curtis, "The 1859 Crisis over Hinton Helper's Book, *The Impending Crisis:* Free Speech, Slavery, and Some Light on the Meaning of the First Section of the Fourteenth Amendment," 68 *Chi.-Kent L. Rev.* 1113, 1123–24, 1133–34 (1993); A. Leon Higginbotham Jr., and Anne F. Jacobs, "The 'Law Only As an Enemy': The Legitimization of Racial Powerlessness Through Colonial and Antebellum Criminal Laws of Virginia," 70 *N.C. L. Rev.* 969 (1992). On some troubling affinities between critical race theory and conspiracy theories, see Jeffrey Rosen, "The Bloods and the Crits," *The New Republic*, Dec. 9, 1996, at 32–33.

20. See Michael Lerner, *The Socialism of Fools: Anti-Semitism on the Left* at 83–84 (Oakland, CA: Tikkun Books, 1992) ("ethnic studies programs rarely include Jewish studies; Jewish contributions are rarely part of multicultural courses; and when teachers are hired to teach these subjects, Jews are lumped with white European males as a group that ought not to be part of the pool from which teachers will be drawn").

21. Renan is quoted in Robert S. Wistrich, *Antisemitism: The Longest Hatred* at 47 (New York: Pantheon, 1991). Renan also said that Jews lacked "creativity." Proudhon is quoted in Joel Carmichael, *The Satanizing of the Jews: Origin and Development of Mystical Anti-Semitism* at 117 (New York: Fromm International, 1992). Wagner is quoted in Wistrich, *Antisemitism: The Longest Hatred* at 56. The American anti-Semite is quoted in Leonard Dinnerstein, *Antisemitism in America* at 64 (New York: Oxford University Press, 1994). De Man is discussed in David Lehman, *Signs of the Times: Deconstruction and the Fall of Paul de Man* (New York: Poseidon, 1991). For a short but interesting discussion of how Nazi propaganda echoed these sentiments, see Geoffrey H. Hartman, "The Book of Destruction," in *Probing the Limits of Representation: Nazism and the "Final Solution"* at 318, 330–31, Saul Friedlander, ed. (Cambridge: Harvard University Press, 1992).

22. John W. Dower, *War Without Mercy: Race and Power in the Pacific War* at 97–98, 302 (New York: Pantheon, 1986) ("no great art," "third-hand culture," "borrowing"); Deborah Woo, "The 'Overrepresentation' of Asian

Americans: Red Herrings and Yellow Perils," in *Race and Ethnic Conflict: Contending Views on Prejudice, Discrimination, and Ethnoviolence* at 314, 323, Fred L. Pincus and Howard J. Ehrlich, eds. (Boulder, CO: Westview Press, 1994) ("not well-rounded"); "Japanese Banking: Mitsubeautiful," *The Economist*, Feb. 9, 1991 at 86; Pat K. Chew, "Asian Americans: The 'Reticent' Minority and Their Paradoxes," 36 *Wm. & Mary L. Rev.* 1, 40 (1994).

23. Gerald Krefetz, *Jews and Money: The Myths and the Reality* at 247 (New Haven: Ticknor & Fields, 1982) ("too successful").

24. Benzion Netanyahu, *The Origins of the Inquisition in Fifteenth Century Spain* (New York: Random House, 1996) ("blood purity"). For a discussion of "middleman minorities," see generally Thomas Sowell, *Migrations and Cultures: A World View* at 27–35, 321–22 (New York: Basic Books, 1996); Joe R. Feagin and Clairece Booher Feagin, "Theoretical Perspectives in Race and Ethnic Relations," in *Race and Ethnic Conflict: Contending Views on Prejudice, Discrimination, and Ethnoviolence* at 29, 41–42, Fred L. Pincus and Howard J. Ehrlich, eds. (Boulder, CO: Westview Press, 1994).

25. Seymour Martin Lipset and Earl Raab, *Jews and the New American Scene* at 106 (Cambridge: Harvard University Press, 1995).

26. Christopher Darden, *In Contempt* at 171 (New York: HarperCollins, 1996); Constance Johnson, "The Hidden Perils of Racial Conformity," *U.S. News & World Report*, Dec. 24, 1990, at p. 42 (characterizing other reviews as describing Steele as a "traitor to his race"); Adolph Reed, "Book Review," *The Nation*, March 4, 1991, at p. 274 ("ratifying"); Ron Suskind, "In Rough City School, Top Students Struggle to Learn—and Escape," *Wall Street Journal*, May 26, 1994, at A8 (quoting gang leader on "disrespect"); Stephen L. Carter, "The Black Table, the Empty Seat, and the Tie," in *Lure and Loathing: Essays on Race, Identity, and the Ambivalence of Assimilation* at 55, 67, Gerald Early, ed. (New York: A. Lane/Penguin, 1993). On the use of peer pressure to prevent success, see, e.g., Rena R. Lindstrom and Sondra Van Sant, "Special Issues in Working with Gifted Minority Adolescents, 64 *J. Counseling & Devel.* 583, 584 (1986) ("students from racial minority groups are often pressured by peers not to leave the group by using the way of the majority culture to gain success, that is, by achieving academically"); Donna Y. Ford, J. John Harris Jr., and James M. Schuerger, "Racial Identity Development Among Gifted Black Students: Counseling Issues and Concerns," 71 *J. Counseling & Devel.* 409 (1993). On derogatory names, see Margaret Beale Spencer and Carol Markstrom-Adams, "Identity Processes Among Racial and Ethnic Minority Children in America," 61 *Child Devel.* 290, 302–3 (1990); Jim Chen, "Unloving," 80 *Iowa L. Rev.* 145, 155–56.

27. On blaming Jews see Karl Marx, *Early Writings* at 34–39, T. B. Bottomore, ed. and trans. (New York: McGraw-Hill, 1963) (blaming capitalism

on Jews); Robert S. Wistrich, *Antisemitism: The Longest Hatred* at 53 (New York: Pantheon, 1991) ("socialists condemned Jews as the embodiment of the 'capitalist spirit' . . . while conservatives pointed to Jews as a source of permanent unrest and revolutionary subversion in European society"); Todd Endelman, "Comparative Perspectives on Modern Anti-Semitism in the West," in *History and Hate: The Dimensions of Anti-Semitism* at 95, 105, David Berger, ed. (Philadelphia: Jewish Publication Society, 1986) ("Jews were associated with all the destructive forces of modernization—capitalism, urbanization, democratization, materialism, socialism"); see also Leonard Dinnerstein, *Antisemitism in America* at 49–50 (New York: Oxford University Press, 1994) (populist anti-Semitism). On American universities, see Deborah Woo, "The 'Overrepresentation' of Asian Americans: Red Herrings and Yellow Perils," in *Race and Ethnic Conflict: Contending Views on Prejudice, Discrimination, and Ethnoviolence* at 314, 319, Fred L. Pincus and Howard J. Ehrlich, eds. (Boulder, CO: Westview Press, 1994). On Germany and Austria, see Wistrich, *Antisemitism* at 61–62; Endelman, "Comparative Perspectives," at 96. On American charges of Jewish influence, see Arnold Forster and Benjamin R. Epstein, *The New Antisemitism* at 111 (New York: McGraw-Hill, 1974).

28. John Rawls, *A Theory of Justice* (Cambridge: Harvard University Press, 1971); John Hart Ely, *Democracy and Distrust: A Theory of Judicial Review* (Cambridge: Harvard University Press, 1980). For criticism of Rawls, see Mari J. Matsuda, "Liberal Jurisprudence and Abstracted Visions of Human Nature: A Feminist Critique of Rawls' Theory of Justice," 16 *N.M. L. Rev.* 613 (1986); Linda R. Hirshman, "Is the Original Position Male-Superior?" 94 *Colum. L. Rev.* 1860 (1994); Chandran Kukathag and Philip Petit, *Rawls' "A Theory of Justice" and Its Critics* (Stanford, CA: Stanford University Press, 1990).

29. Shulamit Volkov, *The Rise of Popular Antimodernism in Germany: The Urban Master Artisans, 1873–1896* at 317 (Princeton: Princeton University Press, 1978) (anti-Semitism as "convenient way of attacking existing order"); Leonard Dinnerstein, *Antisemitism in America* at 223 (New York: Oxford University Press, 1994) (blacks "venting their frustrations" on Jews); Michael Lerner, *The Socialism of Fools: Anti-Semitism on the Left* (Oakland, CA: Tikkun Books, 1992). For other discussions of black anti-Semitism see, e.g., Dinnerstein, *Antisemitism* at 209–10; Jonathan Kaufman, *Broken Alliance: The Turbulent Times Between Blacks and Jews in America* at 273–74 (New York: Charles Scribner's Sons, 1988); Seymour Martin Lipset and Earl Raab, *Jews and the New American Scene* at 100–7 (1995); Gregory Martire and Ruth Clark, *Anti-Semitism in the United States: A Study of Prejudice in the 1980s* at 40–43 (New York: Praeger, 1982); Robert S. Wistrich, *Antisemitism: The Longest Hatred* at 123 (New York: Pantheon, 1991); Harold E. Quinley and Charles Y. Glock, *Anti-Semitism in America* at 54–72 (New York: Free Press, 1979); Gertrude J.

Selznick and Stephen Steinberg, *The Tenacity of Prejudice: Anti-Semitism in Contemporary America* at 117–31 (New York: Harper & Row, 1969); Charles E. Silberman, *A Certain People: American Jews and Their Lives Today* at 339–41 (New York: Summit Books, 1985); Stephen L. Carter, "Loving the Messenger," 1 *J.L. & Humanities* 317 (1989); William G. Ortner, "Jews, African-Americans, and the Crown Heights Riots: Applying Matsuda's Proposal to Restrict Racist Speech," 73 *B.U. L. Rev.* 897, 898–900 (1993).

30. Alain Finkielkraut, *The Defeat of the Mind* at 21 (New York: Columbia University Press, 1995) (quoting J.G. Herder) ("most ignorant nation"). On de Maistre, see Stephen Holmes, *The Anatomy of Antiliberalism* at 86, 281 n.62 (Cambridge: Harvard University Press, 1993).

31. On Schmitt, see Stephen Holmes, *The Anatomy of Antiliberalism* at 2, 37–39, 50–53.

32. David Hollinger, *Science, Jews, and Secular Culture: Studies in Mid-Twentieth Century American Intellectual History* at 171 (Princeton: Princeton University Press, 1996). For an example of a radical multiculturalist defense of creationism, see Frederick M. Gedicks, "Public Life and Hostility to Religion," 78 *Va. L. Rev.* 671 (1992).

33. All of the quotations in this paragraph, including Eliot's, are taken from David Hollinger, *Science, Jews, and Secular Culture: Studies in Mid-Twentieth Century American Intellectual History* at 18–19, 22, 24 (Princeton: Princeton University Press, 1996). See also David A. Hollinger, "The 'Tough-Minded' Justice Holmes, Jewish Intellectuals, and the Making of an American Icon," in *The Legacy of Oliver Wendell Holmes Jr.* at 216, 224–27, Robert W. Gordon, ed. (Palo Alto, CA: Stanford University Press, 1992).

34. Alain Finkielkraut, *The Imaginary Jew* at 73, Kevin O'Neill and David Suchoff, trans. (Lincoln: University of Nebraska Press, 1994).

35. Thomas Keneally, *Schindler's List* at 167–69 (New York: Simon & Schuster, 1982).

Chapter 4

1. For discussion of some of these trends (which have some resemblance to legal storytelling), see Wendy Kaminer, *I'm Dysfunctional, You're Dysfunctional: The Recovery Movement and Other Self-Help Fashions* at 29–43, 156–60 (1992); Ronald K. L. Collins and David M. Skover, *The Death of Discourse* (Boulder, CO: Westview Press, 1996).

2. Derrick Bell, "Foreword: The Civil Rights Chronicles," 99 *Harv. L. Rev.* 4, 40–42, 51 (1985).

3. See Anne M. Coughlin, "Regulating the Self: Autobiographical Performances in Outsider Scholarship," 81 *Va. L. Rev.* 1229, 1303–10 (1996).

4. Patricia J. Williams, *The Alchemy of Race and Rights: Diary of a Law Professor* at 5 (Cambridge: Harvard University Press, 1991).

5. Id.

6. Richard Delgado, "Storytelling for Oppositionists and Others: A Plea for Narrative," 87 *Mich. L. Rev.* 2411, 2416–34 (1988).

7. See Richard A. White, "Statistical Report on the Gender and Minority Composition of New Law Teachers and AALS Faculty Appointments Register Candidates," 44 *J. Legal. Educ.* 424, 429–30 (1994); James Lindgren, "Measuring Diversity," unpublished manuscript. Derrick Bell incorrectly asserts that minority women "have had a disproportionately hard time gaining entry into law school faculties." Derrick Bell, *Confronting Authority: Reflections of an Ardent Protestor* at 168 n.1 (Boston: Beacon, 1994).

8. See Jonathan Baron, *Thinking and Deciding* at 204–212 (New York: Cambridge University Press, 1988); Roger G. Noll and James E. Krier, "Some Implications of Cognitive Psychology for Risk Regulation," 19 *J. Legal Stud.* 747, 754–55 (1990); Elizabeth F. Loftus and Lee Roy Beach, "Human Inference and Judgment: Is the Glass Half Empty or Half Full?" 34 *Stan. L. Rev.* 939, 941–45 (1982).

9. See William N. Eskridge Jr., "Gaylegal Narratives," 46 *Stan. L. Rev.* 607, 625 (1994) (scholarship as community building).

10. Id. at 611–12, 621–22.

11. Id. at 627; Diane H. Mazur, "The Unknown Soldier: A Critique of 'Gays in the Military' Scholarship," 29 *U.C. Davis L. Rev.* 223, 251–54, 265–73, 281 (1996).

12. William N. Eskridge Jr., "Gaylegal Narratives," 46 *Stan. L. Rev.* at 634, 643–44 (1994). On the general issue of defining gay identity, see Daniel R. Ortiz, "Creating Controversy: Essentialism and Constructivism and the Politics of Gay Identity," 79 *Va. L. Rev.* 1833 (1993).

13. Jerome M. Culp Jr., "Black People in White Face: Assimilation, Culture, and the Brown Case," 36 *Wm. & Mary L. Rev.* 665, 670 (1995); Alex M. Johnson Jr., "Defending the Use of Narrative and Giving Content to the Voice of Color: Rejecting the Imposition of Process Theory in Legal Scholarship," 79 *Iowa L. Rev.* 803, 845 (1994) ("duality inherent"); id. at 835–37 (discussing the importance of a race-conscious perspective). As Susan Bandes puts it in her thoughtful article, "Empathy, Narrative, and Victim Impact Statements," 63 *U. Chi. L. Rev.* 361, 386 (1996), "for the alternative story to be heard, sometimes the dominant story must be excluded."

14. Charles Rothfeld, "Minority Critic Stirs Debate on Minority Writing," *New York Times*, Jan. 5, 1990, at B6; Scott Brewer, "Introduction: Choosing Sides in the Racial Critiques Debate," 103 *Harv. L. Rev.* 1844, 1845–47 (1990) (motives and sincerity); id. at 1846 n.10 (quoting Native

American Robert Williams); Derrick Bell, "Who's Afraid of Critical Race Theory?" 1995 *U. Ill. L. Rev.* 893, 908 (1995) (also calling Kennedy the "most politically damaging critic" of critical race theory.).

15. Alfred C. Yen, "Unhelpful," 81 *Iowa L. Rev.* 1573, 1574 (1996) ("attack ad"); Garrett Epps, "What's *Loving* Got to Do With It?" 81 *Iowa L. Rev.* 1489, 1491, 1500 (1996) (all remaining quotations).

16. Catharine A. MacKinnon, *Feminism Unmodified: Discourses on Life and Law* at 205 (Cambridge: Harvard University Press, 1987).

17. Fred Strebeigh, "Defining Law on the Feminist Frontier," *New York Times Magazine*, Oct. 6, 1991, at 28, 56 ("fronting," "Uncle Toms"); Dan Greenberg and Thomas H. Tobiason, "The New Legal Puritanism of Catharine MacKinnon," 54 *Ohio St. L.J.* 1375, 1420 (1993) ("Vichy").

18. David Margolick, "At the Bar," *New York Times*, Nov. 5, 1993, at B12 (nat'l ed.). See also Catharine A. MacKinnon, *Feminism Unmodified: Discourses on Life and Law* at 133 (Cambridge: Harvard University Press, 1987) (complaining that she had been forced to go along with including a representative of the opposing view on a panel: "When world hunger is addressed, is it necessary to have the pro-hunger side presented?").

19. Martha Minow, "Surviving Victim Talk," 40 *U.C.L.A. L. Rev.* 1411, 1427, 1430, 1433, 1437 (1993); Henry Louis Gates Jr., *Loose Canons: Notes on the Culture Wars* at 185 (New York: Oxford University Press, 1992).

20. Mary Louise Fellows and Sherene Razack, "Seeking Relations: Law and Feminism Roundtables," 19 *Signs* 1048, 1069–75 (1994).

21. Marie Ashe, "Zig-Zag Stitching and the Seamless Web: Thoughts on 'Reproduction' and the Law," 13 *Nova L. Rev.* 355 (1989); Kathryn Abrams, "Hearing the Call of Stories," 79 *Cal. L. Rev.* 971, 1040 (1991).

22. Patricia J. Williams, *The Alchemy of Race and Rights: Diary of a Law Professor* at 44–51 (Cambridge: Harvard University Press, 1991).

23. Jerome McCristal Culp Jr., "You Can Take Them to Water But You Can't Make Them Drink: Black Legal Scholarship and White Legal Scholars," 1992 *U. Ill. L. Rev.* 1021, 1031–32.

24. Richard Delgado, "On Telling Stories in School: A Reply to Farber and Sherry," 46 *Vand. L. Rev.* 665, 675 (1993); Alex M. Johnson Jr., "Defending the Use of Narrative and Giving Content to the Voice of Color: Rejecting the Imposition of Process Theory in Legal Scholarship," 79 *Iowa L. Rev.* 803, 826–29 (1994). For yet another interpretation, see Clark Freshman, "Were Patricia Williams and Ronald Dworkin Separated at Birth?" 95 *Colum. L. Rev.* 1568, 1605–6 (1995). See also Arthur Austin, "Evaluating Storytelling as a Type of Nontraditional Scholarship," 74 *Neb. L. Rev.* 479, 526 (1995) (suggesting that the story is implausible).

25. Alex M. Johnson Jr., "Defending the Use of Narrative and Giving Content to the Voice of Color: Rejecting the Imposition of Process Theory

in Legal Scholarship," 79 *Iowa L. Rev.* 803, 830 (1994); Kathryn Abrams, "Hearing the Call of Stories," 79 *Cal. L. Rev.* 971, 1041, 1048–51; Mary I. Coombs, "Outsider Scholarship: The Law Review Stories," 63 *U. Colo. L. Rev.* 683, 714–15 and n.125 (1992); Richard Delgado, "On Telling Stories in School: A Reply to Farber and Sherry," 46 *Vand. L. Rev.* 665, 670 (1993).

26. Jane Baron, "Resistance to Stories," 67 *S. Cal. L. Rev.* 255, 279 (1994).

27. Lucinda M. Finley, "Breaking Women's Silence in Law: The Dilemma of the Gendered Nature of Legal Reasoning," 64 *Notre Dame L. Rev.* 886, 893 (1989); Mari J. Matsuda, "Liberal Jurisprudence and Abstracted Visions of Human Nature: A Feminist Critique of Rawls' Theory of Justice," 16 *N.M. L. Rev.* 613, 619 (1986) (abstraction is "the first step down the road of androcentric ignorance"); Robin West, "Jurisprudence and Gender," 55 *U. Chi. L. Rev.* 1, 26–28 (1988); Ann Scales, "Feminist Legal Method: Not So Scary," 2 *U.C.L.A. Women's L.J.* 1, 4 (1992).

28. Alex M. Johnson Jr., "Defending the Use of Narrative and Giving Content to the Voice of Color: Rejecting the Imposition of Process Theory in Legal Scholarship," 79 *Iowa L. Rev.* 803, 851–52 (1994).

29. Id. at 811.

30. Derrick Bell, "Who's Afraid of Critical Race Theory?" 1995 *U. Ill. L. Rev.* 893, 907–8, 910.

31. Douglas E. Litowitz, "Some Critical Thoughts on Critical Race Theory," 72 *Notre Dame L. Rev.* 515, 521 (1996) ("*all* reasonable perspectives"); Daphne Patai and Noretta Koertge, *Professing Feminism: Cautionary Tales From the Strange World of Women's Studies* at 118 (New York: Basic Books, 1994) ("dismissive sneer").

32. Trina Grillo and Stephanie M. Wildman, "Obscuring the Importance of Race: The Implications of Making Comparisons Between Racism and Sexism (Or Other -Isms)," 1991 *Duke L.J.* 397, 408 n.34.

33. Anne M. Coughlin, "Regulating the Self: Autobiographical Performances in Outsider Scholarship," 81 *Va. L. Rev.* 1229 (1995).

34. Jerome McCristal Culp Jr., "Telling a Black Legal Story: Privilege, Authenticity, 'Blunders,' and Transformation in Outsider Narratives," 82 *Va. L. Rev.* 69, 90–92 (1996); Richard Delgado, "Coughlin's Complaint: How to Disparage Outsider Writing, One Year Later," 82 *Va. L. Rev.* 95, 107 (1996).

35. For another example, see the exchange between Freshman and Posner about whether Posner's appraisals of female and minority scholars were racist and sexist. Clark Freshman, "Were Patricia Williams and Ronald Dworkin Separated at Birth?" 95 *Colum. L. Rev.* 1568, 1590–91 (1995); Richard A. Posner, "Response to Clark Freshman, Were Patricia Williams and Ronald Dworkin Separated at Birth?" 95 *Colum. L. Rev.* 1610 (1995).

36. Mark Tushnet, "The Degradation of Constitutional Discourse," 81 *Geo. L.J.* 251, 268–69 (1992).

37. Gary Peller, "The Discourse of Constitutional Degradation," 81 *Geo. L.J.* 313, 326–27 (1992).
38. Id. at 320–30, 337–41.
39. Mark Tushnet, "Reply," 81 *Geo. L.J.* 350, 350 (1992).
40. Gary Peller, "The Discourse of Constitutional Degradation," 81 *Geo. L.J.* 313, 329, 334 (1992).

Chapter 5

1. Patricia J. Williams, *The Alchemy of Race and Rights: Diary of a Law Professor* at 169–70 (Cambridge: Harvard University Press, 1991). (The sentence we have deleted [marked by the ellipsis] reads: "No matter how she got there." We thought it was redundant.) For a detailed account of the entire Brawley incident, see Robert D. McFadden, Ralph Blumenthal, M. A. Farber, E. R. Shipp, Charles Strum, and Craig Wolf, *Outrage: The Story Behind the Tawana Brawley Hoax* (New York: Bantam, 1990).
2. Anne M. Coughlin, "Regulating the Self: Autobiographical Performances in Outsider Scholarship," 81 *Va. L. Rev.* 1229, 1279 (1995).
3. Kim Lane Scheppele, "Just the Facts, Ma'am: Sexualized Violence, Evidentiary Habits, and the Revision of Truth," 37 *N.Y.L. Sch. L. Rev.* 123, 125–26 (1992) ("Facts must be constructed").
4. Kathryn Abrams, "Hearing the Call of Stories," 79 *Cal. L. Rev.* 971, 1025 (1991); Alex M. Johnson Jr., "Defending the Use of Narrative and Giving Content to the Voice of Color: Rejecting the Imposition of Process Theory in Legal Scholarship," 79 *Iowa L. Rev.* 803, 816 n.65 (1994); Jane B. Baron, "Resistance to Stories," 67 *S. Cal. L. Rev.* 255, 283 (1994) ("cast doubt"); see also Stuart Alan Clarke, "Color-Blind Prophets and Bootstrap Philosophies: Straw Men, Shell Games and Social Criticism," 3 *Yale J.L. & Human.* 83, 91 (1991) ("It is naive if not disingenuous to suggest that all that matters is the promotion of truth"); William N. Eskridge Jr., "Gaylegal Narratives," 46 *Stan. L. Rev.* 607, 625 (1994) ("community building," rather than the search for truth, "provides the best understanding of law"); Michel Foucault, *Discipline and Punish* at 27, A. M. Sheridan-Smith, trans. (London: Penguin, 1979); John 8:32 (American Standard ed.).
5. For Williams's reaction to disbelief, see Patricia J. Williams, *The Alchemy of Race and Rights: Diary of a Law Professor* at 44–51, 242 n.5 (Cambridge: Harvard University Press, 1991). Delgado's reaction is in Richard Delgado, "Coughlin's Complaint: How to Disparage Outsider Writing, One Year Later," 82 *Va. L. Rev.* 95, 105–6 (1996).
6. Alex M. Johnson Jr., "Defending the Use of Narrative and Giving Content to the Voice of Color: Rejecting the Imposition of Process Theory

in Legal Scholarship," 79 *Iowa L. Rev.* 803, 806 (1994). Our initial article is Daniel A. Farber and Suzanna Sherry, "Telling Stories Out of School: An Essay on Legal Narratives," 45 *Stan. L. Rev.* 807 (1993).

7. Jerome McCristal Culp Jr., "Telling Tales in School: Black Legal Scholarship, Race, and Authenticity," unpublished paper presented at the 1993 meeting of the Association of American Law Schools; Jane B. Baron, "Resistance to Stories," 67 *S. Cal. L. Rev.* 255 (1994); Alex M. Johnson Jr., "Defending the Use of Narrative and Giving Content to the Voice of Color: Rejecting the Imposition of Process Theory in Legal Scholarship," 79 *Iowa L. Rev.* 803, 816 (1994); William N. Eskridge Jr., "Gaylegal Narratives," 46 *Stan. L. Rev.* 607, 610, 613, 644 (1994); Gary Peller, "The Discourse of Constitutional Degradation," 81 *Geo. L.J.* 313, 335 (1992).

8. Patricia J. Williams, *The Alchemy of Race and Rights: Diary of a Law Professor* at 47, 242 n.3 (Cambridge: Harvard University Press, 1991). The case is *Blyew v. United States*, 80 U.S. (13 Wall.) 581 (1871), which held that a federal statute allowing cases to be removed from state to federal court in some circumstances could not be applied simply on the basis of a state rule forbidding such testimony. This is a quintessential jurisdictional ruling. The difference between substantive and jurisdictional rulings is one of the first things that law students learn. It is also one of the legal distinctions that radical multiculturalists criticize. Nevertheless, more attention to factual detail might have produced a fuller explanation—rather than a bare citation—of why the case should be interpreted as a substantive holding.

9. Mari J. Matsuda, "Looking to the Bottom: Critical Legal Studies and Reparation," 22 *Harv. C.R.-C.L. L. Rev.* 323, 354 n.132 (1987); Ann C. Scales, "Feminists in the Field of Time," 42 *Fla. L. Rev.* 95, 107 and n.37 (1990); Patricia J. Williams, *The Alchemy of Race and Rights: Diary of a Law Professor* at 110–15 (Cambridge: Harvard University Press, 1991); Richard A. Posner, *Overcoming Law* at 375 (Cambridge: Harvard University Press, 1995). For a discussion of Shaw, see Peter Burchard, *One Gallant Rush: Robert Gould Shaw and His Brave Black Regiment* (New York: St. Martin's Press, 1965); for the computataion of Easter, see "Easter" in Unabridged Random House Dictionary of the English Language (New York: Random House, 1971); on Beethoven's race, see Dominique-Rene de Lerma, "Beethoven as a Black Composer," 10 *Black Music Res. J.* 118 (1990). The computation of Easter is somewhat different in the Eastern Orthodox Church.

10. For defenses of single parenthood, see, e.g., Susan B. Apel, "Communitarianism and Feminism: The Case Against the Preference for the Two-Parent Family," 10 *Wis. Women's L.J.* 1 (1995); Regina Austin, "Sapphire Bound!" 1989 *Wis. L. Rev.* 539; Nancy E. Dowd, "Stigmatizing Single Parents," 18 *Harv. Women's L.J.* 19 (1995); Lucy A. Williams, "The Ideology of

Division: Behavior Modification Welfare Reform Proposals," 102 *Yale L.J.* 719 (1992). The quotation in the text is from National Research Council, *A Common Destiny: Blacks and American Society* at 525, Gerald David Jaynes and Robin M. Williams Jr., eds. (Washington, DC: National Academy Press, 1989). Other support for the disadvantages of single parenthood include id. at 290, 523–26, 543–46; Sara McLanahan, *Growing Up with a Single Parent: What Hurts, What Helps* (Cambridge: Harvard University Press, 1994); William Julius Wilson, *The Truly Disadvantaged: The Inner City, The Underclass, and Public Policy* at 71–72 (Chicago and London: University of Chicago Press, 1987); Marian Wright Edelman, *Families in Peril: An Agenda for Social Change* at 3–6, 52–53, 56–57 (Cambridge: Harvard University Press, 1987); Mary Jo Bane and David T. Ellwood, "One Fifth of the Nation's Children: Why Are They Poor?" 245 *Science* 1047, 1051 (Sept. 8, 1989). In chapter 6 we will examine a number of other myths of radical multiculturalism.

11. Jeanne L. Schroeder, "The Taming of the Shrew: The Liberal Attempt to Mainstream Radical Feminist Theory," 5 *Yale J.L. & Feminism* 123, 123 (1992).

12. Richard Delgado, "On Telling Stories in School: A Reply to Farber and Sherry," 46 *Vand. L. Rev.* 665 (1993); Richard Delgado, "Storytelling for Oppositionists and Others: A Plea for Narrative," 87 *Mich. L. Rev.* 2411 (1989); Robert Chang, "Toward an Asian American Legal Scholarship: Critical Race Theory, Post-structuralism, and Narrative Space," 81 *Cal. L. Rev.* 1241, 1286 (1993).

13. Albert S. Lindemann, *The Jew Accused: Three Anti-Semitic Affairs (Dreyfus, Beilis, Frank) 1894–1915* at 121–22 (Cambridge: Cambridge University Press, 1991) (emphasis in original).

14. The story of General Volkogonov is taken from David Remnick, *Lenin's Tomb: The Last Days of the Soviet Empire* at 401–11 (New York: Random House, 1993). The quotation from Volkogonov is at page 410.

15. For a moving account of Lester's ordeal, see Julius Lester, *Lovesong: Becoming a Jew* (New York: Henry Holt, 1988); for a less personal account, see "Editorial: Ambush at Amherst," *The New Republic*, June 27, 1988 at 9.

16. The case is reported at 839 F.2d 302 (7th Cir. 1988). For a discussion of the case and its aftermath, and an explanation of the statistical issues, see Thomas Haskell and Sanford Levinson, "Academic Freedom and Expert Witnessing: Historians and the *Sears* Case," 66 *Tex. L. Rev.* 1629, 1636–48 (1988).

17. Peter Novick, *That Noble Dream: The "Objectivity Question" and the American Historical Profession* at 502–16 (Cambridge: Cambridge University Press, 1988) (describing Rosenberg). Kessler-Harris's perspective on the case can be found in "Academic Freedom and Expert Witnessing: A Response to

Haskell and Levinson," 67 *Tex. L. Rev.* 429 (1988); the quotation in the text is at p. 430. The "archive" is in the Summer 1986 issue of *Signs*. For a description of *Signs* as "the premier feminist periodical," see Daphne Patai and Noretta Koertge, *Professing Feminism: Cautionary Tales From the Strange World of Women's Studies* at 161 (New York: Basic Books, 1994).

18. See Peter Novick, *That Noble Dream: The "Objectivity Question" and the American Historical Profession* at 508–9 (Cambridge: Cambridge University Press, 1988); Thomas S. Haskell and Sanford Levinson, "Academic Freedom and Expert Witnessing: Historians and the *Sears* Case," 66 *Tex. L. Rev.* 1629, 1631 (1988) ("women struggling"); id. at 1630 ("no other historian").

19. We are not the first to point out radical multiculturalism's totalitarian potential. See, e.g., Joel F. Handler, "Postmodernism, Protest, and the New Social Movements," 26 *Law & Soc. Rev.* 697 (1992); Peter Dews, *Logics of Disintegration: Post-structuralist Thought and the Claims of Critical Theory* (London and New York: Verso, 1987).

20. Eric Blumenson, "Mapping the Limits of Skepticism in Law and Morals," 74 *Tex. L. Rev.* 523, 529 (1996); Richard Rorty, *Consequences of Pragmatism* at xlii (Minneapolis: University of Minnesota Press, 1982).

21. Eric Blumenson, "Mapping the Limits of Skepticism in Law and Morals," 74 *Tex. L. Rev.* 523, 536 (1996) ("clitoridectomy"); id. at 566 ("whose ox is gored"). The other examples in the text are taken from the following cases: *People v. Kimura*, Record of Court Proceedings, No. A-091133 (Super. Ct. L.A. County Nov. 21, 1985) (mother-child suicide); *People v. Moua*, Record of Court Proceedings, No. 315972-0 (Super. Ct. Freson County Feb. 7, 1985) (marriage-by-capture); *State v. Lee*, 494 N.W.2d 475 (Minn. 1992) (same). For a careful discussion of the issues raised by these and similar cases, see Doriane Lambelet Coleman, "Individualizing Justice Through Multiculturalism: The Liberals' Dilemma," 96 *Colum. L. Rev.* 1093 (1996).

22. See Michel Foucault, *Politics, Philosophy, Culture: Interviews and Other Writings 1977–1984* at 215, Lawrence D. Kritzman, ed. (New York: Routledge, 1988); Didier Eribon, *Michel Foucault* at 244, Betsy Wing, trans. (Cambridge: Harvard University Press, 1991). See also William Ewald, "Unger's Philosophy: A Critical Legal Study," 97 *Yale L.J.* 665 (1988).

23. John Dewey, *Freedom and Culture* at 148 (New York: G. P. Putnam's Sons, 1939); Steven C. Rockefeller, "Comment," in Charles Taylor, Amy Gutmann, Michael Walzer, Steven Rockefeller, and Susan Wolf, *Multiculturalism: Examining the Politics of Recognition* at 87, 91 (Princeton: Princeton University Press, 1994) ("unalterably opposed"); Robert K. Merton, "Science and the Social Order," 5 *Philos. of Science* 321, 327 (1938). For more on Dewey and democracy, see Hilary Putnam, "A Reconsideration of Deweyan Democracy," 63 *S. Cal. L. Rev.* 1671 (1990). On Merton, see David A. Hollinger,

Science, Jews, and Secular Culture: Studies in Mid-Twentieth-Century American Intellectual History at 80–96 (Princeton: Princeton University Press, 1996).

24. William P. Marshall, "In Defense of the Search for Truth as a First Amendment Justification," 30 *Ga. L. Rev.* 1, 31–32 (1995).

25. Kathryn Abrams, "Law's Republicanism," 97 *Yale L.J.* 1591, 1591 (1988). On historians' struggle with objectivity questions, see Joyce Appleby, Lynn Hunt, and Margaret Jacob, *Telling the Truth About History* (New York and London: W. W. Norton, 1994); Peter Novick, *That Noble Dream: The "Objectivity Question" and the American Historical Profession* (Cambridge: Cambridge University Press, 1988). On the blurring of fact and fiction, see Gordon S. Wood, "Novel History," *New York Review of Books* 12 (June 27, 1991).

26. Hayden White, *The Content of the Form: Narrative Discourse and Historical Representation* at 74 (Baltimore: Johns Hopkins University Press, 1987); Saul Friedlander, "Introduction," in *Probing the Limits of Representation: Nazism and the "Final Solution"* at 1, 9, Saul Friedlander, ed. (Cambridge: Harvard University Press, 1992) ("compromise"); Hayden White, "Historical Emplotment and the Problem of Truth," in *Probing the Limits of Representation: Nazism and the "Final Solution"* at 37, Saul Friedlander, ed. (Cambridge: Harvard University Press, 1992). For an overview of historians' confrontation with objectivity, see Peter Novick, *That Noble Dream: The "Objectivity Question" and the American Historical Profession* (Cambridge: Cambridge University Press, 1988).

27. Saul Friedlander, "Introduction," in *Probing the Limits of Representation: Nazism and the "Final Solution"* at 3, 4–5, Saul Friedlander, ed. (Cambridge: Harvard University Press, 1992).

28. Mari J. Matsuda, "Public Response to Racist Speech: Considering the Victim's Story," 87 *Mich. L. Rev.* 2320, 2366–67 (1989).

29. Deborah E. Lipstadt, *Denying the Holocaust: The Growing Assault on Truth and Memory* at 1–2, 18 (New York: Free Press, 1993).

30. The account in this paragraph is taken from Lynne V. Cheney, *Telling the Truth: Why Our Culture and Our Country Have Stopped Making Sense— And What We Can Do About It* at 80 (New York: Simon & Schuster, 1995). She notes that "the Duke editor's decision may well have revealed less about her misunderstanding of ideas that are now common on campuses than it did about what can happen when truth and reason are dismissed." Id. at 81.

31. Eric Muller, e-mail posting to Lawprof List, June 18, 1996 (used with the author's permission).

32. Eugene D. Genovese, *Roll, Jordan, Roll; The World the Slaves Made* (New York: Vintage, 1976); Eugene D. Genovese, *The Southern Tradition: The Achievement and Limitations of an American Conservatism* (Cambridge: Harvard University Press, 1994). Legal cases on the Confederate flag con-

troversy include *NAACP v. Hunt,* 89 F.2d 1555 (11th Cir. 1990); *Augustus v. School Board of Escambia County,* 507 F.2d 152 (5th Cir. 1975); *Melton v. Young,* 465 F.2d 1332 (6th Cir. 1972), *cert. denied* 411 U.S. 951 (1973); *Smith v. St. Tammany Parish School Board,* 316 F. Supp. 1174 (E.D. La. 1970). For radical multiculturalist condemnations of the confederate flag as a purely racist symbol, see, e.g., Richard Delgado, "Rodrigo's Tenth Chronicle: Merit and Affirmative Action," 83 *Geo. L.J.* 1711, 1718 n.25 (1995); Robin D. Barnes, "Standing Guard for the P.C. Militia, or Fighting Hatred and Indifference: Some Thoughts on Expressive Hate-Conduct and Political Correctness," 1992 *U. Ill. L. Rev.* 979, 979–80; James Forman Jr., "Driving Dixie Down: Removing the Confederate Flag from Southern State Capitols," 101 *Yale L.J.* 505 (1991). See also *Doe v. University of Michigan,* 721 F. Supp. 852, 851–58 (E.D. Mich. 1989) (invalidating University of Michigan ban on hate speech, which had been supported by many of the radical multiculturalists; ban was accompanied by a "Guide" that suggested that it would be prohibited harassment for a student to "display a confederate flag" on a dormitory room door). The radicals might argue that the perspective of the victims of slavery is better or more valid than the perspective of proud southerners, but that implies external criteria of validity. If they maintain that it is more politically effective to take the victims' perspective, why should proud southerners in power listen to them?

A number of scholars have recognized the ambiguous symbolism represented by the confederate flag. See, e.g., Viktor Mayer-Schöberger and Teree E. Foster, "More Speech, Less Noise: Amplifying Content-Based Speech Regulations Through Binding International Law," 18 *B.C. Int'l & Comp. L. Rev.* 59, 131 n.301 (1995). For more nuanced and thoughtful discussions of the legal issues raised by display of the confederate flag, see Sanford Levinson, "They Whisper: Reflections on Flags, Monuments, and State Holidays, and the Construction of Social Meaning in a Multicultural Society," 70 *Chi.-Kent L. Rev.* 1079 (1995); Beattie I. Butler, "Muzzling Leviathan: Limiting State Powers of Speech and Expression," 5 *Kan. J.L. & Pub. Pol'y* 153 (Winter 1996).

33. Henry Louis Gates Jr., "Truth or Consequences: Putting Limits on Limits," in *The Limits of Expression in American Intellectual Life* at 15, 27 (New York: American Council of Learned Societies, 1993).

34. Patricia J. Williams, *The Rooster's Egg* at 130 (Cambridge: Harvard University Press, 1995).

35. Ian Hacking, *Rewriting the Soul: Multiple Personality and the Sciences of Memory* at 267 (Princeton: Princeton University Press, 1995).

36. Albert Camus, *The Plague* at 132, Stuart Gilbert, trans. (New York: Vintage International, 1991).

Chapter 6

1. On the fundamental nature of the critique of truth, see Neil Hamilton, *Zealotry and Academic Freedom: A Legal and Historical Perspective* at 56 (New Brunswick, NJ: Transaction Publishers, 1995). On the views of individual thinkers, see Mark V. Tushnet, "Following the Rules Laid Down: A Critique of Interpretivism and Neutral Principles," 96 *Harv. L. Rev.* 781 (1983); Mark Tushnet, "The Degradation of Constitutional Discourse," 81 *Geo. L.J.* 251 (1992); Duncan Kennedy, "A Cultural Pluralist Case for Affirmative Action in Academia," 1990 *Duke L.J.* 705; Catharine A. MacKinnon, *Toward a Feminist Theory of the State* (Cambridge: Harvard University Press, 1989).

2. Catharine A. MacKinnon, *Only Words* (Cambridge: Harvard University Press, 1993).

3. Id.; Richard Delgado, "Rodrigo's Eleventh Chronicle: Empathy and False Empathy," 84 *Cal. L. Rev.* 61, 96–97 (1996). See also Jerome McCristal Culp Jr., "Voice, Perspective, Truth, and Justice: Race and the Mountain in the Legal Academy," 38 *Loy. L. Rev.* 61 (1992) (many white scholars believe in white supremacy). Martha Mahoney tells of a scholar who compiled a list of forty-six ways in which she enjoyed the daily benefits of white privilege, including "things that happen because she is white and things that do not happen because she is white"—an "invisible" package of special privileges. Reportedly, she found these forms of privilege "extremely subtle and forgot them repeatedly until she wrote them down." Eternal vigilance is the price of ideological purity, it would seem. Martha R. Mahoney, "Whiteness and Women, In Practice and Theory: A Reply To Catharine MacKinnon," 5 *Yale J.L. & Feminism* 217, 234 (1993).

4. On the predictive ability of standardized tests for blacks, see Stephen L. Carter, *Reflections of an Affirmative Action Baby* at 92–94 (New York: Basic Books, 1991); Stephen P. Klein, *Summary of Research on the Multistate Bar Examination* at 38–39, 61 (National Conference of Bar Examiners, 1993); June O'Neill, "The Role of Human Capital in Earning Differences Between Black and White Men," 4 *J. Econ. Persp.* 25, 32, 40–41 (Fall 1990).

5. See Christopher T. Wonnell, "Circumventing Racism: Confronting the Problem of Affirmative Action," 1989 *B.Y.U. L. Rev.* 95, 119–141.

6. "The First Amendment, Under Fire From the Left," *New York Times Magazine* 40, 57, 68, Anthony Lewis, mod., Mar. 13, 1994.

7. Jerome McCristal Culp Jr., "Black People in White Face: Assimilation, Culture, and the Brown Case," 36 *Wm. & Mary L. Rev.* 665, 670 (1995); Derrick Bell, "Racial Realism," 24 *Conn. L. Rev.* 363, 370 (1992); Derrick Bell, *Faces at the Bottom of the Well: The Permanence of Racism* at 115–16 (New York: Basic Books, 1992). For Carter's views on affirmative action, see Stephen L. Carter, *Reflections of an Affirmative Action Baby* (New York: Basic

Books, 1991); for Thomas's views on affirmative action see "'Gods Law' Required Him to Vote Against Affirmative Action, says Justice Thomas," *Jet,* Sept. 11, 1995, at 8.

8. For an example of the radical claim, consider Derrick Bell, who believes that blacks are worse off than at any time since slavery. Linda Greenhouse, "The End of Racism, and Other Fables," *New York Times,* Sept. 20, 1992, at 7 (telephone interview). For statistics on Asians, see chapter 3. On the Hispanic situation, see Peter Skerry, "Not Much Cooking: Why the Voting Rights Act Is Not Empowering Mexican Americans," 11 *Brookings Rev.* 43 (Summer 1993).

9. See *A Common Destiny: Blacks and American Society* at 14–17, 335–48, Gerald D. Jaynes and Robin M. Williams Jr., eds. (Washington, DC: National Academy Press, 1989) ("significant improvements" in black economic status over the past fifty years; rise in number of black elected officials "from a few dozen in 1940 to over 6800 in 1988"; also rising test scores and improved graduation rates); Christopher Jencks, *Rethinking Social Policy: Race, Poverty, and the Underclass* at 177–81 (Cambridge: Harvard University Press, 1992) (lower dropout rate and other improved educational indicia for black students); john a. powell, "Racial Realism or Racial Despair?" 24 *Conn. L. Rev.* 533, 544 (1992) (improvement in just about every category).

10. For an example of this claim, see Judy Scales-Trent, "Black Women and the Constitution: Finding Our Place, Asserting Our Rights," 24 *Harv. C.R.-C.L. L. Rev.* 9 (1989). For its refutation, see Reynolds Farley, "The Common Destiny of Blacks and Whites: Observations about the Social and Economic Status of the Races," in *Race in America: The Struggle for Equality* at 197, 204–7, Herbert Hill and James E. Jones Jr., eds. (Madison: University of Wisconsin Press, 1993); *A Common Destiny: Blacks and American Society* at 297–301, Gerald D. Jaynes and Robin M. Williams Jr., eds. (Washington, DC: National Academy Press, 1989); James Lindgren, "Measuring Diversity," unpublished manuscript (black women over-represented in law teaching).

11. "Why the Erosion in Black Wage Gains?" 17 *Rand. Res. J.* 1, 4 (Summer 1993) ("rise in the income returns"). See also *A Common Destiny: Blacks and American Society* at 353–54, Gerald D. Jaynes and Robin M. Williams Jr., eds. (Washington, DC: National Academy Press, 1989); see Thomas B. Edsall amd Mary D. Edsall, *Chain Reaction: The Impact of Race, Rights, and Taxes on American Politics* at 241 (New York: Norton, 1991); James P. Smith, "Affirmative Action and the Racial Wage Gap," *Am. Econ. Rev.* 79, 84 (May 1993) (proceedings volume).

12. The statistics in this paragraph are taken from the following sources: "First Annual Report" (special section), "Minorities in Science: The Pipeline Problem," 258 *Science* 1175, Elizabeth Culotta and Ann Gibbons, eds.

(1992); Walter E. Massey, "A Success Story Amid Decades of Disappointment," 258 *Science* 1177, 1178 (1992); Dinesh D'Souza, *Illiberal Education: The Politics of Race and Sex on Campus* at 168 (New York: Free Press, 1991) (providing statistics).

13. The Justices' views can be gleaned from the majority, concurring, and dissenting opinions in *Bush v. Vera*, 116 S. Ct. 1941 (1996); *Shaw v. Hunt*, 116 S. Ct. 1894 (1996); *Miller v. Johnson*, 115 S. Ct. 2475 (1995); and *Adarand Constructors v. Pena*, 115 S. Ct. 2097 (1995).

14. For an overview of legal pragmatism, citations to the voluminous literature, and responses to some criticisms of pragmatism, see Daniel A. Farber, "Reinventing Brandeis: Legal Pragmatism for the Twenty-First Century," 1995 *U. Ill. L. Rev.* 163, 167–72. See also Scott Brewer, "Exemplary Reasoning: Semantics, Pragmatics, and the Rational Force of Legal Argument by Analogy," 109 *Harv. L. Rev.* 923 (1996).

15. Cass R. Sunstein, *Legal Reasoning and Political Conflict* at 25 (New York: Oxford University Press, 1996) ("familiar and exceedingly unfortunate"); id. at 130 ("complex set"); see also id. at 75–76.

16. See Cass R. Sunstein, "Republicanism and the Preference Problem," 66 *Chi.-Kent L. Rev.* 181 (1990). For typical radical views, see Alex M. Johnson Jr., "Defending the Use of Narrative and Giving Content to the Voice of Color: Rejecting the Imposition of Process Theory in Legal Scholarship," 79 *Iowa L. Rev.* 803, 840 (1994) (voice of color is anti-individualistic); John O. Calmore, "Critical Race Theory, Archie Shepp, and Fire Music: Securing an Authentic Intellectual Life in a Multicultural World," 65 *S. Cal. L. Rev.* 2129, 2194 (1992) (because of racial integration, people of color too often "assume the voice of a distinct *individual*, one separated in an operational sense from colored community, culture, and peoplehood").

17. On Holmes, see Thomas C. Grey, "Holmes and Legal Pragmatism," 41 *Stan. L. Rev.* 787 (1989). On Brandeis, see Daniel A. Farber, "Reinventing Brandeis: Legal Pragmatism for the Twenty-First Century," 1995 *U. Ill. L. Rev.* 163.

18. Martha C. Nussbaum, "Skepticism About Practical Reason in Literature and the Law," 107 *Harv. L. Rev.* 714, 730 (1994). We should note that Fish does not always appear to take this approach. We should also note that we are not making a similar argument in this book. While we hope to show that the radical multiculturalists are wrong, this does not necessarily mean that our own favored approach (legal pragmatism) is correct.

19. Keith Aoki, "The Scholarship of Reconstruction and the Politics of Backlash," 81 *Iowa L. Rev.* 1467 (1996) ("backlash scholarship"); Leti Volpp, "Talking 'Culture': Gender, Race, Nation, and the Politics of Multiculturalism," 96 *Colum. L. Rev.* 1573, 1573 (1996) ("backlash scholarship"; "preempt

debate"); Alex M. Johnson Jr., "Defending the Use of Narrative and Giving Content to the Voice of Color: Rejecting the Imposition of Process Theory in Legal Scholarship," 79 *Iowa L. Rev.* 803, 811, 152 (1994). Catharine A. MacKinnon, *Feminism Unmodified: Discourses on Life and Law* at 145 (Cambridge: Harvard University Press, 1987). See also Jerome McCristal Culp Jr., "Posner on Duncan Kennedy and Racial Difference: White Authority in the Legal Academy," 41 *Duke L.J.* 1095, 1096–97 (1992) (characterizing Posner's article as "the pious, solipsistic demand of white authority and the right of ultimate control"); Marc H. Fajer, "Authority, Credibility and Pre-Understanding: A Defense of Outsider Narratives in Legal Scholarship," 82 *Geo. L.J.* 1845, 1865 (1994) ("Despite their . . . protestations of friendliness, I experienced a large part of Farber and Sherry's and Tushnet's critiques as attacks. . . . I felt discouraged from telling the stories of my own life").

20. Mari J. Matsuda, "Voices of America: Accent, Antidiscrimination Law, and a Jurisprudence for the Last Reconstruction," 100 *Yale L.J.* 1329, 1394 (1991); Katharine Bartlett, "Tradition, Change, and the Idea of Progress in Feminist Legal Thought," 1995 *Wis. L. Rev.* 303, 323–24.

21. Blatantly paranoid conspiracy theories seem to be on the rise in all parts of the ideological spectrum. See Michael Kelly, "The Road to Paranoia," 71 *New Yorker,* June 19, 1995, at 60.

22. The response to criticism is exemplified by the Johnson, Bell, and Culp quotes earlier. The co-optation fear is exemplified by an article attacking Sunstein's "domestication" of MacKinnon's ideas. Jeanne L. Schroeder, "The Taming of the Shrew: The Liberal Attempt to Mainstream Radical Feminist Theory," 5 *Yale J.L. & Feminism* 123, 130 (1992) (Sunstein "cross dresses" as a feminist). See also William N. Eskridge Jr. and Gary Peller, "The New Public Law Movement: Moderation as a Postmodern Cultural Form," 89 *Mich. L. Rev.* 707 (1991). On the collaboration point, see, e.g., Book Note, "And We Will Not Be Saved," 106 *Harv. L. Rev.* 1358, 1363 and n.18 (1993) (Bell seemingly includes Randall Kennedy and Stephen Carter as black "opportunists").

Conclusion

1. Harlon L. Dalton, "The Clouded Prism," 22 *Harv. C.R.-C.L. L. Rev.* 435, 437 (1987).

2. See *A Common Destiny: Blacks and American Society* at 372, Gerald D. Jaynes and Robin M. Williams Jr., eds. (Washington, DC: National Academy Press, 1989) (a study recently done at a predominantly black high school in Washington, DC, demonstrates that "many behaviors associated with high achievement—speaking standard English, studying long hours, striving

to get good grades—were regarded as 'acting white'"; students engaged in such behaviors were stigmatized as "braniacs").

3. Derrick Bell, "Who's Afraid of Critical Race Theory?" 1995 *U. Ill. L. Rev.* 893, 899.

4. Stanley Fish, *There's No Such Thing as Free Speech And It's a Good Thing, Too* at 271 (New York: Oxford University Press, 1994). See also Rebecca L. Brown, "Tradition and Insight," 103 *Yale L.J.* 177 (1993).

5. Katharine T. Bartlett, "Tradition, Change, and the Idea of Progress in Feminist Legal Thought," 1995 *Wis. L. Rev.* 303, 334–35 (1995); Margaret Jane Radin, "The Pragmatist and the Feminist," 63 *S. Cal. L. Rev.* 1699 (1990).

6. William N. Eskridge Jr., *Dynamic Statutory Interpretation* (Cambridge: Harvard University Press, 1994); Mari J. Matsuda, "Voices of America: Accent, Antidiscrimination Law, and a Jurisprudence for the Last Reconstruction," 100 *Yale L.J.* 1329, 1403–4 (1991) ("Enlightenment"); Mari J. Matsuda, "When the First Quail Calls: Multiple Consciousness of Jurisprudential Method," 14 *Women's Rts. L. Rep.* 297, 300 (1992) ("Anzio").

7. For a somewhat different vision of reconciliation between opposing modes of scholarship, see Edward L. Rubin, "The New Legal Process, the Synthesis of Discourse, and the Microanalysis of Institutions," 109 *Harv. L. Rev.* 1393 (1996).

8. *DiSanto v. Pennsylvania*, 273 U.S. 34, 43 (1927) (Brandeis, J., dissenting) ("logic of words"); Oliver Wendell Holmes Jr., *The Common Law* at 1 (1881) (Boston: Little, Brown, 1943); Henry Louis Gates Jr., "Let Them Talk: Why Civil Liberties Pose No Threat to Civil Rights," *The New Republic*, Sept. 20 and 27, at 48; *New State Ice Co. v. Liebmann*, 285 U.S. 262, 311 (1932) (Brandeis, J., dissenting) ("light of reason"). On the role of imagination in law, see also Anthony T. Kronman, "Living in the Law," 54 *U. Chi. L. Rev.* 835, 853 (1987).

9. Amy Gutmann and Dennis Thompson, *Democracy and Disagreement* at 83–84 (Cambridge: Belknap Press, 1996). Stanley Fish makes a similar point: In an uncertain world, "one avoids the Scylla of prideful self-assertion and the Charybdis of paralysis by stepping out provisionally, with a sense of limitation, with a sense of style." Stanley Fish, *There's No Such Thing as Free Speech And It's a Good Thing, Too* at 272 (New York: Oxford University Press, 1994).

Index